I AM NOT IN THIS BOOK PG: 0*

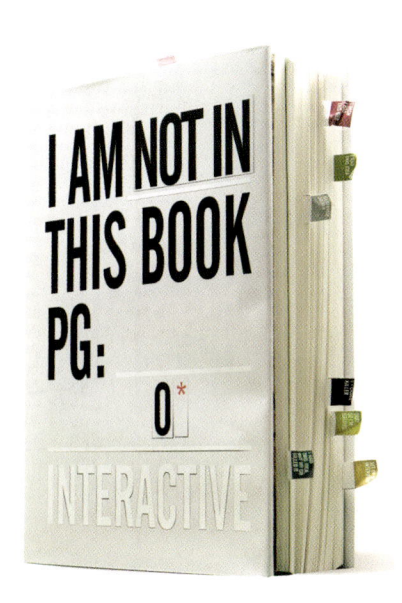

THE ONE SHOW INTERACTIVE VOLUME 10
Advertising's best interactive and new media

$4-

Chief Executive Officer
Mary Warlick

President
Kevin Swanepoel

Editor
Audrey N. Carpio

Contributing Editor
Tiffany Edwards

Designer
Francisco Hui

Cover and Divider Page Design
Arnold/Boston

Published by
One Club Publishing LLC
21 E. 26th Street, 5th Floor
New York, NY 10010
Tel: (212) 979 1900
Fax: (212) 979 5006
Email: publishing@oneclub.org
Web: www.oneclub.org

First Printing
One Show Interactive, Volume X
ISBN-13: 978-0-929837-32-1
ISBN-10: 0-929837-32-0
EAN: 9-78092983732-1
UPC: 0-80665-00298-4

Sponsors
Media Temple
Wall Street Journal
Yahoo!

Distribution (USA and International)
Rockport Publishers, a member of
Quayside Publishing Group
100 Cummings Center
Suite 406-L
Beverly, Massachusetts 01915-6101
Telephone: (978) 282-9590
Fax: (978) 283-2742
www.rockpub.com

10 9 8 7 6 5 4 3 2 1

© 2007 by One Club Publishing
All rights reserved. No part of this book may be reproduced in any form without written permission of the copyright owners. All images in this book have been reproduced with the knowledge and prior consent of the artists concerned, and no responsibility is accepted by producer, publisher, or printer for any infringement of copyright or otherwise, arising from the contents of this publication. Every effort has been made to ensure that credits accurately comply with information supplied. We apologize for any inaccuracies that may have occurred and will resolve inaccurate or missing information in a subsequent reprinting of the book.

INTRODUCTION

002 The One Club
003 Board of Directors
004 Message from the President
005 Message from the Jury Chair
007 Judges' Choice

PENCIL WINNERS

025 Banners: Fixed Space
035 Banners: Dynamic
042 Microsites
058 Web Sites
080 Brand Gaming
084 Wireless/Mobile Marketing
092 Email Marketing
098 Online Branded Content
104 New Media Innovation & Development
116 Other Interactive Digital Media
122 Integrated Branding Campaign
134 Self-Promotion

MERIT WINNERS

141 Banners: Fixed Space
152 Banners: Dynamic
163 Microsites
185 Web Sites
199 Brand Gaming
204 Wireless/Mobile Marketing
205 Email Marketing
207 Online Branded Content
217 New Media Innovation & Development
223 Other Interactive Digital Media
225 Integrated Branding Campaign
230 Self-Promotion

INDEX

235

THE ONE CLUB

The One Club exists to champion and promote excellence in advertising and design in all its forms. It is the world's foremost non-profit organization devoted to elevating creative work in the industry. It seeks to celebrate the legacy of creative advertising and to use that legacy to inspire future generations. The One Club is the 'keeper of the flame' for advertising creatives. The One Show remains the pinnacle of achievement by providing a showcase of the world's best work, and by inviting collaboration among individuals that are actively developing outstanding work.

The One Club exists to educate and inspire students of the business, and benefit the next generation through scholarships, portfolio reviews and annual student exhibitions and competitions.

And finally, The One Club exists to inspire clients to seek the rewards that come with calculated risks and new ideas. As long as great ideas are allowed to take form, The One Club will continue to exist to encourage and promote them.

BOARD OF DIRECTORS

David Baldwin (Chairman of the Board)
McKinney/Durham

Arthur Bijur (Vice Chairman)
Cliff Freeman and Partners/New York

Kevin Roddy (Treasurer/Corporate Secretary)
Bartle Bogle Hegarty/New York

David Apicella
Ogilvy & Mather/New York

Rossana Bardales
Mother/London

Jeff Benjamin
Crispin Porter + Bogusky/Miami

Rick Boyko
VCU Adcenter/Richmond

Joe Duffy
Duffy & Partners/Minneapolis

Kara Goodrich
BBDO/New York

Norm Grey
The Creative Circus/Atlanta

Jan Leth
Ogilvy & Mather/New York

Kerri Martin
Auburn Hills, Michigan

José Mollá
la comunidad/Miami

Deborah Morrison
University of Oregon/Eugene

Jim Mountjoy
Loeffler Ketchum Mountjoy/Charlotte

Kevin Proudfoot
Wieden + Kennedy/New York

Steve Sandstrom
Sandstrom Design/Portland

Luke Sullivan
GSD&M/Austin

Joyce King Thomas
McCann Erickson/New York

MESSAGE FROM THE PRESIDENT

KEVIN SWANEPOEL
President/The One Club

We are working in one of the most exciting but uncharted periods in advertising.

More than ever, today's advertising needs to be engaging, entertaining and relevant, or it will succumb to the attention deficit disorder of today's multitasking consumer.

New media outlets and channels are coming to market more frequently than ever before, making it possible for advertisers to create branded content in the form of games, videos and movies. This new communication entertains and allows one-on-one interaction with the consumer and the brand.

The new generation of tech-savvy consumers has a firm grip on the remote control. They are able to customize and program the content they want to have pushed to them in this changing media landscape.

The One Club recognizes the very best of good advertising in whatever form it is presented. As an organization, we are constantly seeking ways to accurately reflect the advertising market and be relevant. In 1998, we were the first organization to introduce a separate awards show dedicated to honoring the very best of interactive advertising. One Show Interactive is the most prestigious new media award in advertising today.

MESSAGE FROM THE JURY CHAIR

PJ PEREIRA
Jury Chair

On the 10th anniversary of One Show Interactive, we celebrate ideas that brought interactive thinking to virtually all forms of communication: traditional advertising, promotions, PR, events.

This was the year when websites controlled shadows on the streets, talked to mobile phones and showed what those robots were doing on the streets.

The year that interactive advertising took the lead and invented stories that changed products, created media opportunities and actually led multi-platform campaigns that would never be possible before the digital age.

After an entire week together, all of us, members of the jury, had the clear impression that we haven't just selected the best work being done around the world.

We actually witnessed ideas that have made history.

JUDGES' CHOICE
PG: 07-23

INTERACTIVE JUDGES

PJ Pereira (Chair)
AKQA/San Francisco

Daniel Bonner
AKQA/London

Heike Brockmann
Scholz & Volkmer/Wiesbaden

Martin Cedergren
AKQA/Amsterdam

Meera Chandra
Tribal DDB/Mumbai

Ben Clapp
Tribal DDB/London

Marco de Boer
Artmiks/Amsterdam

Sam de Volder
These Days/Antwerp

Pedro Gravena
DDB Brasil/ São Paulo

Ken Hamm
Manner Maker Media/New York

Naoki Ito
GT/Tokyo

Ian Kovalik
Mekanism/San Francisco

Nick Law
R/GA/New York

Stefan Lindfors
Stefan Lindfors/Helsinki

Gustav Martner
Daddy/Gothenburg

Will McGinness
Goodby Silverstein & Partners/San Francisco

Peter Moss
Ogilvy Worldwide/Singapore

Edu Pou
Crispin Porter + Bogusky/Miami

Robert Rasmussen
R/GA/New York

Fernanda Romano
Lowe/New York

Liz Sivell
Profero/London

Rafa Soto
Herraiz Soto & Co./Barcelona

Ulises Valencia
Grupo W/Saltillo

Adam Whitehouse
Stonewall/Cape Town

Robert Wong
Arnold/Boston

JUDGES' CHOICE

DANIEL BONNER
AKQA/London

Cisco Systems/Cisco Booming
This was a breath of fresh air. A simple, single-minded experience and a genuinely inspired and inventive demonstration of engaging the user with the input device—your voice. Many have attempted this territory with what can only be described as a clunky and plonky series of dialogue boxes and pop-ups to activate microphones and test if it works and blah blah blah. But this was executed with charm, elegance and it worked. More so that I told people about it, it must have been good.

Audi/Control Email
Aaahhh yes the 'make a compelling and engaging email' brief. I'm all for championing the underdog, the detail, the overlooked and the easily dismissed, and so in an interactive world of rich media, video branded content and the broadband revolution, it was good to see some attention being paid to what is still the most used, and in some part, most underrated media—the humble email. This scroll-fest for Audi caught me off guard and made me smile. A simple message, handled beautifully.

JUDGES' CHOICE

MARTIN CEDERGREN
AKQA/Amsterdam

Optimo/Form::Process
E-commerce hasn't yet reached the same standard of quality as seen in many other categories. It plays a very essential role though.

The work for Optimo is a good push forward for the whole industry. It´s an online shop selling records mainly to club DJs and the website does not only sell music, but lets the visitor enjoy it as well.

It´s an excellent piece of work and a given bookmark for every music lover around!

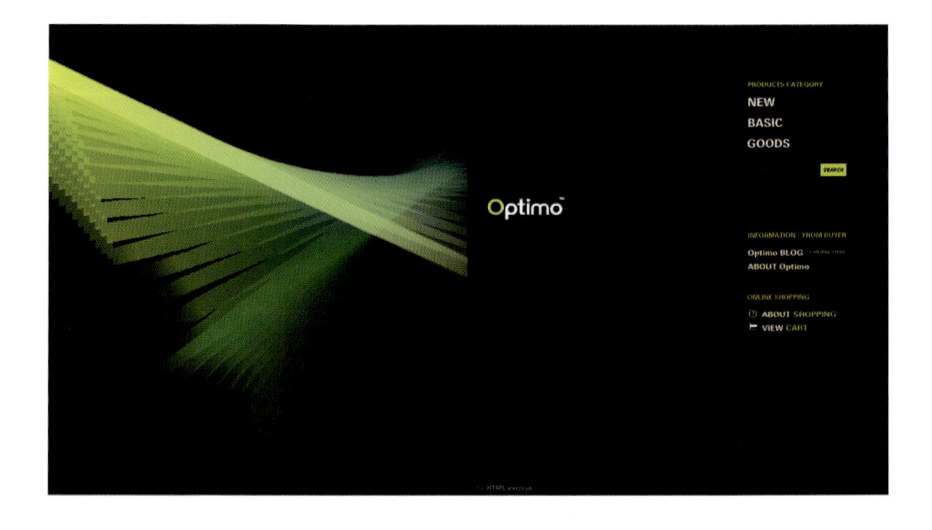

JUDGES' CHOICE

MEERA CHANDRA
Tribal DDB/Mumbai

Nike/Nike+

To me by far the most seamless integration of technology, user-friendliness and sticky experience is Nike+. I think it took a lot of guts and effort to straddle technologies in order that the runner could compete with his own best, with those who run the same circuit and indeed strangers across the world who share the same passion. The brand values captured are so core to the Nike DNA that it all just adds up beautifully. You just have no excuses to … well … run out of!

Burger King/Whopperettes

Burger King's Whopperettes is a personal favorite—the execution has done complete justice to an idea so simple and yet so brilliant in thought.

The opera is just the right setting for a high-appetite-appeal performance that reaches a crescendo in the form of a perfect Whopperette.

Have it your way, to my mind, is simply crafted but layered with a lot of attitude.

Diesel/Heidies

Another example of disruptive techniques working well in the interactive space is the Heidies. The creative leap of hijacking one's own brand site and making it into a multi-camera-enabled, reality-show-style, user-interface-area boggles the mind. What a wacky web idea and what a brilliant demonstration of brand attitude!

An observation: I do believe three brands really hit the high notes this year: Nike, Burger King and VW. It has been a showing of consistent quality across geographies and variants and it can be only attributed to a firm belief in the interactive space and a passion to own it with brand presence.

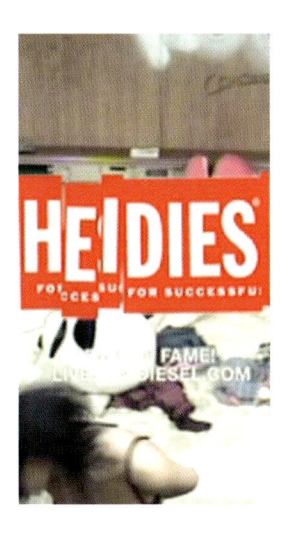

JUDGES' CHOICE

BEN CLAPP
Tribal DDB/London

Microsoft/Clearification
One of advertising's key roles is changing brand perception. And when it comes to that challenge, I can't think of many harder tasks than that of changing the perception of Microsoft to cynical hardware techies. Yet somehow, through its wit, humanity and charm, this digital campaign does exactly that. Fantastic stuff.

ROBERT RASMUSSEN
R/GA/New York

Microsoft/Clearification
My Judge's Choice for 2007 is Clearification.com for Microsoft Vista. This multiple Merit winner failed to Pencil in our show, which is a shame in my opinion. Judging Interactive can be a dreary process. Long days are spent in dark rooms rooms sifing through entry after entry hoping to find gold. For every Nike+ there are fifty executions that barely deserve a minus much less a plus.

Clearification stood out. While it does little to explain the benefits of the new fantabulous Windows Vista operating system, it did what it needed to. It convinced me to spend some time with a brand I had yet been unwilling to unless forced. And I am better for it. The entire site is beautiful, functions well and is full of content I enjoyed. Demetri Martin, the center of the Clearification universe, is charismatic, both animated and as an actual person.

So did I learn more about their software? No, but I already know all about Vista because I do not live under a rock and have seen many elements of the media blitz. But did I enjoy the time I spent and think better of them for creating it to entertain me, yes. If that wasn't the brief it should have been. Nice job McCann/Mekanism.

JUDGES' CHOICE

MARCO DE BOER
Artmiks/Amsterdam

Diesel/Heidies

How on Earth do you get young people to get excited over a new brand of underwear, when they've been tired of seeing Marky Mark-like six packs for years?

By adding a healthy dose of naughty fantasies to a smart, YouTube-like approach for a fake guerrilla campaign.

Ingredients: two very hot exotic girls, one not too unattractive male model, a hotel room, a camcorder and an internet connection. At times it feels a bit over arranged, but the tension just jumps off the screen. The Heidies, a showcase for a well thought out, online campaign for the youngsters. That's how.

JUDGES' CHOICE

SAM DE VOLDER
These Days/Antwerp

Burger King/HuckinChicken.com
OK. So chicken burgers are for pussies and beef burgers are for real men. But how to convince those men to try a chicken burger anyway? Throw in a wet T-shirt competition for chicks? Too obvious. Organize a chicken fight? Done that. But hey, somebody thought, let's go for a stunt chicken on a motorbike, that'll get the testosterone flowing. And so it went, and the site aired clip after clip of the chicken performing amazing stunts, each video making you curious about the next one. To top it off they came up with a smart viral (ouch—ugly word) approach: the most spectacular stunt would only be released if the Huckin' Chicken managed to entertain an audience of one million viewers.

Weave Toshi/Daydream
In a world full of user-generated content, Web 2.0 and flash-movies that take an hour to load, this small site feels like a poem. A wonderful and beautifully crafted piece for Weave Toshi, a headwear manufacturer/retailer based in Tokyo and London. With a very simple interface they showcase their hats in a piece called "Daydream." It's as simple as that. Intriguing, clever and definitely a different way to show people what a product is about.

Unilever, Dove/Daughters
Year after year most of the emotional pieces in award shows appear in the charity category. But for consumer brands, you don't see them as often (to say the least). This piece for Dove certainly struck a chord. It's a small film (part of a series) in which girls talk about the pressure of growing up in a beauty-obsessed society. Maybe it's because I have a daughter? Hey, maybe my female side is over-developed? Who knows. But it sure shut me up while watching it, goose-pimples included.

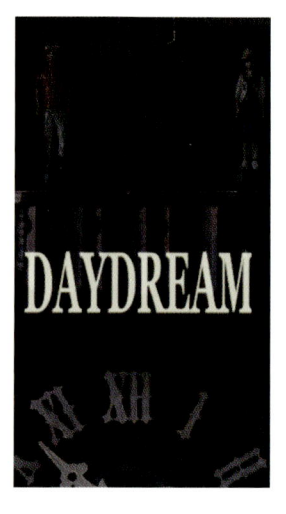

JUDGES' CHOICE

PEDRO GRAVENA
DDB Brasil/São Paulo

Nike/Nike+
Somebody once said "the magic is in the product," but it is not enough for good advertising today. The products are very similar and it is becoming more and more difficult to find that magic.

But the Nike+ project goes much further. They created one product to sell another and good advertising to sell both. This is really new and it is great entertainment with great interactivity (and that is the point). The shoes interact with the iPod, the iPod interacts with the website, the website interacts with people, and people interact with each other. It looks great.

NASP/Unflinching Triumph
It is a very brave project. The brand is everywhere, but neither the product or the logo ever appear. The surprising fact is that the consumers make that connection. Yeah. They connected that strange sport with the Red Bull brand without any help.

JUDGES' CHOICE

NAOKI ITO
GT/Tokyo

Nike/Nike+
I run every week.
I have watched the visual image and I like how it works, I love the idea, design, and the flash movement.

The purpose of the interaction is to visualize one's body sensation, and so to me the work is very physical.

The Coca-Cola Company/Burning Calories - Sleeping
Sleeping is "loading" and "burning".
The banner is so funny but very intelligent.

JUDGES' CHOICE

IAN KOVALIK
Mekanism/San Francisco

Nike/Nike+
Nike+ deserves every bit of praise it's received. It's beautiful, easy to use, and is arguably the first website designed for humans. Specifically, the ones that need to go outside, get sunburned, get sweaty, and run around. When I go there, I'm in the comfort zone. The designers have somehow wrangled a lot of information and displayed it in an efficient little window. At the same time, they've managed to distill the goodness of the two brands into a digital component that is as critical to the overall system of Nike+ as the two famous physical ones.

Uniqlo/Uniqlo.com
Without having heard of the brand before, I became an instant fan of Uniqlo thanks to the site's focused design, lightning-fast download, and rich user experience. Not many other fashion/clothing brands can boast of a site that turns their wares into pixel-based fine art. It's a must-see. The blend of commerce and technical coolness spoke volumes, and the grandness of the 'Experience' module made me want to keep exploring. With so much on the web to choose from, Uniqlo found an unforgettable way to sell clothes and dimensionalize a brand online.

Weave Toshi/Daydream
Any site that combines live-action models wearing hats and living in a darkly lit, Kafka-esque giant cuckoo clock deserves attention. I also like how focused the site is—no heavy text to wade through or navigation to size up. Just a mad-hatter's hat show. An excellent, immersive experience that delivers an unexpected level of imagination and production value.

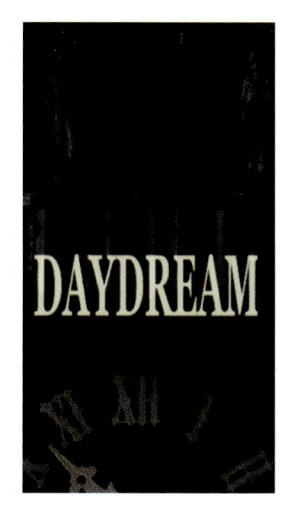

JUDGES' CHOICE

NICK LAW
R/GA/New York

Burger King/Xbox Games
I'm not much of a gamer, and I've never actually played any of the BK games; but it's pretty hard to ignore this entry's ingenious success. We belong to an industry that makes a habit of getting in people's way and annoying them; so it's quite a feat to get customers to actually buy and enjoy marketing.

Smirnoff/Tea Partay
Unlike with traditional interruptive media, narrative on the web exists as a destination in itself; thus it needs to be uncommonly compelling. This preppy rap video made me laugh so much I peed lemon tea.

Uniqlo/Uniqlo.com
Ah, websites. Remember them? Since the traditional agencies have hijacked the award shows, interactive pieces deep enough to require a site map have slowly disappeared. This beautifully crafted site is not some feeble extension of an offline campaign, has no "viral" punch line and actually has the audacity to reward exploration.

JUDGES' CHOICE

GUSTAV MARTNER
Daddy/Gothenburg

RememberSegregation.org/White and Black Banner
My time as a One Show Interactive 2007 juror got me a bit confused. The stuff I've been going on about since we started Daddy seemed to be fixed. As we went through thousands of entries from around the world, no one could avoid noticing that the ideas were cleverly using all of the medium's features, the budgets have grown huge and production values are off the chart. And digital campaigns are not only well integrated with the rest of the world—they are actually going beyond digital and changing the real world. Just look at Nike+ by R/GA: Where does the product end and the marketing start? Or how about the King Games by Crispin Porter + Bogusky, Xbox-games selling burgers in the real world—using characters from their previous online campaigns. What's digital? What's IRL?

Time has caught up with online advertising. And maybe that is why I feel so strong about the remembersegregation.org banner. No fancy interactive stuff. No big budgets. Just plain black on white copy. I guess traditional advertising has caught up with me.

JUDGES' CHOICE

PETE MOSS
Ogilvy Worldwide/Singapore

Audi/Control Email
Odd, that of all the wonderful work, it was an email that really caught my attention. Like most people, I write so many that I don't stop to think about the possibilities.

This piece of work for Audi is inspired. It was a communication sent out to Audi owners inviting them to register for the Audi Driving Experience in Finland. Basically, how to drive on ice. The email is a continual line of tire-tracks in the snow. Like most people, I started scrolling down in the hope of finding something and shot right past the message.

Point made. Stopping on ice isn't easy. It quickly, simply and effectively demonstrates the product. Fabulous.

The Coca-Cola Company/SubLYMONal
From the incredibly simple to the incredibly complex—that was the Sublymonal campaign, an arsenal of subliminal advertising and conspiracy theories. I think the campaign touched on almost every online channel (radio, podcasts, blogs, sites, banners). Quite simply, a roller-coaster challenge that was thrown out and picked up on by the audience.

The interesting thing about this campaign is that it probably could not have been solved by any one person and put its faith in the strength of online communities and natural collaboration to make it a success. Smart stuff.

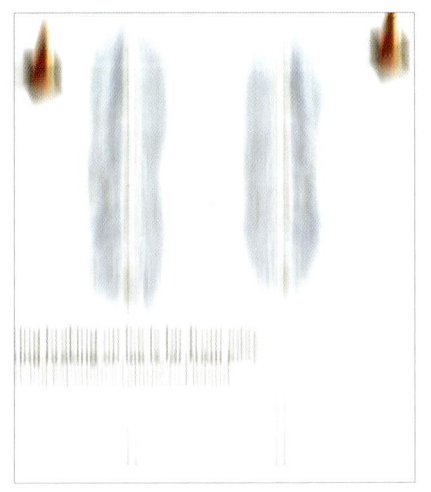

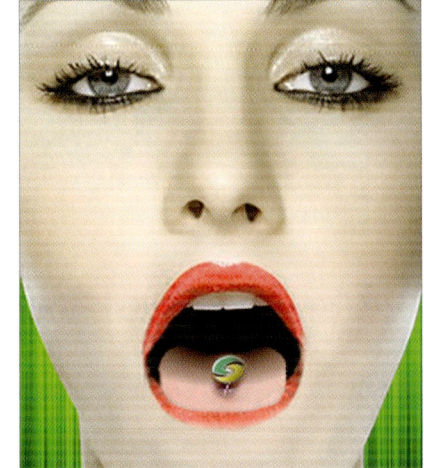

JUDGES' CHOICE

LIZ SIVELL
Profero/London

Microsoft/Big Shadow
Well, what can I say? I felt like a kid in a candy store judging at this year's One Show Interactive Awards. I was so inspired by the work, often kicking myself thinking "Damn, I wish I had thought of that!"

Given my obsession for Nike and Apple, you'd expect my obvious choice to be Nike+, an outstanding user experience that goes beyond the computer—a complex platform with a simple interface. However, my actual choice would definitely have to be "Big Shadow," Microsoft's Interactive Wall for their Xbox 360 game, Blue Dragon. I am a real evangelist when it comes to digital experiences that break away from traditional mediums, and this was a fantastic example. It's playful and offers a deep engagement by having magnified shadows of ordinary people in town projected onto the Shibuya Prime building, a vast 40 meter tall wall—just a bigger monitor really!

I hope next year brings some more exciting projects like these.

JUDGES' CHOICE

RAFA SOTO
Herraiz Soto & Co./Barcelona

Weave Toshi/Daydream

Interactivity should reinvent the narrative. And advertising has always been a narrative laboratory. So I'm relieved to see someone exploring and trying out new ideas as with the weavetoshi.co.jp piece. My immediate impression was: "Hey, there's something different here!" Then you really dive into a new and evocative world. Not a word. Not an instruction. You just turn the mouse clockwise, and the poetry comes to you even if you are not in the mood for poetry (which is the 99.99% of the time). Sensitive production, great idea, and what's best: inventing narrative. And that—changing your mood, making you travel and connecting you with the brand on an emotional level—is what advertising is all about.

ULISES VALENCIA
Grupo W/Saltillo

Weave Toshi/Daydream

I love this case because it represents an ideal of advertising. A great idea, wonderful production, and a powerful and very convincing message. The site works very simply without any menu, and the concept of TIME is a gorgeous element to play with. The user just moves the mouse in circles in a clockwise direction to move forward in a dreamlike way; or the other way around to go backward in time.

The product, a beautiful hat collection, is shown to be appreciated. There is no copy, no button or any additional information. There are no logos, prices, or shopping carts. Just an experience full of magic that grabs the user's attention and generates desire.

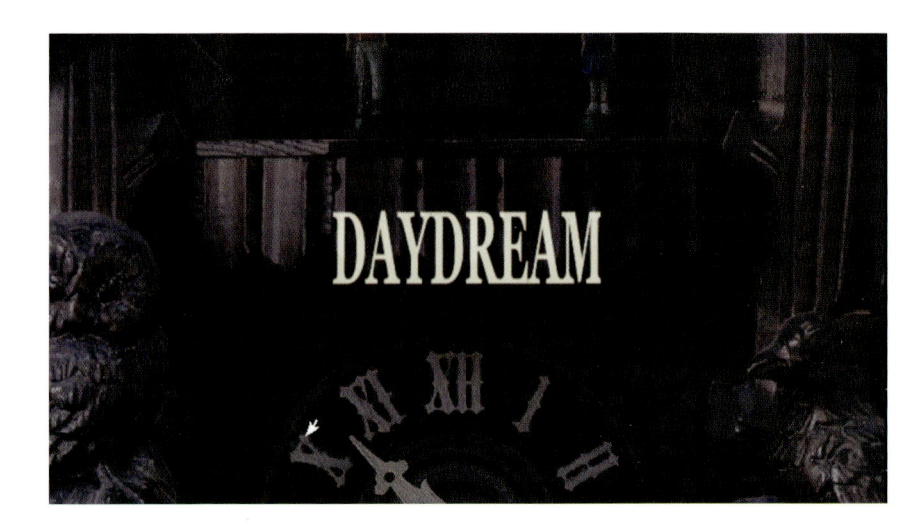

JUDGES' CHOICE

ADAM WHITEHOUSE
Stonewall /Cape Town

Nike/The Chain

Consumer generated content has become a must-have in any big brand's arsenal of marketing tools, yet most CGC campaigns backfire in some way, or miss the point completely.

This is a fantastic example of a brand taking its strategy and turning it into a community-building platform that engages and connects its consumers (literally). Through this campaign, Nike has achieved the perfect mix of brand engagement and viral buzz, and the beauty of it is that it's so SIMPLE!

Creativity in an interactive context is about more than awesome design and amazing technology—ANYTHING is possible. The beauty lies in the simple creative concept and using these tools to make the concept come to life. Congrats to Nike and Framfab for coming up with such a great idea and bringing it to life.

ROBERT WONG
Arnold/Boston

Nike/The Chain

Of everything I saw this year, Nike Chain touched me the deepest. It made me feel part of something bigger. It made me feel part of something more beautiful. It made me feel good about being a human being. Mainly, it made me feel happy.

To the beautiful people who came up with this, thank you.

PENCIL WINNERS
PG:025-139

BANNERS - FIXED SPACE: BUSINESS TO CONSUMER - SINGLE

THE SWEDE LIFE

Sven, Inga, a giant meatball and a wandering discoball lead you through the land of endless days.

GOLD

AGENCY
Farfar/Stockholm

CLIENT
Visit Sweden

ART DIRECTOR
Johan Ohrn

WRITER
Tom Eriksen

DESIGNER
Per Hansson

PROGRAMMER
Bo Gustavsson

INFORMATION ARCHITECT
Marielle Lundqvist

PRODUCTION COMPANIES
Colony
Freecloud
Harakiri

CREATIVE DIRECTOR
Nicke Bergstrom

ANNUAL ID
07001N

URL
www.farfar.se/awards/oneshow2007/stockholm2/

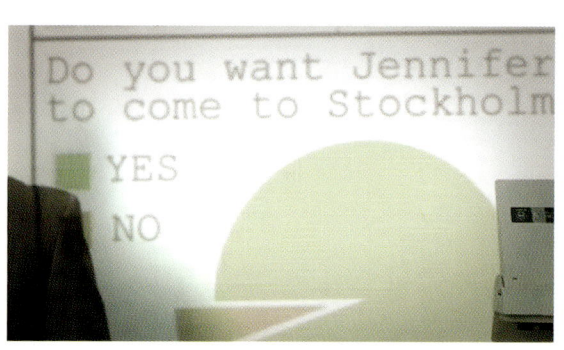

"Stockholm the Musical" lures the British into taking a trip to Sweden through song and dance, rhapsodizing about the nation's great food, architecture, nightlife and shopping. The musical is customizable, with most English names available to be sung into the video. If your name isn't on the list, you can always choose from other monikers like "Tight-fisted Brit," or "Sexyhunk." And if that isn't enough to get you going, the secret weapon is brought out: a Swedish bikini model.

An infectiously cheery and slightly nostalgic jaunt through a Sweden both traditional and modern, wholesome and sexy, "Stockholm" indeed shows how Swede it is.

BANNERS - FIXED SPACE: BUSINESS TO CONSUMER - SINGLE

GUTTER FINGER
Germophobes, this one's for you.

SILVER

AGENCY
*AgênciaClick/
São Paulo*

CLIENT
Brastemp

ART DIRECTOR
Fabiano de Queiroz

WRITER
Jones Krahl Jr.

PROGRAMMERS
*Andre Brunetta
Andre Cardozo*

CREATIVE DIRECTOR
Ricardo Figueira

ANNUAL ID
07002N

URL
*www.kodoish.com/
2006/multibras/
purificador/en*

The new water purifier from Brastemp has a modern triple-filtering system that eliminates all bacteria, serving utterly clean water. This banner lets you play with a stream of running water, trying to catch what is written behind: "This water was 100% bacteria free til you put your finger in it."

BANNERS - FIXED SPACE: BUSINESS TO CONSUMER - SINGLE

FRANKS OF FURY
Non-stick pan helps even the wurst player.

BRONZE

AGENCY
F/Nazca Saatchi & Saatchi/
São Paulo

CLIENT
Arno

ART DIRECTOR
Vagner Godoi

WRITER
Cristiane Gribel

DESIGNER
William Queen

PROGRAMMER
Paulo Pacheco
André Cinicola

INFORMATION ARCHITECTS
Alexandre Bessa
Paula Obata

CREATIVE DIRECTORS
Fabio Simões Pinto
Fabio Fernandes

ANNUAL ID
07003N

URL
www.adversiting.net/2006/18/

The idea came during a fun late night cooking session. We mixed it with an old Pong obsession and the concept came through naturally.

BANNERS - FIXED SPACE: BUSINESS TO CONSUMER - SINGLE

LOOSING FACE
The G-force is with you.

BRONZE

AGENCY
glue/London

CLIENT
MINI

ART DIRECTORS
Simon Lloyd
Christine Tuner

WRITERS
Simon Lloyd
Christine Turner

DESIGNERS
Leon Ostle
Matt Verity

MULTIMEDIA ARTIST
Simon Cam

CONTENT STRATEGIST
Miranda Ross

PRODUCTION COMPANY
Upset TV

CREATIVE DIRECTOR
Seb Royce

ANNUAL ID
07004N

URL
www.bestofg.com/oneshow/mini_overboost.php

The brief was to launch the new generation of MINI's online as part of an overall campaign. November is a tricky month to launch a car, and the challenge was to ensure that the audience understand the key product differences between the new model and the current—whilst delivering a strong brand building solution.

"Boost" uses cutting edge interactive video to again give immensely satisfying interaction, while also using incredibly funny characters.

BANNERS - FIXED SPACE: BUSINESS TO CONSUMER - SINGLE

FOOL HOUSE

A cast of characters ups the ante on online gambling ads.

SILVER

AGENCY
Lean Mean Fighting Machine/London

CLIENT
Virgin Games

WRITERS
Zoe Hough
Claire Baker

DESIGNERS
Jonas Persson
Mark Beacock

PROGRAMMER
Dave Cox

CREATIVE DIRECTORS
Sam Ball
Dave Bedwood

ANNUAL ID
07005N

URL
www.leanmean
fightingmachine.co.uk/
oneshow/virgin/

Virgin Casino wanted their online advertising to look different from the competition, with a feeling of fun and irreverent 'Virgin-ness' that is present in much of their brand work. Furthermore they were interested in the prospect of people interacting with the advertising and getting a bit of fun out of it for their trouble.

We started by looking at their competition. Flashing 'WIN WIN' signs; coins raining down from the sky; cherries and bells everywhere. Every ad looked the same but was promoting a different Casino. It was remarkable. We were witnessing possibly the worst advertising on planet Earth and all we had to do was stand out from it. We had hit the jackpot.

BANNERS - FIXED SPACE: BUSINESS TO CONSUMER - SINGLE

SILENCING THE SQUEAKS
What to do when noise annoys.

BRONZE

AGENCY
DDB Brasil/
São Paulo

CLIENT
Henkel

ART DIRECTOR
Sandro Rosa

WRITER
Rafael Taiar

PROGRAMMER
Wagner Nunes

CREATIVE DIRECTORS
Sergio Valente
Mauricio Mazzariol

ANNUAL ID
07006N

URL
www.judgehere.com/
soundoff/honeymoon/
index.html

These banners employ the very standard and almost inconspicuous "sound off" button that appears on most interactive pieces with an audio track. The noises—the annoying creaks of an old bed, the grating hack of a rusty swing, and the interminable drone of an electric fan—will drive you to click that button pronto lest you try to jump out the window. As always, Lub—no, Super Lub, will save the day.

BANNERS - FIXED SPACE: PUBLIC SERVICE/NON-PROFIT/EDUCATIONAL - SINGLE

DEFOREST FOR THE TREES

A classic board game wherein the only solution is to stop playing (with nature).

GOLD

AGENCY
AlmapBBDO/
São Paulo

CLIENT
Greenpeace

ART DIRECTOR
Guiga Giacomo

WRITER
Moacyr Netto

MULTIMEDIA ARTISTS
Marcelo Mandaji
Z4

PROGRAMMER
Rodrigo França

CREATIVE DIRECTOR
Sergio Mugnaini

ANNUAL ID
07007N

URL
200.185.34.146/
awards/2007/
greenpeace/peg/arq/
index.html

What has man made with his intelligence?

Every day 3,700,000 tree ploughs are cut and removed from the Amazon. This piece was created to alert the population about the dangers of human interference in nature, which has led to the extinction of important species, and is the main cause of climate change.

The banner works as a game well known in Brazil, called "Peg Solitaire." The game's objective is to eliminate all the pegs on the board, until there is only one left.

Greenpeace was very satisfied with the result of this ad. This banner was adapted in many countries and was also executed into other formats, like mobile phone games and touchscreen monitors in Brazil airports.

WHEN JIM CROW FLEW
Black and white brings the message home, again.

> **WHITE READERS** — CLICK HERE —   **COLORED READERS** — CLICK HERE —

> **WHITE READERS** — CLICK HERE —   RememberSegregation.org   **COLORED READERS** — CLICK HERE —

Memory of Dr. Martin Luther King and the civil rights struggle in the U.S. has been fading. The goal was to revive a visceral connection to the civil rights era and engage people in the reason for honoring the legacy of Dr. King. The solution: the world's first segregated advertising campaign which allows our audience to experience discrimination firsthand and feel the sting of "separate but equal."

SILVER

AGENCY
DDB/Seattle

CLIENT
Remember Segregation.org

ART DIRECTORS
Jason Stanfield
Ray Page

WRITER
Keith Anderson

PROGRAMMER
Mike Swartz

CONTENT STRATEGIST
Aaron Rosenstein

CREATIVE DIRECTORS
John Livengood
Eric Gutierrez

ANNUAL ID
07008N

URL
w3.sea.ddb.com/clientdoor/mlk/mlk_bannerad.html

BANNERS - FIXED SPACE: PUBLIC SERVICE/NON-PROFIT/EDUCATIONAL - SINGLE

SEE CREATURES
...while they're real.

BRONZE

AGENCY
Leo Burnett/
Sydney

CLIENT
World Wildlife Fund

ART DIRECTORS
Kieran Ots
Michael Spirkovski

WRITERS
Vicky Burrough
Grant McAloon

CREATIVE DIRECTOR
Mark Collis

ANNUAL ID
07009N

URL
www.leoburnett.com.au/awards/work/digital/turtle.html

"The Future is Man Made" campaign asks us to imagine a world where many endangered animals are extinct, and all we can see are artificial replicas. The banner opens with a turtle in what appears to be a natural photograph. But when we drag across the banner, our perspective changes—we look behind the scenes and see that the turtle is no more than a wooden prop on a barren ocean floor. The message: we're all responsible for the world we leave for the next generation—the future we make is up to us.

BANNERS - DYNAMIC: BUSINESS TO CONSUMER - SINGLE

POSITIONS GALORE
Get creative, shake things up.

GOLD

AGENCY
Jung von Matt/
Stuttgart

CLIENT
Kabel Deutschland
RedX Club

WRITER
Matthias Kubitz

MULTIMEDIA ARTIST
Kaspar Zwirner

PROGRAMMERS
Oliver Mueller
Stefanie Hezinger

CREATIVE DIRECTORS
Michael Zoelch
Holger Oehrlich

ANNUAL ID
07010N

URL
www.jvm.de/oneshow/
interactive/kamasutra

Sex used to sell. Unfortunately, the more sex there is, the less it is a guaranteed bestseller. Even more: since sex these days is virtually everywhere, it obviously has an even harder time selling itself. And that is how we come into the picture. With an idea for an online banner that was not only fun to play with, but also made sex the seller it used to be. And so, for the adult movie program of our client the RedX Club, ideas are simply the new Viagra.

BANNERS - DYNAMIC: BUSINESS TO CONSUMER - SINGLE

SNOOZE CONTROL
FedEx is about time.

BRONZE

AGENCY
Atmosphere BBDO/
New York

CLIENT
FedEx

ART DIRECTOR
Brett Simon

WRITER
John Heath

DESIGNER
Rob Seale

CREATIVE DIRECTOR
Cabot Norton

ANNUAL ID
07011N

URL
www.atmosphere
bbdo.comwork/2006/
assets/powernap_
728x90_v10.html

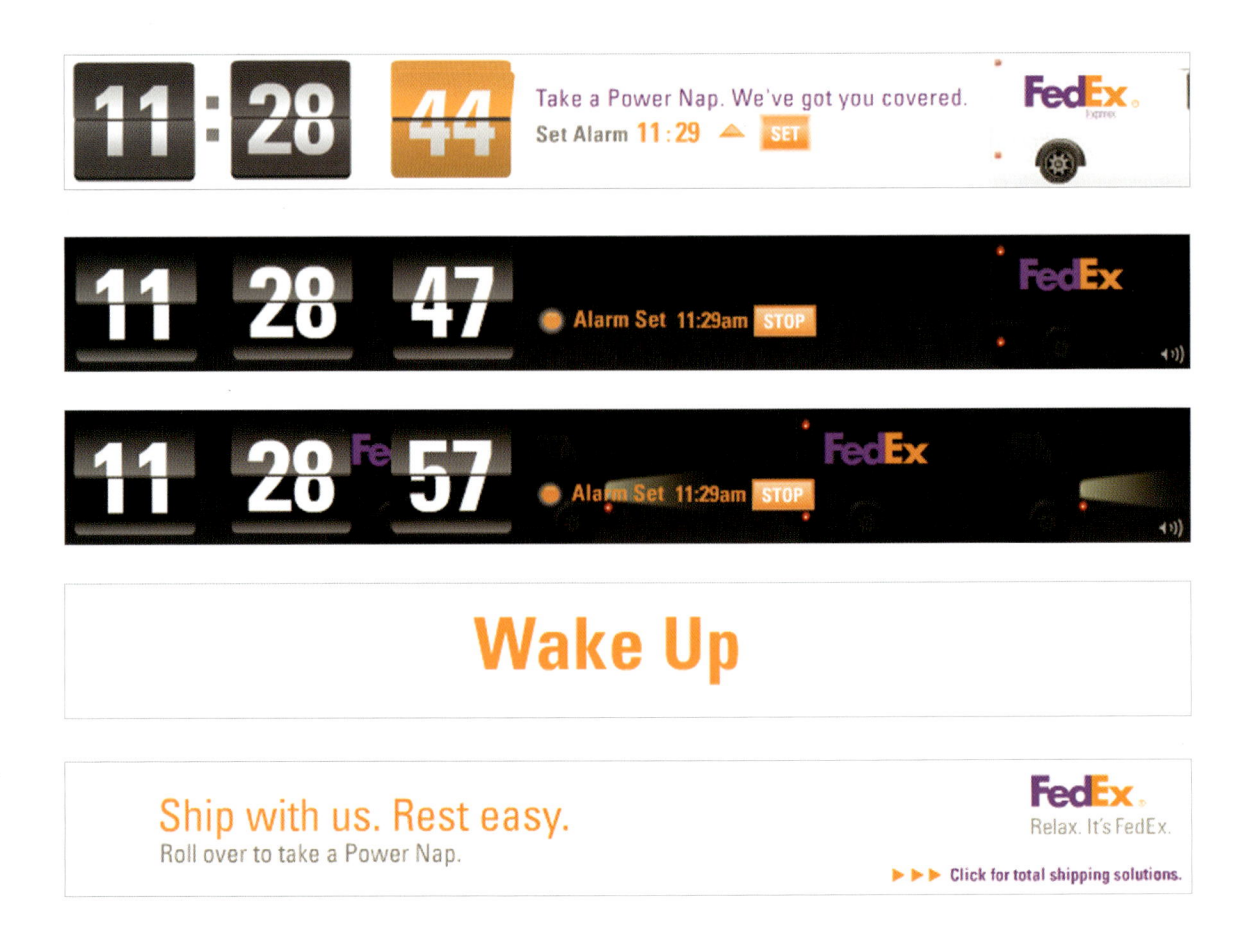

A clever little device, this banner takes the time from your computer's clock and lets you set an alarm, for say, when you're taking those micronaps at your desk. Just when you're dreamily lounging on a white sand beach, about to take that first sip of your piña colada, a truck comes and backs up all over your feet. Wake up.

BANNERS - DYNAMIC: BUSINESS TO CONSUMER - CAMPAIGN

AUTOBAHNDITS
Crispin playfully shows that these cars are mad fun, German Heritage or not.

GOLD

AGENCY
Crispin Porter + Bogusky/Miami

CLIENT
Volkswagen

ART DIRECTORS
DaYoung Ewart
James Martis
Thomas Rodgers

WRITER
Mike Howard

PRODUCTION COMPANIES
Zugara
Domani Studios

CREATIVE DIRECTORS
Alex Bogusky
Andrew Keller
Jeff Benjamin
Tony Calcao
Rob Strasberg

ANNUAL ID
07012N

URL
www.cpbgroup.com/awards/vwgtibanners.html

This banner campaign brought the Volkswagen GTI and its features to life and put the German pre-tuned car into the hands of users. Banners also featured headlines referencing the German Heritage, and performance of the GTI with lines such as "Fast as schnell," "German engineering in da haus," and "Auf Wiedersehen, sucka." During the first month of the campaign alone, GTI sales were nearly 80 percent above VW sales forecasts. In "Smoke Banner," users bring to life a simple and exhilerating burnout. In "Pinball," users launch themselves across the information superhighway quickly traveling out of the site they're on—and across sites like Yahoo, Maxim, eBay, MySpace—and then return to the site they started from. The "Paddleshifter Banner" puts the paddleshifting feature in the hands of users so they can race their GTI. The "Unpimp Banner" let users unpimp an auto.

BANNERS - DYNAMIC: BUSINESS TO CONSUMER - CAMPAIGN

CRASH TEST FUNNIES
Jetta makes accidents happy.

SILVER

AGENCY
Crispin Porter + Bogusky/Miami

CLIENT
Volkswagen

ART DIRECTORS
Kevin Koller
Da young Ewart

WRITER
Carl Corbitt

DESIGNER
Conor McCann

MULTIMEDIA ARTISTS
James Martis
Luis Santi

PRODUCTION COMPANY
Domani

CREATIVE DIRECTORS
Alex Bogusky
Andrew Keller
Jeff Benjamin
Tony Calcao
Rob Strasberg

ANNUAL ID
07013N

URL
www.cpbgroup.com/awards/vwjetta banners.html

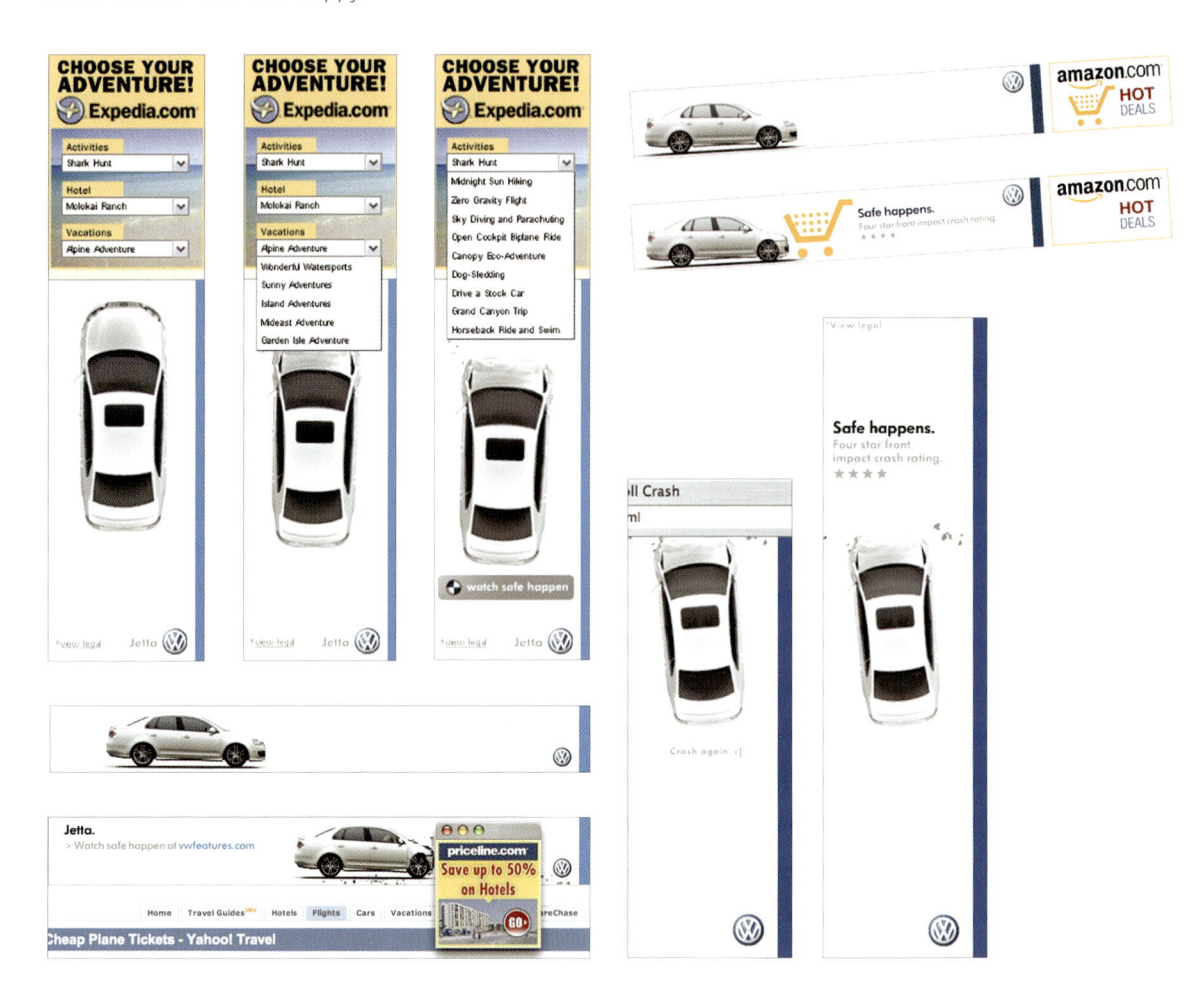

As a compliment to the "Safe Happens" campaign, these web banners appeared on the Internet providing unexpected impacts of their own. The impacts on the screen caught the attention of our target audience and left them with a singular message, "The Volkswagen Jetta ranks high in crash testing." This message struck a chord with prospective buyers. Sales jumped over 35 percent compared with a year earlier.

In "Pop-up," users get a quick demonstration of Jetta's 4-star rating in front impact crash testing. In the "Pull-Down Crash Banner," enticed by thrilling vacations like Shark Hunting, viewers are given a surprise demonstration of the safety features of a Jetta. With "Scroll", users create a crash test as they scroll down the page, offering yet another interactive example of how Volkswagen prepares for surprises by equipping every Jetta with class leading safety features. In "Shopping Cart," users are surprised when a Jetta rolls up, tilling the banner, and causing the shopping cart icon from the adjacent Amazon.com banner to roll into the front of the Jetta. A surprise with a message.

BANNERS - DYNAMIC: BUSINESS TO CONSUMER - CAMPAIGN

CLOSER
Familiar movie genres, just six times more familiar.

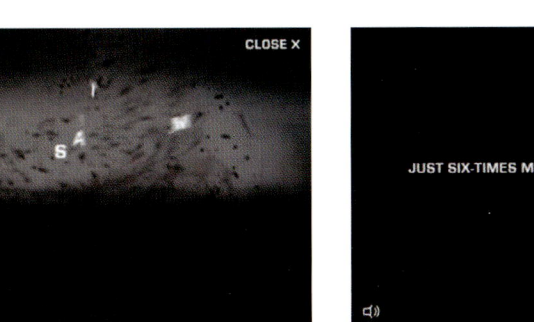

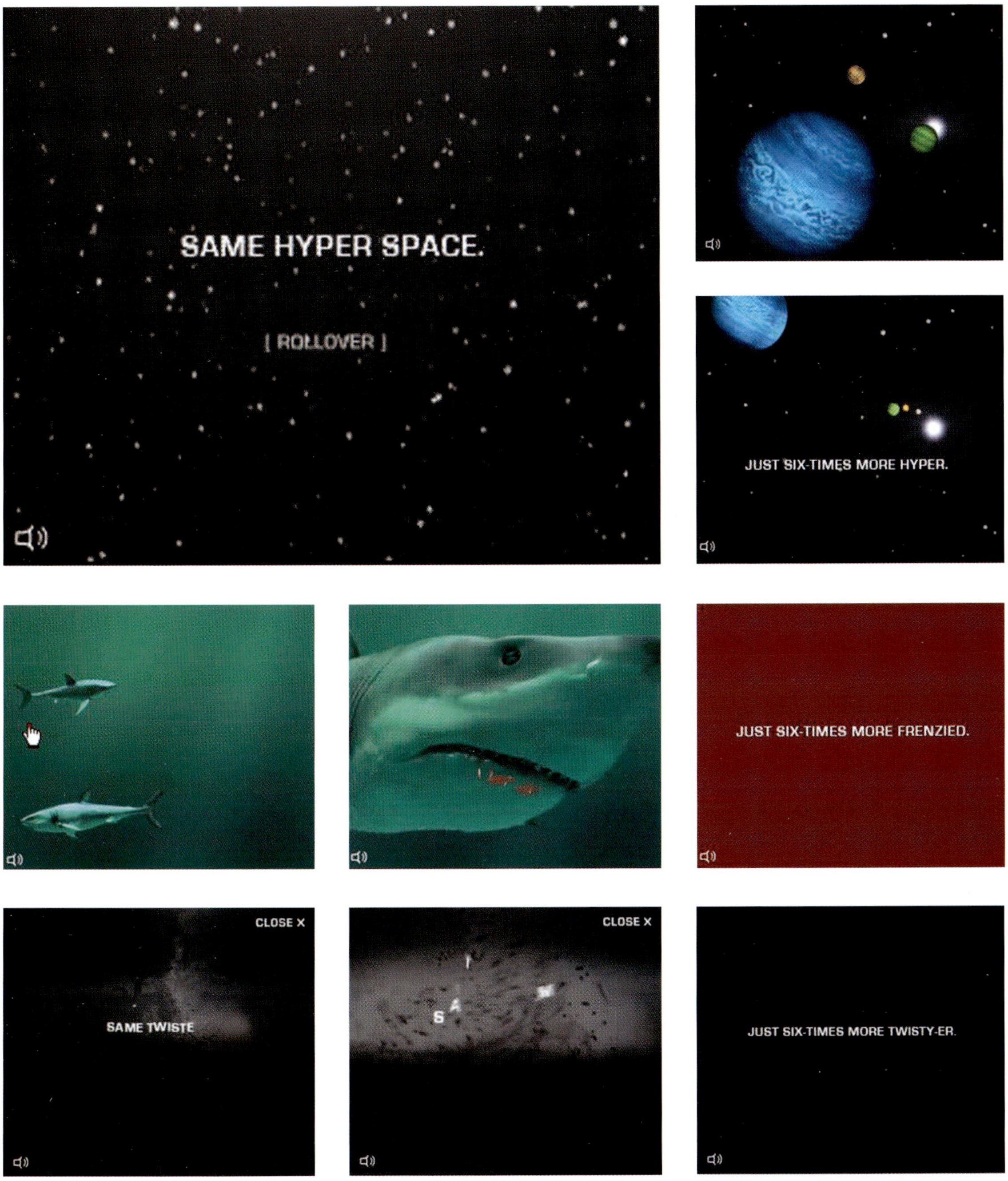

BRONZE

AGENCY
Goodby, Silverstein & Partners/San Francisco

CLIENT
HD DVD

ART DIRECTOR
Michael Coyne

WRITER
Spencer Riviera

CONTENT STRATEGISTS
Mike Geiger
Brit Charlebois

PRODUCTION COMPANY
Unit-9

CREATIVE DIRECTORS
Will McGinness
Ronny Northrop

ANNUAL ID
07014N

URL
www.unit9.com/banners/gsp/hddvd/

Remember the first time you watched Captain EO, and there were all these lasers shooting at the audience, and Michael Jackson dancing right up in your face was not as scary as the alien Supreme Leader who looked like she was about to jump off the screen and grab you with her wicked claws? Well, these banners for HD DVD kind of remind you of that.

BANNERS - DYNAMIC: PUBLIC SERVICE/NON-PROFIT/EDUCATIONAL - SINGLE

GORILLA WARFARE
A collective beast's call to action.

SILVER

AGENCY
CONTRAPUNTO/
Madrid

CLIENT
World Wildlife Fund

ART DIRECTOR
Alberto Barragán

WRITERS
Jaime Chávarri
Lis Torrón

PRODUCTION COMPANY
Booker

CREATIVE DIRECTORS
Antonio Montero
Juan Corrales
Iván de Dios
Jaime Chávarri

ANNUAL ID
07015N

URL
www.contrapunto.es/
oneshow2007/

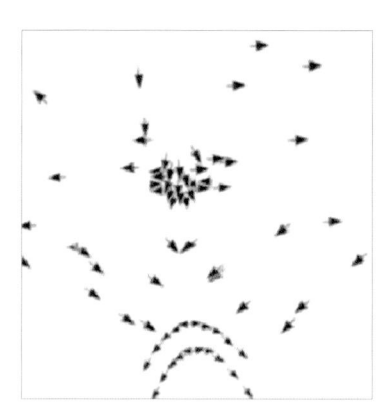

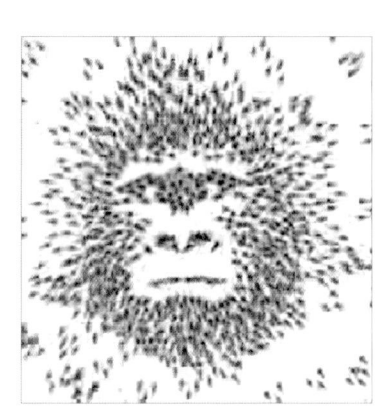

The World Wildlife Fund is an organization that fights for wildlife on a worldwide scale. Its basic strength is coordinating the action and energy of individuals who share the same vision. Its most recognized icon is the gorilla. This animation represents how the union of separate individuals can make the wildlife cause stronger. It requires only minimal interaction, a small effort that, combined with others, can generate great strength and power.

BANNERS - DYNAMIC: PUBLIC SERVICE/NON-PROFIT/EDUCATIONAL - SINGLE

IM A STRANGER
Online predators are no LOL matter.

BRONZE

AGENCY
Profero/London

CLIENT
COI/Home Office

ART DIRECTOR
Ian Owen

WRITER
James Taylor

DESIGNER
Stuart Peddie

CREATIVE DIRECTOR
Matt Powell

ANNUAL ID
07016N

URL
www.profero.com/cpoi_athome

The Home Office decided to take a completely new approach to child protection on the Internet, as research highlighted teenagers are aware of risks online but often do not adhere to safety rules promoted in previous campaigns. The key insight that came out of research is that children put themselves at risk of being targeted by paedophiles by treating "virtual friends" they meet online in the same way as close friends they know offline, without taking account of their age, personality and intentions. Therefore, the campaign aimed to change behaviour by getting children to start treating the Internet as part of the real world, with real consequences. It was vital to demonstrate why they should follow advice and not just to dictate to them.

COI reappointed Profero on behalf of the Home Office to develop a concept conveying a strong message of safety and awareness, to remind children of the potentially harsh consequences when giving out their personal information online. Profero created a campaign revolving around the strapline, "smart online, safe offline." Finding creative solutions that could be integrated into the Internet activity of 11 to 14 year olds, the ads appeared in environments where children chat with friends and socialize, such as mykindaplace.co.uk and Messenger.

Featuring a creepy figure with the face of an emoticon (a yellow smiley face) lurking menacingly, the campaign illustrates how easy it is for people to disguise their intentions and identity by hiding behind the writing style and iconography that children use online.

MICROSITES: BUSINESS TO CONSUMER

WEAVE DREAMER
Qubibi puts on his mad cap to create this dark and disorienting time piece.

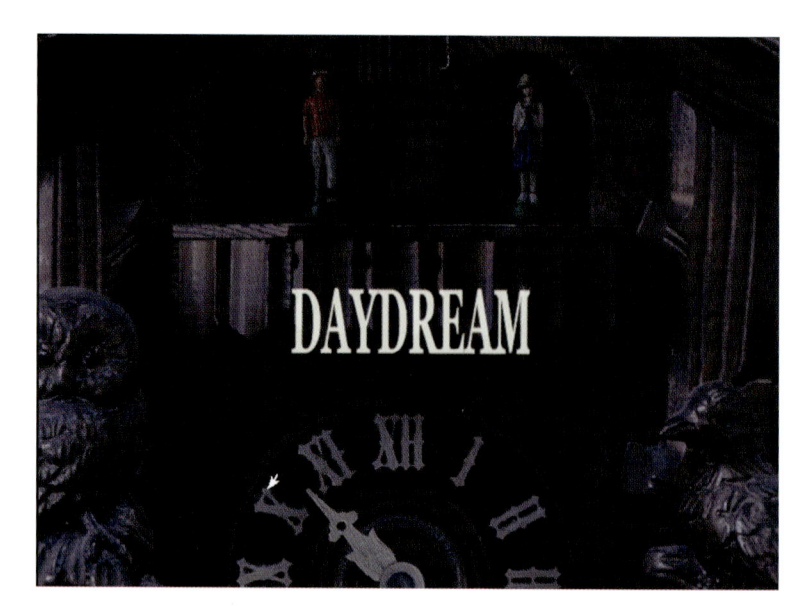

MICROSITES: BUSINESS TO CONSUMER

GOLD

AGENCY
qubibi/Tokyo

CLIENT
Weave Toshi

ART DIRECTOR
Kazumasa Teshigawara

PROGRAMMER
Kazumasa Teshigawara

CREATIVE DIRECTOR
Kazumasa Teshigawara

ANNUAL ID
07017N

URL
www.weavetoshi.co.jp/webc3/index.html

This is for a Japanese hat maker Weave Toshi's third annual collection. I intended not to focus on merely introducing the products, but rather tried to raise its brand value. That was my task as a web designer.

The basic idea stemmed from the feeling of being in a nightmare—wet, eerie, lukewarm, repetitive and dizzy. I came up with a solution to visualize this feeling by adapting a clock-like development. What if dolls in a cuckoo clock moved like real human beings? This must be a kind of idea everyone had when they were children. The clock's trick is connected to the clock's hands. Move hands and the trick starts to work. Hands of the clock move and time goes. Everyone knows that. DAYDREAM is created by combining several, ordinary elements in this mechanism.

The interface with the mouse isn't for the user to view the hats better. The whole point is to roll the mouse. By the time users get used to the action, an animation starts to peek in between the male and female character. Each animated image relates to the idea that inspired the hat. For example, the image of a flame for the hat with a motif of flames; the white pigeon for a hat created with a motif of the pigeon, a symbol of freedom.

At the end, the story re-starts from the beginning. The elder character keeps rolling the clock. Users keep rolling the mouse. This action of "rolling" is also a very intriguing element for me personally.

MICROSITES: BUSINESS TO CONSUMER

THE GREAT MANSCAPE
Wield a razor on your back, sack and crack.

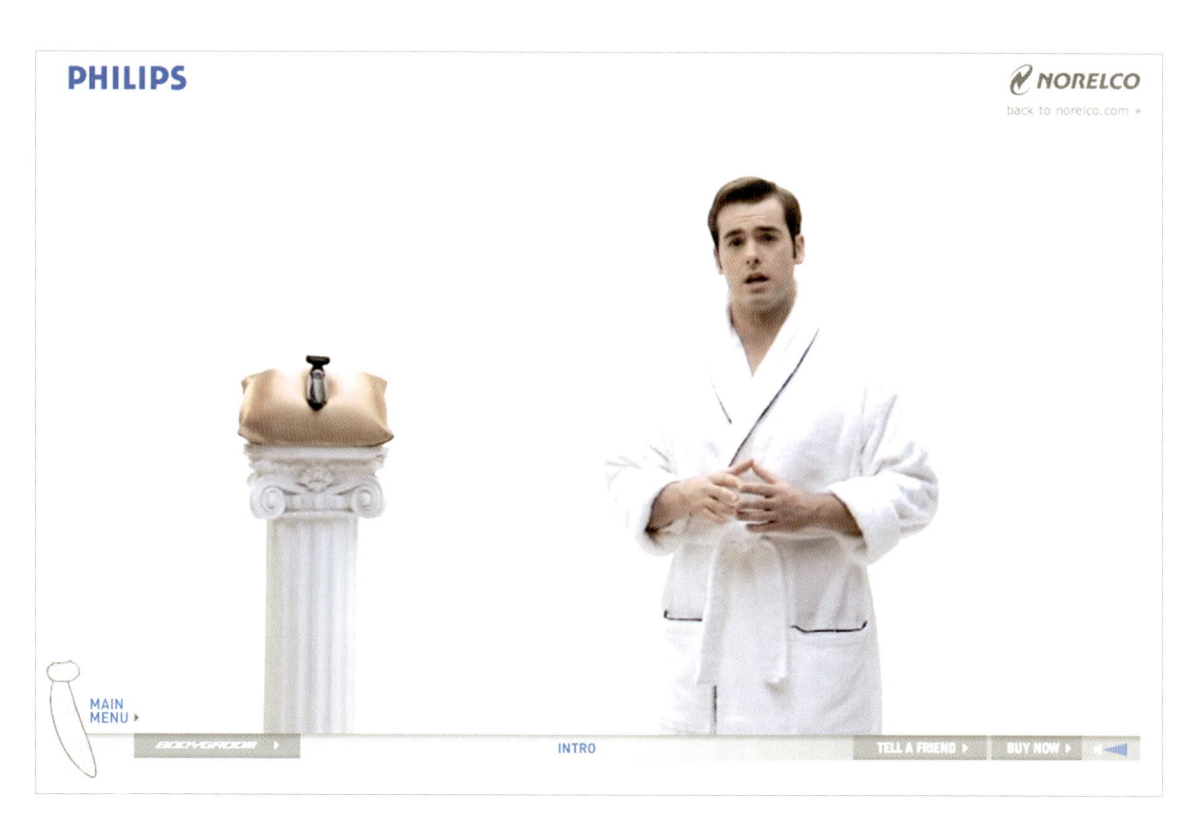

MICROSITES: BUSINESS TO CONSUMER

GOLD

AGENCY
*Tribal DDB/
New York*

CLIENT
Philips Norelco

ART DIRECTORS
*Daniel Modell
January Vernon*

WRITERS
*Brook Lundy
Scott Ginsberg*

PRODUCTION COMPANY
Struck Design

CREATIVE DIRECTORS
*Stephen Nesle
Brook Lundy*

ANNUAL ID
07018N

URL
*www.shave
everywhere.com*

We addressed the potential sensitivity and awkwardness of talking about "male grooming" by creating a character who is so (ridiculously) comfortable discussing the topic, he makes the audience comfortable talking about it as well. In addition to website, blog and video sharing sites, the program also included a music video, talking urinals and 13" rulers emblazoned with the URL that were left in bars and clubs around the country.

The campaign exceeded 12-month sales target within The first four weeks. The company had to quadruple manufacturing capacity to respond to demand. Exclusive retail relationships were cemented due to outstanding sales performance.

By taking a consumer insight and translating It into a communicative viral piece of advertising that exceeded sales expectations, the creative set a new benchmark in the industry.

MICROSITES: BUSINESS TO CONSUMER

BURGERS OVER BROADWAY
Women are not just meat, they're veggies and condiments too.

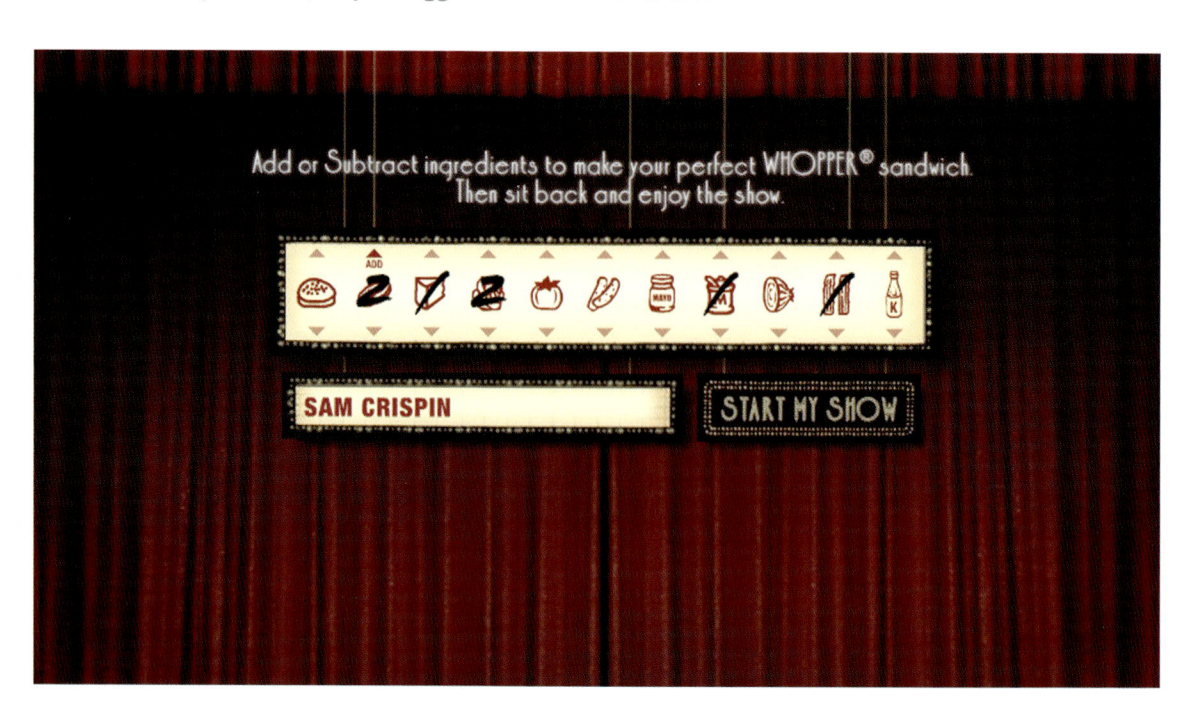

MICROSITES: BUSINESS TO CONSUMER

SILVER

AGENCY
Crispin Porter + Bogusky/Miami

CLIENT
Burger King

ART DIRECTORS
John Parker
Mark Taylor

WRITERS
Evan Fry
Bob Cianfrone

DESIGNERS
Chean Wei Law
Thomas Rodgers

PROGRAMMERS
Lucas Shuman
John Mastri

PRODUCTION COMPANY
EVB

CREATIVE DIRECTORS
Alex Bogusky
Andrew Keller
Rob Reilly
Jeff Benjamin

ANNUAL ID
07019N

URL
www.cpbgroup.com/awards/whopperettesoneshow.html

To compliment BK's Superbowl commercial, Whopperettes.com lets you have it your way with the Whopperettes—a troupe of 92 dancing ladies dressed as Whopper toppings. Visitors order a Whopper the way they want it...and see it built right before their very eyes as the Whopperettes dance, then jump on top of each other forming the burger you ordered. The show you create also features an announcer who yells out visitors names and details of what they ordered. The website features behind the scenes footage, cast bios, ringtones, marching band sheet music, garage band files of all music, lyrics, mp3s, costume gallery, desktop calendar, and more.

MICROSITES: BUSINESS TO CONSUMER

BOVINE INTERVENTION
When two space operatives from Brittlelactica trek to Earth to get milk, udder hilarity ensues.

MICROSITES: BUSINESS TO CONSUMER

SILVER

AGENCY
*Goodby, Silverstein & Partners/
San Francisco*

CLIENT
California Milk Processor Fluid Advisory Board

ART DIRECTORS
*Robert Lindstrom
Feh Tarty*

WRITERS
*Ronny Northrop
Pat McKay
Paul Charney*

PROGRAMMER
Klas Kroon

CONTETN STRATEGISTS
*Mike Geiger
David Eriksson
Roger Stighall*

PRODUCTION COMPANY
North Kingdom

CREATIVE DIRECTORS
*Jeff Goodby
Will McGinness*

ANNUAL ID
07020N

URL
www.goodbysilverstein.com/planetinneed

While Will and the crew were busy in San Francisco readying this site for launch, Feh and I were invited to speak at the International UFO Congress in Laughlin, Nevada. Essentially, to get up in front of a crowd of people who believe, I mean BELIEVE, in aliens, and show them the work. Our ambiguously-gay, frail-bodied, spoof-driven race of Brittleacticans who do nothing if not totally make fun of people who BELIEVE in aliens.

We were scared.

We wrote our presentation driving through the desert. We show up, and the room is packed. Big, huge screen facing the audience. I thought we were dead. I was marking off exits and calculating steps-per-second. They called our names and I almost didn't go out there. Feh nearly dragged me onstage.

But, to our surprise, they loved the work. They got it, maybe even related a little to the brittle-boned interlopers with no milk on their planet. So Feh coaxed me out from under the AV table—my back sore from coiling in the fetal position—and we got to walk around the room shaking hands. It was totally unexpected.

Planetinneed.com chronicles the entire aliens story. It's all there. Da Iry. The history of Brittleactica. The explorers' search for the 'white wonder tonic.' We tried pretty hard to do it all justice. Although, at the conference, one of the attendees did tell us how we screwed up. Said we should've used little green men. They're much more believable. *- Pat McKay*

MICROSITES: BUSINESS TO CONSUMER

COLLISION COURSE
Customize your car, then customize your crash.

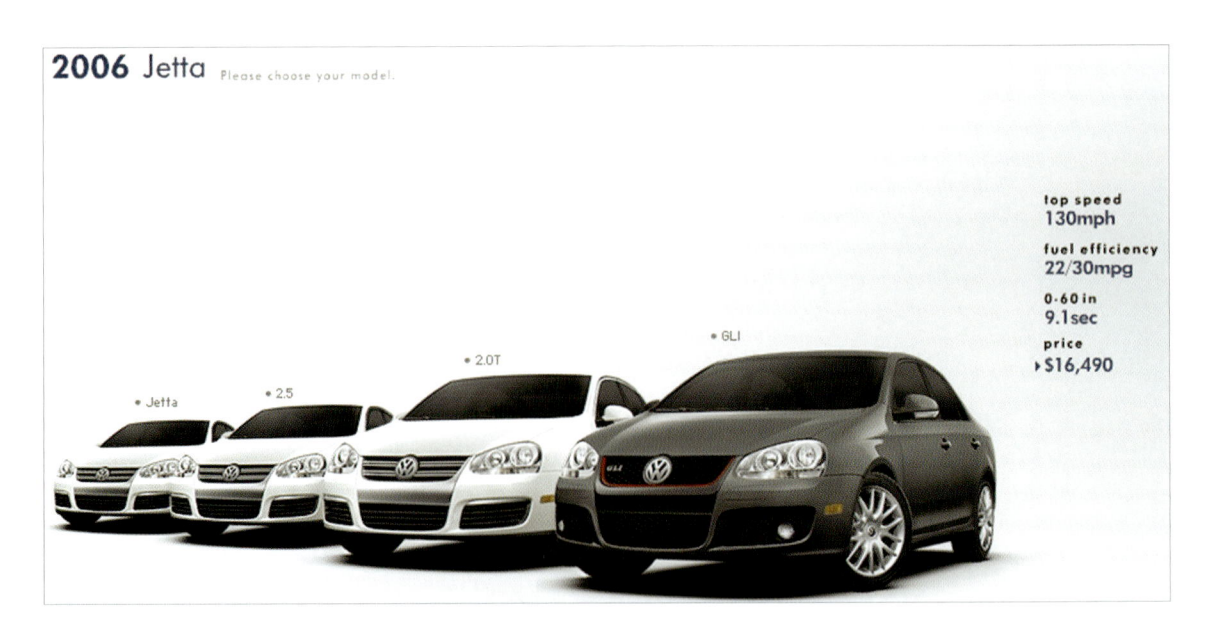

2006 Jetta Please choose your model.

- Jetta
- 2.5
- 2.0T
- GLI

top speed
130mph

fuel efficiency
22/30mpg

0-60 in
9.1sec

price
▸ **$16,490**

---

top speed
130mph

fuel efficiency
23/32mpg

0-60 in
7sec

price
▸ **$23,990** view summary

take a joyride
print brochure
email this car
dealer locator
get a quote

- xenon headlights
- chrome mirror caps
- heated washer nozzles adds package 2
- full body kit

- Gorilla-Gear™ trunk liner
- cargo organizer with VW logo
- trunk liner carbon plastic
- roller blind for rear window
- cargo net

- iPod adapter
- DVD voyager – two screens
- nav system w/CD/DVD
- aluminum pedal caps
- AM/FM 6 CD and satellite radio

50

MICROSITES: BUSINESS TO CONSUMER

BRONZE

AGENCY
Crispin Porter + Bogusky/Miami

CLIENT
Volkswagen

ART DIRECTORS
Dawn Yemma
Mike Ferrare

WRITERS
Yutaka Tsujino
Jason Wolske

DESIGNER
Conor McCann

MULTIMEDIA ARTISTS
Thomas Rodgers
James Martis

PRODUCTION COMPANIES
Hanson Dodge
Motive

CREATIVE DIRECTORS
Alex Bogusky
Andrew Keller
Jeff Benjamin
Rob Strasberg
Tony Calcao

ANNUAL ID
07021N

URL
www.cpbgroup.com/
awards/vwfeaturesjetta.
html

The "Safe Happens" campaign brought to life a singular message: "The Volkswagen Jetta ranks high in crash testing." Online consumers got to have fun in a crash facility, crashing the cars they configured into a wall with Humpty Dumpty, giant lizards, UFOs, and more. This message struck a chord with prospective buyers. Sales jumped over 35 percent compared with a year earlier.

MICROSITES: BUSINESS TO BUSINESS

KICK VOX
Cisco scores with penalty shout-offs over the Internet.

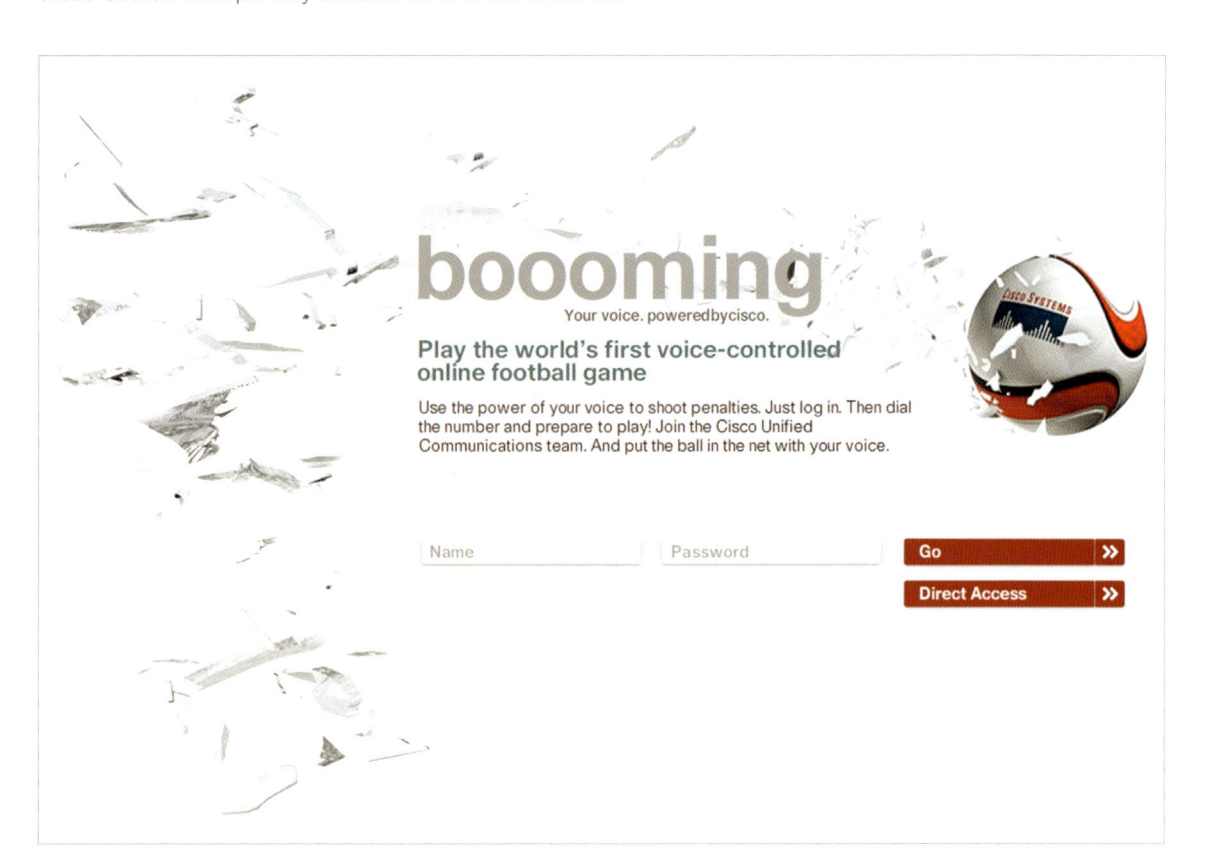

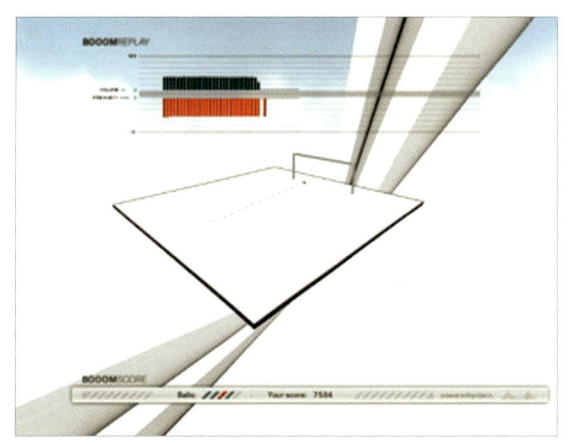

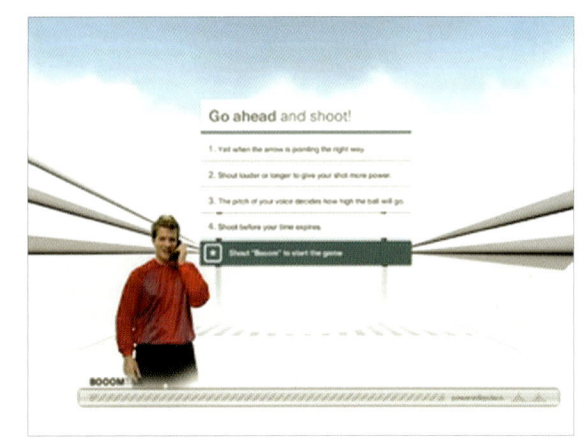

MICROSITES: BUSINESS TO BUSINESS

SILVER

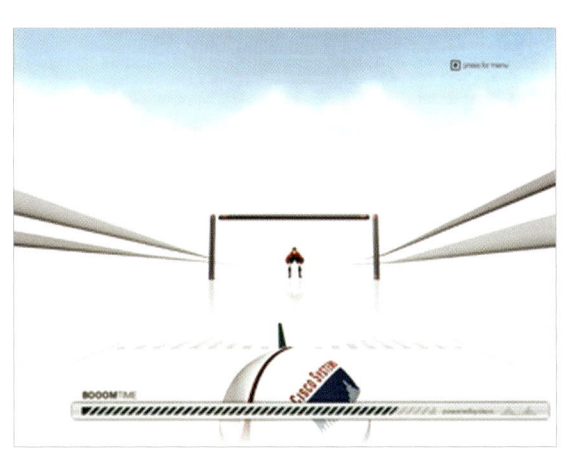

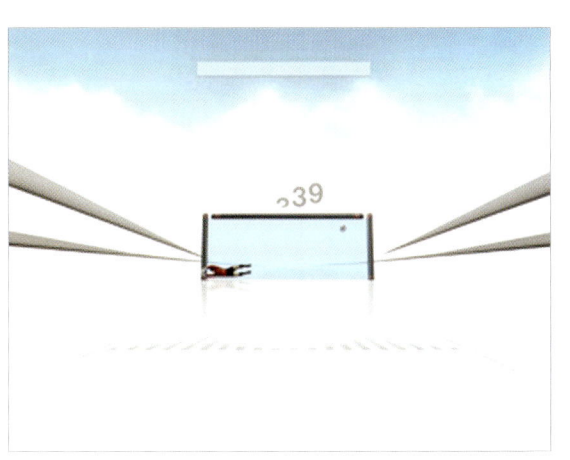

AGENCY
OgilvyOne Worldwide/
Frankfurt

CLIENT
Cisco Systems

ART DIRECTOR
Uwe Jakob

DESIGNERS
Nicole Holzenkamp
Serena Stoerlein

CREATIVE DIRECTORS
Michael Kutschinski
Ulf Dr. Schmidt

ANNUAL ID
07022N

URL
www.ourwork.de/
cisco/boooming/

The task: Tell technical and business decision makers in enterprises that they can integrate all their telephones into their data network with Cisco Unified Communications. Do this during the World Cup in June, and make the target group aware of Cisco as an innovator.

The solution: Call a website with your telephone and "booom" penalties with your voice on the Internet, changing the volume and pitch of your voice to control the ball in the field and to score a goal. We established a connection between the users' telephone and his individual PC using a session-based telephone number. For the first time in the world, users could shake the net by shouting into their telephones. They literally felt the power of a united telephone-and-data network. Booom!

53

MICROSITES: PUBLIC SERVICE/NON-PROFIT/EDUCATIONAL

RIGHT HEAR
Test your visual deafness and discover your aural blindspots.

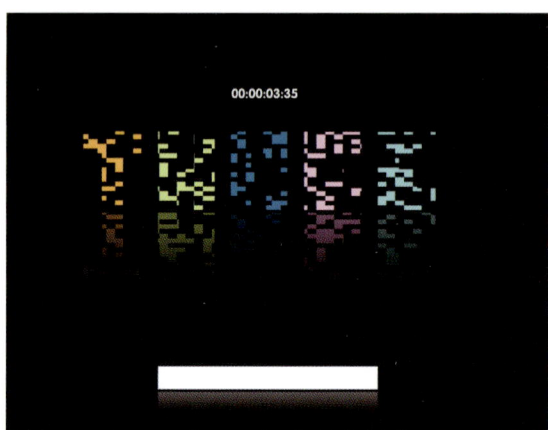

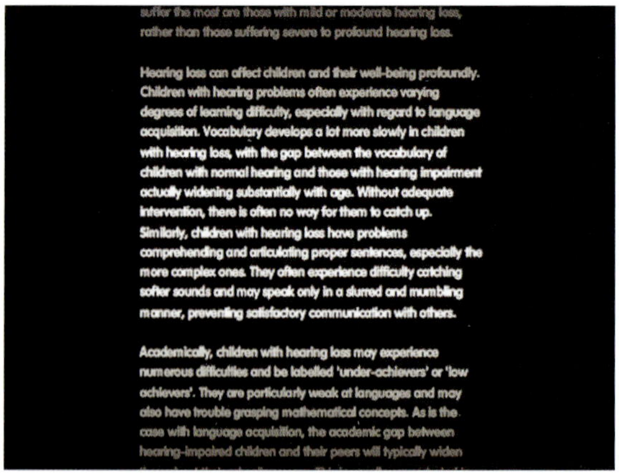

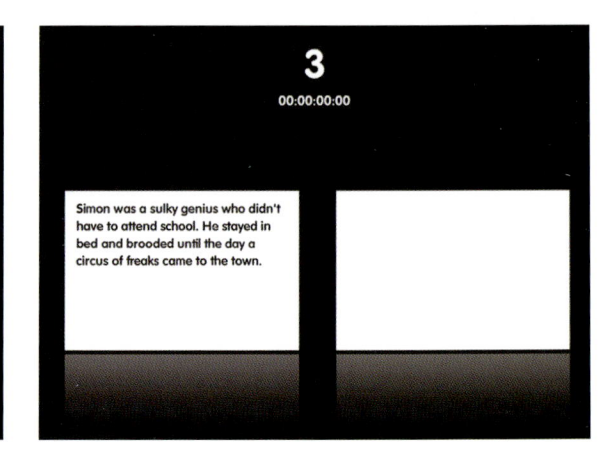

MICROSITES: PUBLIC SERVICE/NON-PROFIT/EDUCATIONAL

SILVER

AGENCY
Kinetic/
Singapore

CLIENT
The Hear and Be Heard Fund Centre for Hearing Intervention & Language Development

ART DIRECTORS
Francis Tan
Sean Lam

WRITER
Alex Goh

MULTIMEDIA ARTIST
Francis Tan

CREATIVE DIRECTOR
Sean Lam

ANNUAL ID
07023N

URL
www.errortypeone.com/awards/whatnoise/

The brief is to create a website for a non-profit initiative that seeks to raise funds for hearing impaired children, particularly those from financially disadvantaged families.

While charity organizations require all the help they can get, we could do with one less run-of-the-mill call for donation website, which could drone on about the plight of the handicapped and needy without giving users a real glimpse of the physical limitations of the disabled.

This website introduces users to the world of the hearing impaired unobtrusively through a road of discovery, and more importantly, self-discovery. The website was designed specifically to draw the user in to discover with an open mind, and guide him along with little intervention, in order to give him as close an experience as possible on how the hearing impaired perceive and cope with their disability. The website consists of three different environments where each user can experience what is like to live without sound and infuses in the user how challenging it can be every day to be hearing-impaired.

MICROSITES: PUBLIC SERVICE/NON-PROFIT/EDUCATIONAL

ON THIN ICE
A real-time campaign that puts the freeze on climate crisis.

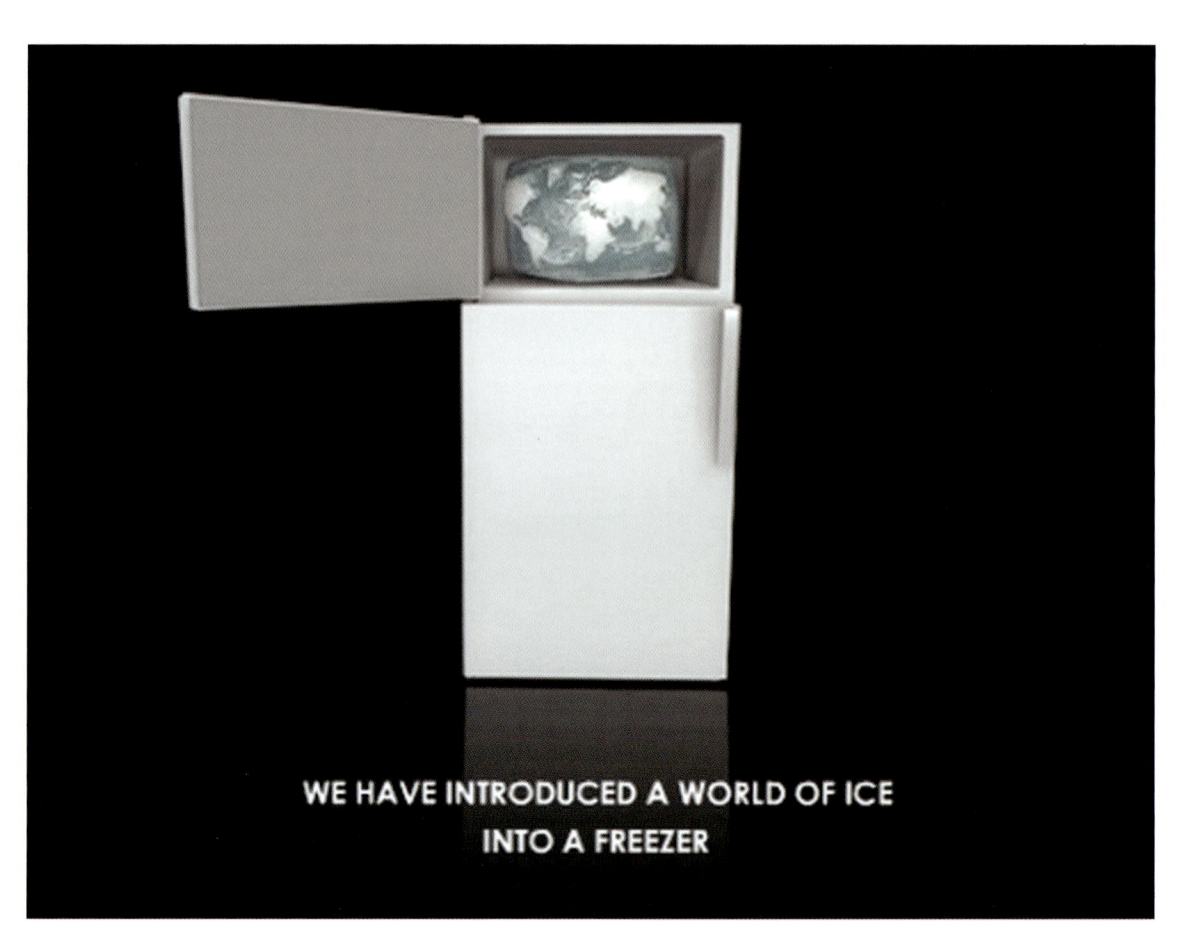

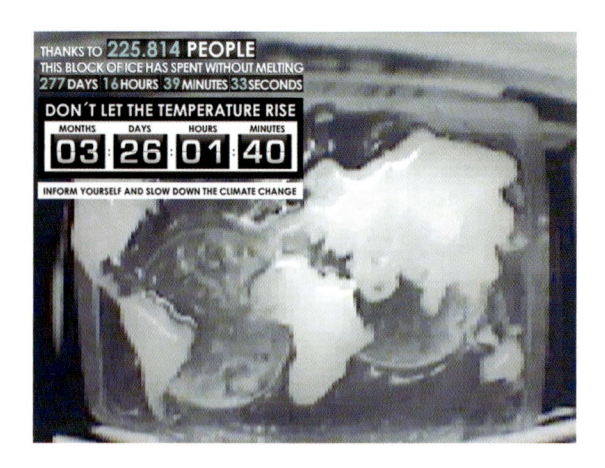

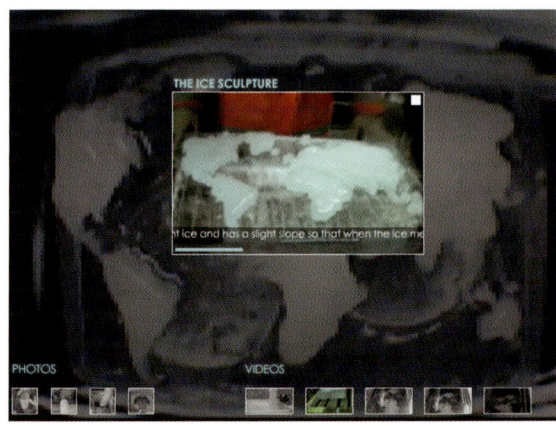

MICROSITES: PUBLIC SERVICE/NON-PROFIT/EDUCATIONAL

BRONZE

AGENCY
CP Proximity/ Barcelona

CLIENT
Fundacion Natura

ART DIRECTORS
*Rubén Martínez
Liliana Tavares
Gloria Joven*

WRITER
Nerea Cierco

PROGRAMMERS
*Marc Martínez
Juan Carlos Moscardo*

CREATIVE DIRECTORS
*Enric Nel-lo
Hugo Olivera*

ANNUAL ID
07024N

URL
www.thisismywork.com/oneshow/frena/

Climate change is a problem whose consequences are already being felt in Spain. Scientists confirm that due to our country's geographic location, the effects of climate change are especially dangerous and will become more pronounced in the next years, even though most of us believe, mistakenly, that we will never live to see that situation.

The non-profit organization Fundacion Natura asked us to create a viral campaign addressed to students to generate awareness about the importance of acting together to slow down the climate change. To raise awareness in our target audience, we needed to make an impact and arouse their interest. We created a live viral campaign that generated interest and at the same time was linked to a blog.

We put a world of ice into a freezer connected to a web-cam in real time. We also created an informative blog on how to slow down climate change. The time that students spent looking at information on the blog added up on a meter. If the meter reached zero, the freezer ceased to work.

As of January 15, 2007, 156,412 users had prevented the temperature of our frozen world from increasing, keeping the freezer always on and with reserves for at least 106 more days. The campaign received national coverage on two television channels, seven radio stations, 21 publications and in over 100 direct references to the website.

WEB SITES: BUSINESS TO CONSUMER

CHAIN REACTION
Splice in your own fancy footwork and be part of something bigger.

WEB SITES: BUSINESS TO CONSUMER

GOLD

AGENCY
Framfab/Copenhagen

CLIENT
Nike

ART DIRECTOR
Rasmus Frandsen

WRITER
Thomas Robson

DESIGNERS
Rasmus Frandsen
Kristian Grove Moeller
Martin Mohr

PROGRAMMER
Martin Ludvigsen

INFORMATION ARCHITECT
Jens Christiansen

CONTENT STRATEGIST
Bettina Sherain

CREATIVE DIRECTOR
Lars Cortsen

ANNUAL ID
07025N

URL
www.nikefootball.com/chain

For the Football World Cup 2006 Nike wanted to unite football crazy kids on a global scale in the fight against ugly football: diving, timewasting, acting, foul play, etc. by celebrating beautiful football—joga bonito.

The challenge was to create an engaging, involving and globally relevant interactive experience. The target audience was football crazy kids, 13–17 years old, but the experience should speak to football lovers more broadly.

We wanted to create an interactive, content-driven experience and let our target audience be the carrier of our message. By creating The Chain, aka "the world's longest football video," we gave them a voice and opportunity to participate in our communications right next to Ronaldinho. We believe that entertainment and advertising is merged and authenticity is brought forward. We are letting consumers borrow our brand values and thereby be connected to them. It is honest and simple. And global by nature.

WEB SITES: BUSINESS TO CONSUMER

HIJACKING WITH THE HEIDIES

Internet killed the TV star, wearing only its skivvies.

WE HIJACKED DIESEL.COM

Mission accomplished. A combination of traditional and traditionally illegal methods (the hostile take over of Diesel.com, theft of an unreleased underwear collection and a hostage situation) gave us what we came for.

Did you miss our show? Enter the site to see it all.

Welcome to our 15 megabytes of fame!

You have to be at least 18 to play.

DISCLAIMER: This site DOES contain people in underwear, bad language, property damage, slight glorification of violence and several giant panda suits.

WEB SITES: BUSINESS TO CONSUMER

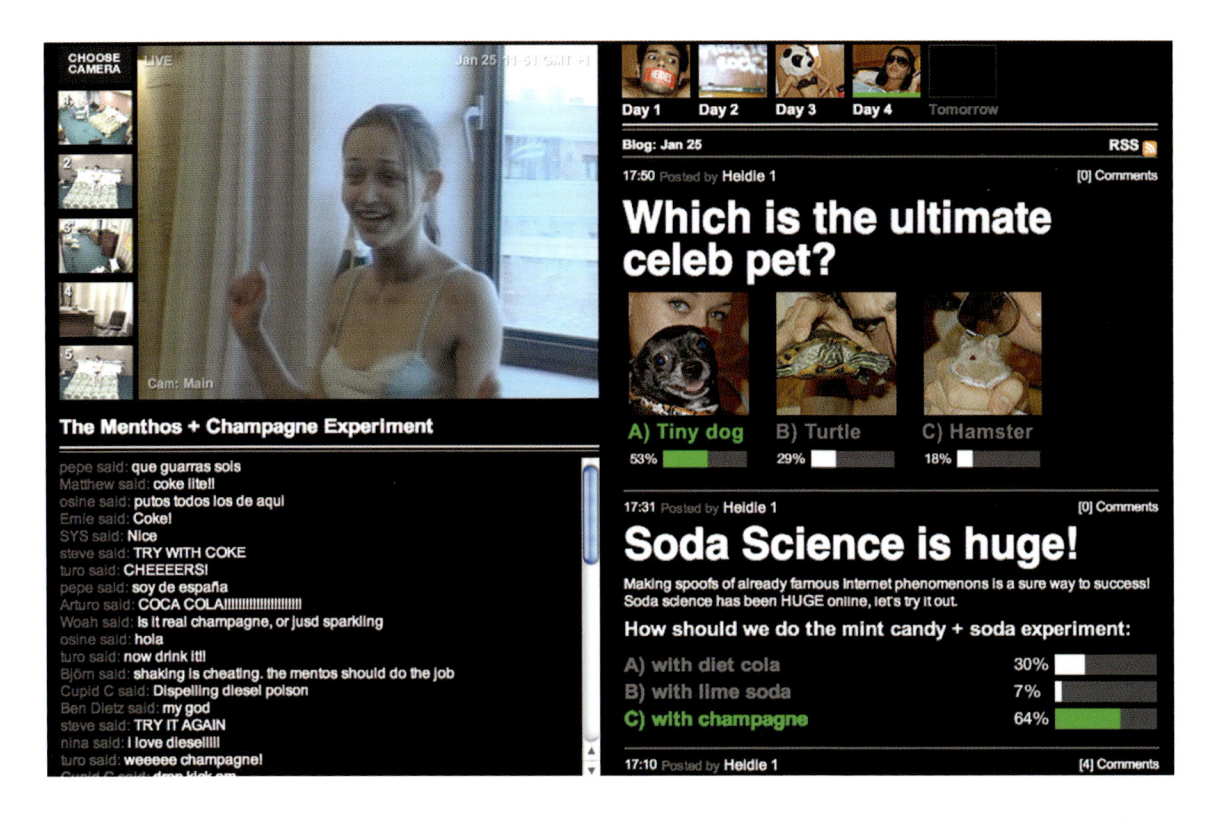

SILVER

AGENCY
Farfar/
Stockholm

CLIENT
Diesel

DIRECTOR
Hobbyfilm

CREATIVE DIRECTORS
Farfar
Diesel Creative Team

ANNUAL ID
07026N

URL
www.farfar.se/awards/
oneshow2007/diesel/

Six video cameras, live 24 hours a day, five days in a row on www.diesel.com.

Two gorgeous and crazy girls wanted to become famous. These two girls, The Heidies, stole the new and unreleased Diesel Intimate collection, kidnapped a sales guy from Diesel, and locked themselves (and him) in a hotel room for five days. They wanted to show the world what they were doing! The Heidies had a plan for their road to stardom, and if Diesel didn't meet their demands the Heidies would destroy the stolen Diesel underwear in a wood-crushing device.

On top of this, Diesel had to hand over the control of their website to the Heidies. With this online power at their mercy, The Heidies interacted and chatted with their growing audience, uploading their shenanigans to the site as well as a chunk load of other popular sites. Fans from all over the world influenced the storyline and the actions as they happened, enjoying everything (and we mean everything) that took place inside this hotel room on the live stream. The Heidies were online between Monday the 22nd and Friday the 26th of January, and during those five days, the people were hooked, some to the point of taking a sick day off work to stay up with the Heidies, and keep interacting with the room.

An ironic but sexy parody of popular TV and online phenomena from Big Brother and other reality shows to MySpace and YouTube, whose core is the desire to be seen and to become famous, is revamped in a Diesel way—humorous, original and provocative.

WEB SITES: BUSINESS TO CONSUMER

LOSE YOUR ILLUSION
Post-production artist Natuh Abootalebi reveals the unreal.

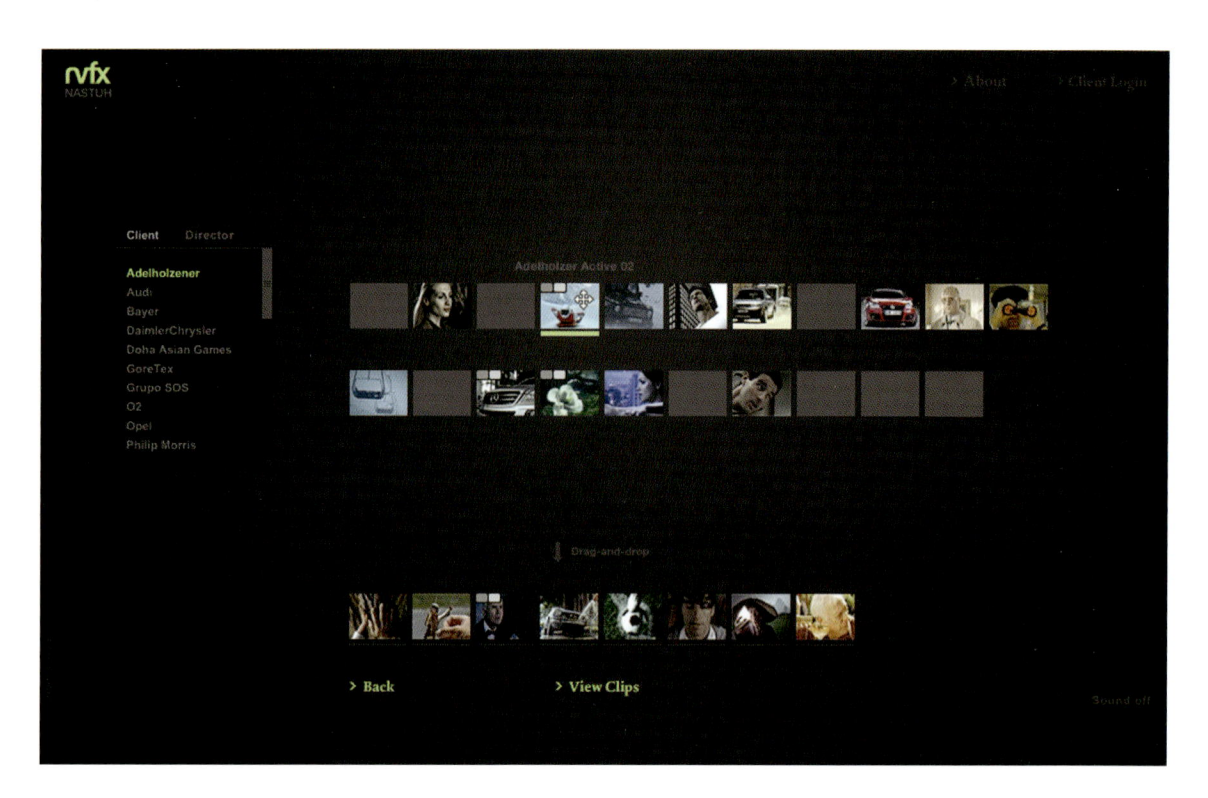

WEB SITES: BUSINESS TO CONSUMER

SILVER

AGENCY
Scholz & Volkmer/
Wiesbaden

CLIENT
Nastuh Abootalebi

ART DIRECTOR
Tobias Kreutzer

WRITER
Tim Sobczak

DESIGNER
Christoph Noe

MULTIMEDIA ARTIST
Jens Fischer

PROGRAMMERS
Kerem Guelensoy
Timm Kreuder
Wolf Rauch
Florian Hermann
Manfred Kraft
Peter Reichard

CONTENT STRATEGISTS
Manfred Kraft
Tobias Kreutzer
Pia Tannenberger

CREATIVE DIRECTOR
Heike Brockmann

ANNUAL ID
07027N

URL
www.s-v.de/
projects/nastuh

The website presents the portfolio of the visual effects artist, and appeals to existing and potential customers such as post-production companies, directors and agencies. The concept was to make the actual service of visual effects visible.

A direct comparison between the pre and the post version for the first time demonstrates how much a film can be vitalized by visual effects. Users can move their mouse over a film clip that was processed by Nastuh, "erase" the visual effects and find out what the film looked like before it was processed. The show reel can be individually configured with clips from the archive. The navigation elements fade as soon as the mouse stops moving, thereby creating a real movie atmosphere.

WEB SITES: BUSINESS TO CONSUMER

DROPPIN CASHMERE
Online catalogs are fresh again.

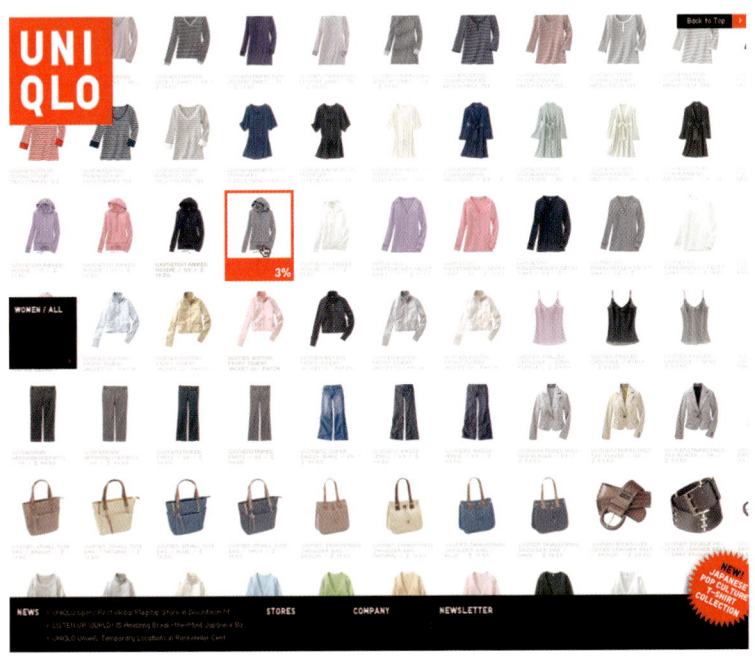

WEB SITES: BUSINESS TO CONSUMER

SILVER

AGENCY
tha/Tokyo

CLIENT
UNIQLO

ART DIRECTOR
Yugo Nakamura

DESIGNERS
Kojiro Futamura
Sayaka Matsukawa

PROGRAMMER
Keita Kitamura

CREATIVE DIRECTOR
Kashiwa Sato

ANNUAL ID
07028N

URL
uniqlo.archive.
tha.jp/index.html

Uniqlo's much anticipated and hyped store opening in New York, which was touted as a trendier, Japanese Gap, met expectations—it was a vast, vertical store, with T-shirts and basics galore.

Their website reflects this prolific, yet graphically clean sensibility. The "Uniqlo Explorer" section of the site lets you skim up and down a page of product thumbnails. Catch one of the items to enlarge it, float it around and turn it into an artful mosaic piece, containing tiny options of related merchandise: entire wardrobe possibilities.

WEB SITES: BUSINESS TO CONSUMER

FROM AIR TO ETERNITY
Visualize your own tripped-out run.

WEB SITES: BUSINESS TO CONSUMER

BRONZE

AGENCY
Big Spaceship/ Brooklyn

CLIENT
Nike

ANNUAL ID
07029N

URL
www.bigspaceship.com/ sizzle/nike/

Can the unique feeling of riding directly on Air translate into a digital experience? We think so, having built a next-generation Flash site controlled entirely by the user. Combining animation, photography, greenscreen video, original sound, and interactive design with simple keystrokes, each user creates and shares a personal vision of what it feels like to run or play basketball on Air. And each user comes away with a unique understanding of the power of the new generation of Air Max.

WEB SITES: BUSINESS TO CONSUMER

10 POINTS OF VIEW

A haunting artistic collaboration delves into the ways an image makes a thousand connections.

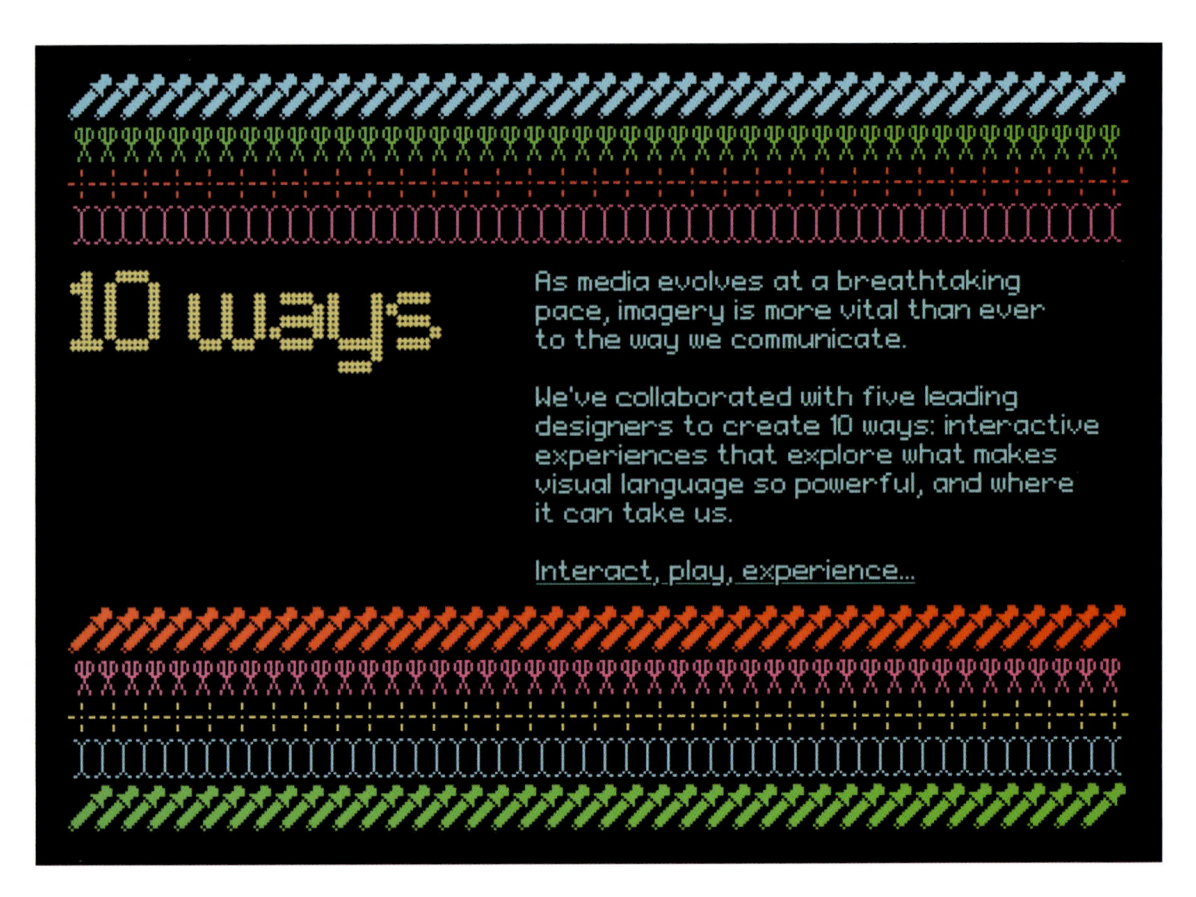

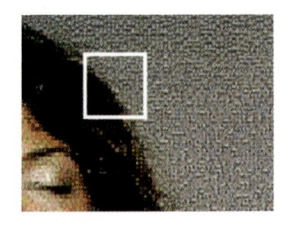

WEB SITES: BUSINESS TO CONSUMER

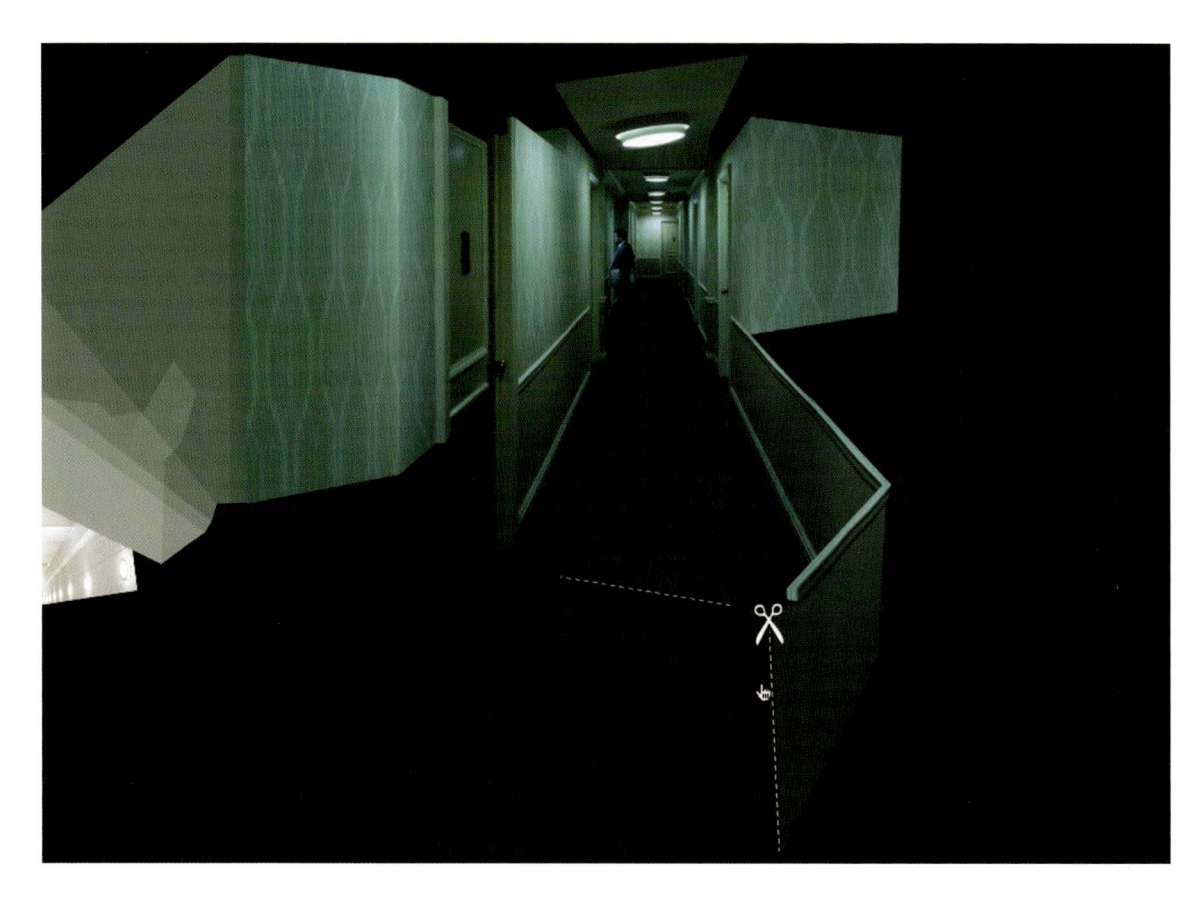

BRONZE

AGENCY
*Great Works/
Stockholm*

CLIENT
Getty Images

ART DIRECTOR
*Max Larsson von
Reybekiel*

PROGRAMMER
Oskar Sundberg

CREATIVE DIRECTOR
Mattias Nyström

ANNUAL ID
07030N

URL
*www.interacttenways.
com/usa/home.asp*

In this interactive art project for Getty Images, Tomato (London), LessRain (London, Berlin), Sumona (South Africa), The Barbarian Group (New York), and Great Works (Sweden) all created interactive applications to explore what makes visual language so powerful.

The ten ways—or themes, concepts, journeys, explorations, revelations—are filters through which you create your own individual stories. See the world through light, information, memory, space, response, emotion, color, truth, time, and transformation—just see.

WEB SITES: E-COMMERCE

WAVE TWISTERS
Retro-futuristic site hypnotizes with light and sound.

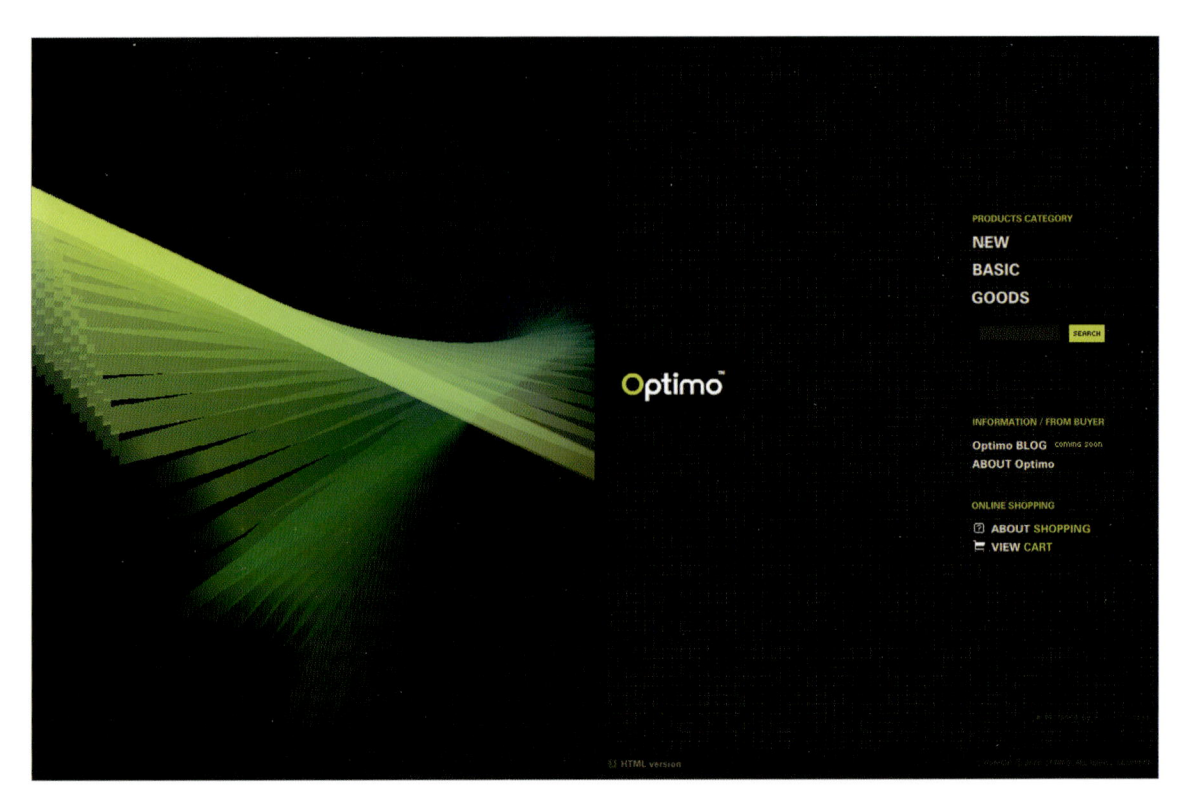

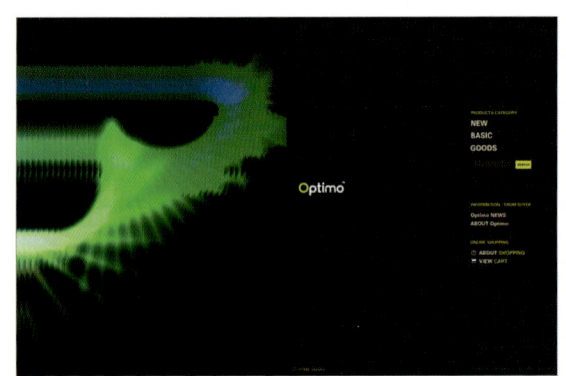

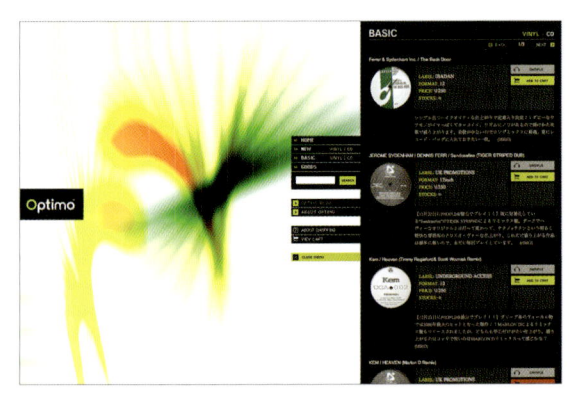

WEB SITES: E-COMMERCE

GOLD

AGENCY
*FORM::PROCESS/
Tokyo*

CLIENT
Optimo

ART DIRECTOR
Takaaki Yagi

DESIGNERS
*Yosuke Seki
Keigo Kurihara
Tomohiro Sato*

MULTIMEDIA ARTIST
DJ Hiro

PROGRAMMER
Tetsuya Mito

PRODUCTION COMPANY
FORM::PROCESS

ANNUAL ID
07031N

URL
*www.form-process.com/
wk/optimo/*

This is an online shop selling records mainly to club DJs. We had to start from scratch in building the brand, beginning with the logo-type design. In order to clearly distinguish our client's business from major record stores which sell mainly CDs, we were asked to create the online shop expressing the client's unique orientation.

The purpose of this website is not simply to sell music, but rather to enjoy it. The site design uses a frame dividing the screen into a left and right side that allows the motion graphics, which appear at the beginning, to continue playing on one side. When a user goes to one of the sample screens to preview a sound clip, he or she can enjoy the music and graphics at the same time, and each enhances the other.

Due to the online shopping system, it was necessary to display product lists and shopping cart pages in HTML, but the motion graphics constantly change shape randomly and continue to play, unrelated to the user shifting between the shop web pages.

Further, these motion graphics are interactive, changing according to the movements of the user's cursor, so we created a site wherein users can have fun while they shop.

WEB SITES: E-COMMERCE

THE SNIFFLE DETECTOR
With a few questions, Sneeze Aid determines a cold's severity.

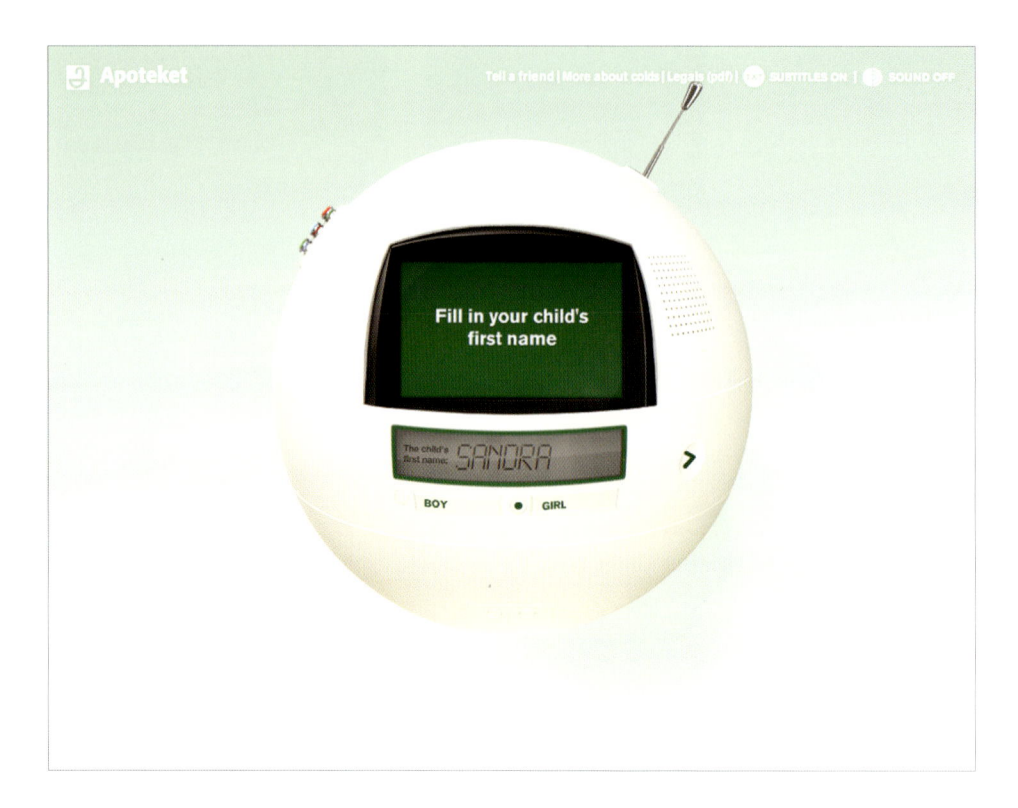

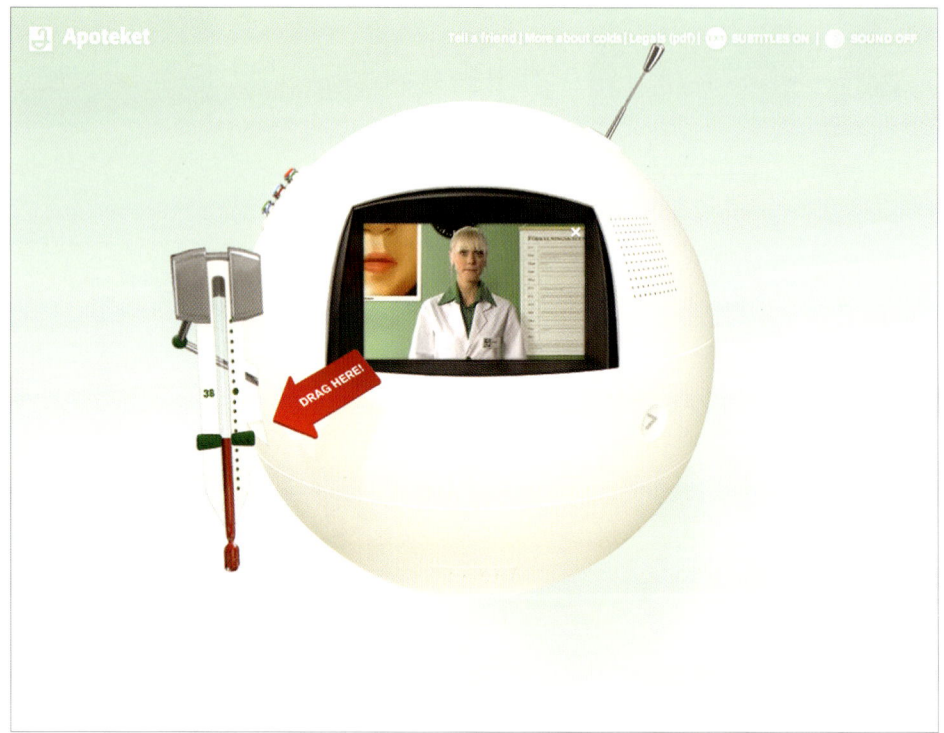

WEB SITES: E-COMMERCE

SILVER

AGENCY
Forsman & Bodenfors/
Gothenburg

CLIENT
Apoteket

ART DIRECTORS
John Bergdahl
Martin Cedergren

WRITERS
Anna Qvennerstedt
Johan Olivero

DESIGNERS
Lotta Dolling
Nina Andersson

PRODUCTION COMPANIES
B-Reel
Kramgo

ANNUAL ID
07032N

URL
demo.fb.se/e/
apoteket/sneezeaid/

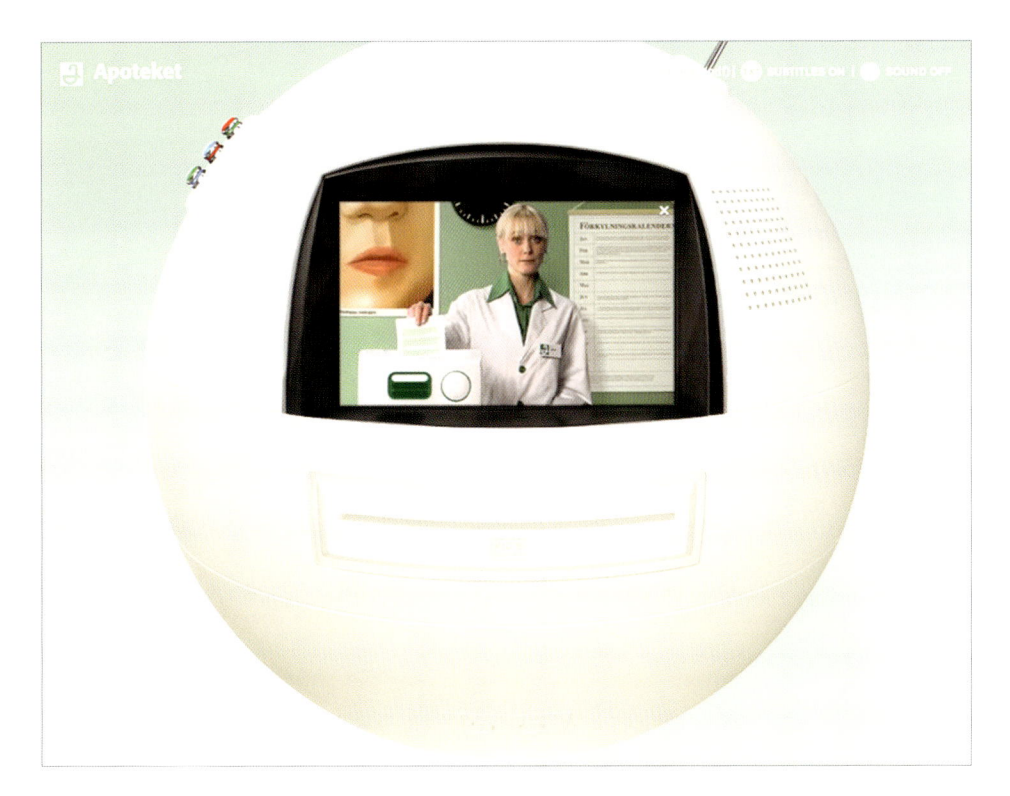

What could really help parents when it comes to children's colds? Mix an advertising agency with a few doctors and see what they'll come up with. Imagine you've got a sick kid at home, and you're not sure if it's the common cold or if you should see a doctor. This tool, developed in collaboration with doctors, helps you decide and offers personalized advice, including a list of relevant products.

WEB SITES: E-COMMERCE

JUST SHOP

Nike goes to Town with the relaunch of its online store.

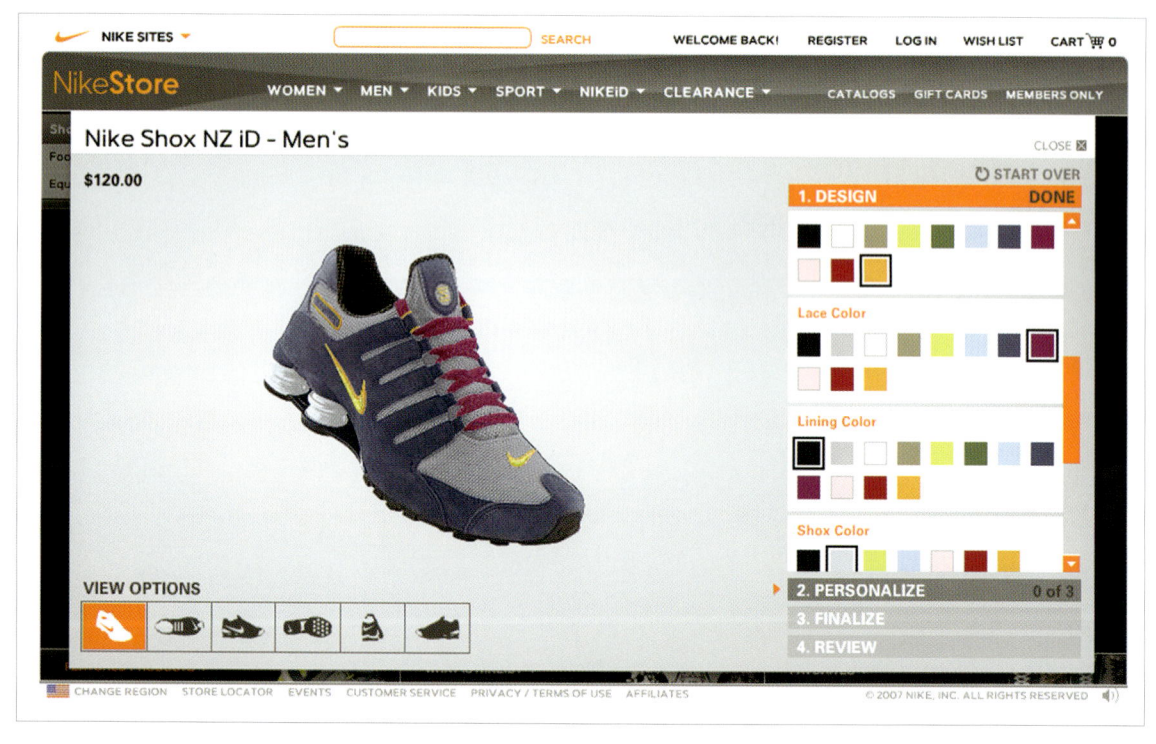

WEB SITES: E-COMMERCE

BRONZE

AGENCY
R/GA/New York

CLIENT
Nike

DESIGNERS
Ben Oderwald
Aya Karpinska
Rachel Abrams
Wade Convay
Jeff Baxter

PROGRAMMERS
Brad Alan
Jens Loeffler
Steve Warren
Aaron Ambrose
Geoffrey Roth
August Yang

AGENCY PRODUCER
Ameer Youssef

INFORMATION ARCHITECT
Heidi Miller

CREATIVE DIRECTORS
Nick Law
Noel Billig

ANNUAL ID
07033N

URL
www.rga.com/award/nikestore.html

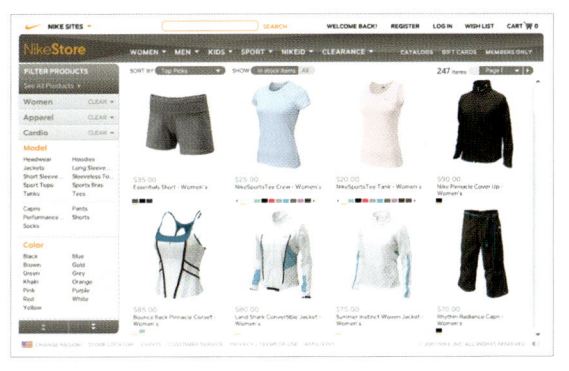

The new retail experience represents a significant evolution of Nike's online commerce capabilities. The changes are designed to introduce deeper product storytelling, enhanced customer service, and additional functionality. It provides a platform for a number of new shopping features that are available on the site now and others that will be activated in the future.

Consumers are able to filter the entire inventory of Nike products. This system puts the customer in control, allowing them to narrow the more than 30,000 products available on the NikeStore to those most relevant to them. Functionality changes include faceted navigation, which allows customers to search by any number of definitive characteristics, such as color, sport category and price of each product.

This is the first end-to-end ecommerce application of its size built in Flash, which results in faster checkout and downloads, among other improvements to the previous HTML site. It is the first major renovation of Nike's online store since its launch in 1999.

WEB SITES: PUBLIC SERVICE/NON-PROFIT/EDUCATIONAL

A TREE GROWS IN MÉXICO
Fresh foliage and whimsical creatures stalk the stars at this school for young creatives.

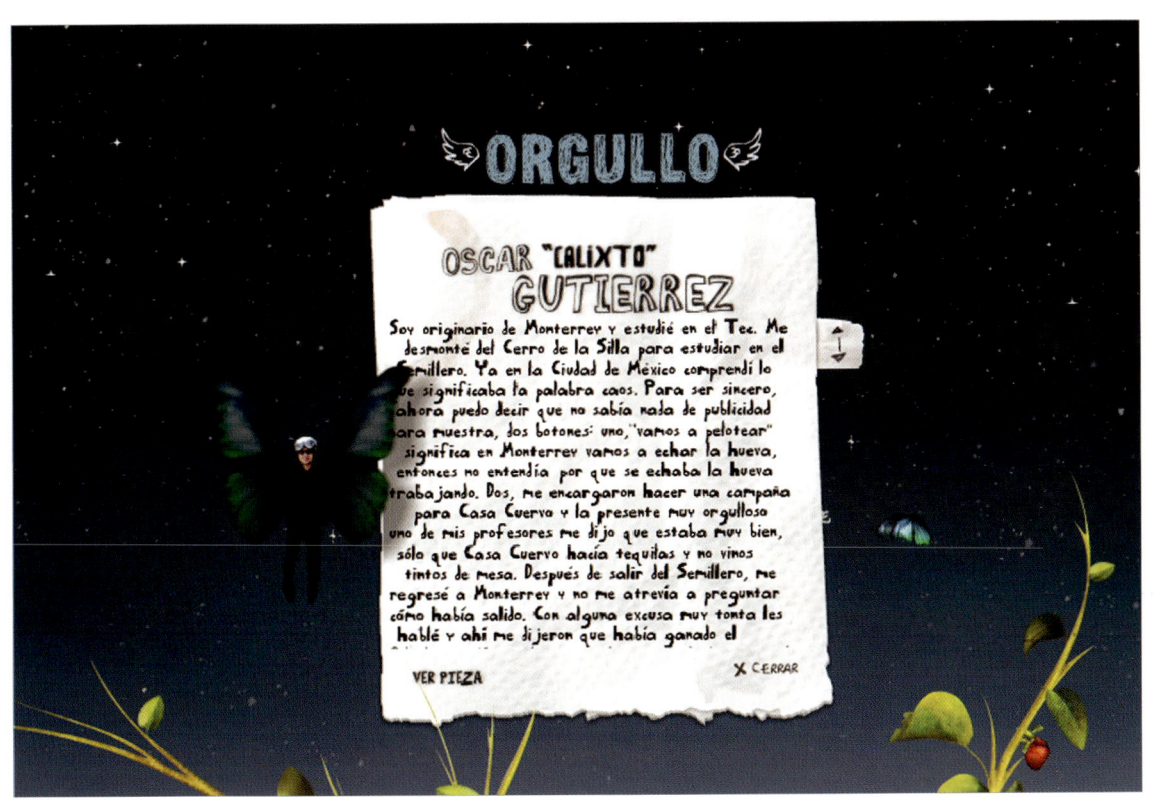

WEB SITES: PUBLIC SERVICE/NON-PROFIT/EDUCATIONAL

SILVER

AGENCY
Grupo W/Saltillo

CLIENT
Semillero Creatives School

ART DIRECTOR
Cesar Moreno

WRITER
Ruben Ruiz

MULTIMEDIA ARTISTS
Ulises Valencia
Cesar Moreno
Sebastian Mariscal

PROGRAMMER
Raul Uranga

CREATIVE DIRECTOR
Miguel Calderon

ANNUAL ID
07034N

URL
www.grupowprojects.com/semillero

Creating the Semillero plant wasn't an easy job. More than three months of drawing and giving life to every one of its details was a truly exhausting assignment. Opposite of what happens in most of the projects made with the newest technologies, Semillero returned to the basics, to the artisanal scheme that made us rethink the whole digital theme.

Every one of the stages of the plant needed to surprise and enrich the user's experience, what at the end became a psychedelic journey with brain-bugs, hand-flowers and hearts with human-caterpillars lodged inside. This has been one of the most beloved projects of our agency, and most of this because although the investment was small, we had complete creative freedom to develop it.

What we like the most about this project is the analogy of how a whole universe can arise from a small seed—the same way big ideas can. - *Miguel Calderon*

WEB SITES: PUBLIC SERVICE/NON-PROFIT/EDUCATIONAL

THE RULES OF RECREATION
Hangover helpers, beer goggles, and other handy drinking devices.

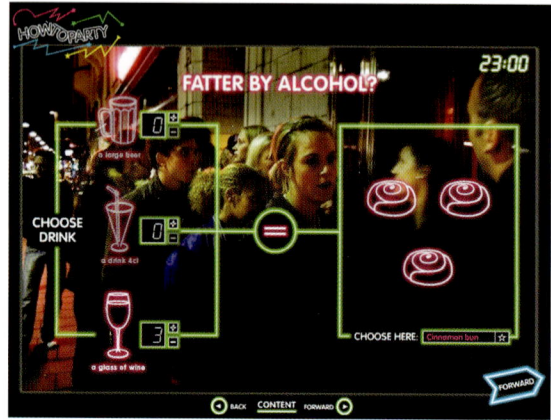

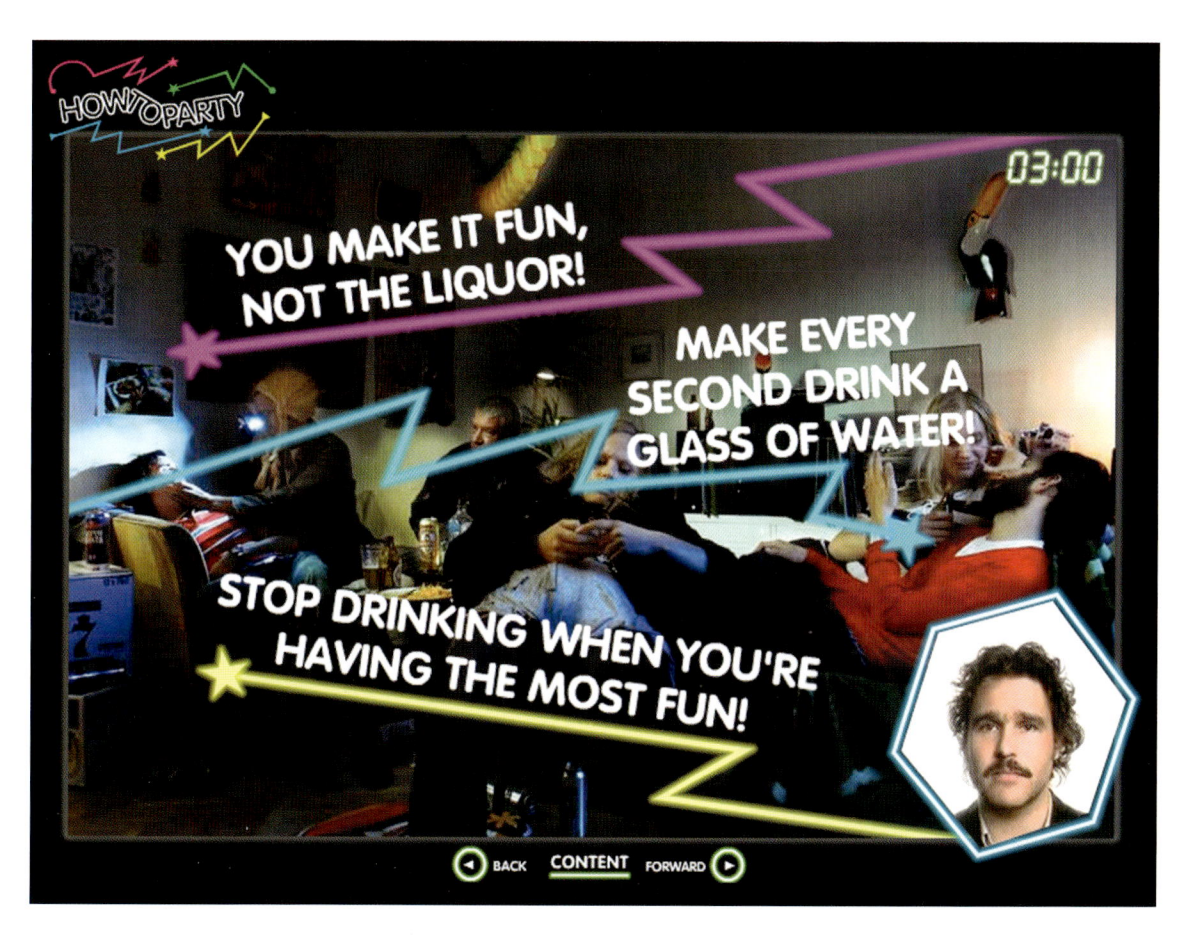

WEB SITES: PUBLIC SERVICE/NON-PROFIT/EDUCATIONAL

BRONZE

AGENCY
Farfar/
Stockholm

CLIENT
The Swedish
Alcohol Committee

ART DIRECTOR
Nicke Bergstrom

WRITER
Henrik Berglof

DESIGNER
Isabelle Funck

MULTIMEDIA ARTIST
Per Hansson

PROGRAMMERS
Bjorn Johansson
Bo Gustavsson

INFORMATION ARCHITECT
Anders Gustavsson

CONTENT STRATEGIST
Jonas Andersson

CREATIVE DIRECTOR
Nicke Bergstrom

ANNUAL ID
07035N

URL
www.farfar.se/
awards/oneshow
2007/howtoparty/

There's nothing more of a buzzkill than learning all the dour facts about alcohol, right? Farfar thinks not, and created this "How to Party" website which treats drinking not as a vice, not as something to shun or be ashamed of, but as reality. The youth will drink, and it's better to arm them with information and not beat them on the head with it, so they can take control of their partying lifestyles.

On a night out with some fun Swedes, drinking myths are debunked, the unfortunate truth about fat content is charted (would you eat four cinnamon buns in one day?), and the science of hangovers is explained with neon-colored chemicals. Now go and have fun, just don't throw up in your purse.

BRAND GAMING/APPLICATIONS: ONLINE

SUPER BAD
Break something with Rexona's no-sweat action hero.

BRAND GAMING/APPLICATIONS: ONLINE

SILVER

AGENCY
Grupo W/Saltillo

CLIENT
Unilever/Rexona

ART DIRECTOR
Miguel Calderon

WRITER
Ivan Gonzalez

DESIGNER
Jezreel Gutierrez

MULTIMEDIA ARTISTS
Ulises Valencia
Sebastian Mariscal
Daniel Bates

PROGRAMMERS
Raul Uranga
Edgar Ortiz

CREATIVE DIRECTORS
Miguel Calderon
Ulises Valencia

ANNUAL ID
07037N

URL
www.grupowprojects.com/rexona/stuntman

Creating "The Stuntman" was a big challenge for the agency; we were entirely devoted to this project for about three months, day and night. This was the first time that we developed a site taken from a shooting session with a model/actor in a studio, so it all was an entire odyssey: from planning the sessions, setting up the screens that we needed to record, then working on them frame by frame and finally taking care of every little detail on the production.

During the making of "Stuntman," we had real problems that cost us many nights of sleep. And when the viral-game was just about to be finished, we had to restructure the movements of the main character and the objects in the scenario; but after all this hard work, we could say that we had grown up a bit more, and that we truly achieved something with this development.

"Stuntman" is one of the projects that has left one of the deepest marks on the agency.

BRAND GAMING/APPLICATIONS: ONLINE

FIND THE SUV, SAVVY?
Unravel the mystery of the pirated SUV on a journey across seven seas.

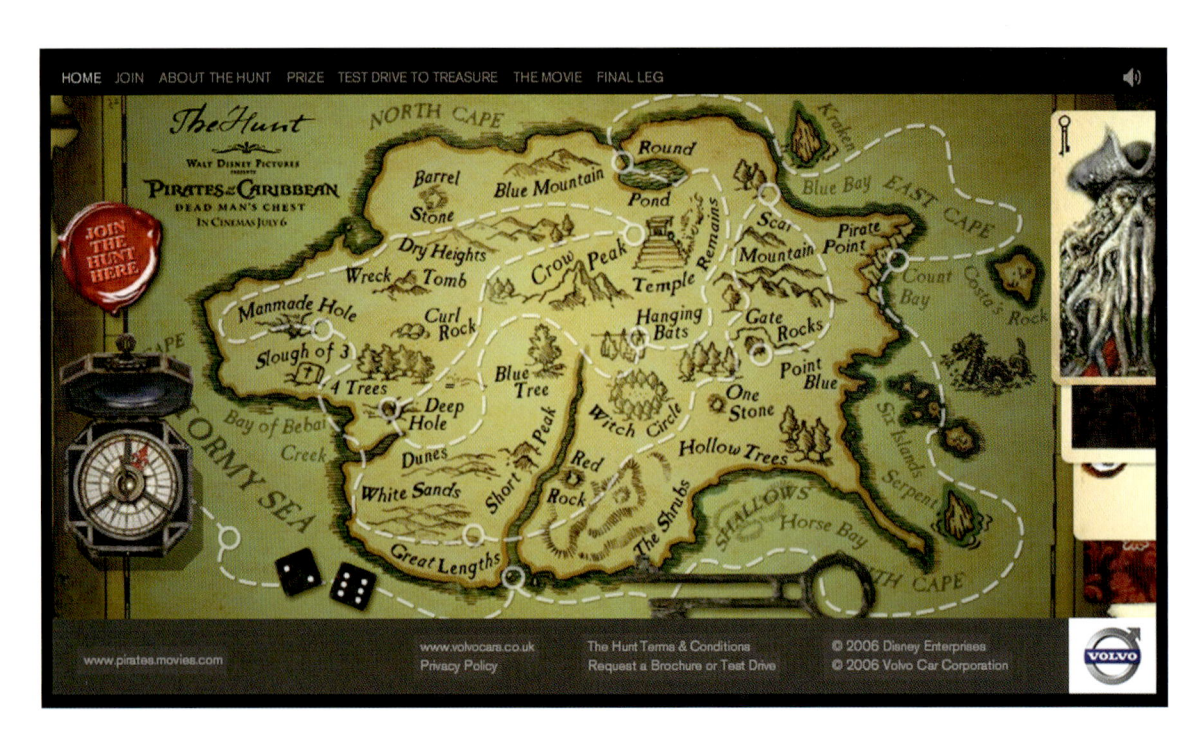

BRAND GAMING/APPLICATIONS: ONLINE

"The Hunt" was an online treasure hunt to find a real buried Volvo XC90. Most of all "The Hunt" was a people's campaign. It wasn't our campaign. It was theirs.

"The Hunt" sparked online communities, going beyond cultural and personal borders. Soccer moms discussed their hunt with math wizards. The folks charting "The Hunt" on their blogs were hailed as heroes by their readers.

Sometimes it was about competition, but in the end it was just men and women from all ages having one of the best times of their lives. And that really was their, and our, biggest prize.

BRONZE

AGENCY
*Euro RSCG 4D/
Amstelveen*

CLIENT
Volvo Cars Corporation

ART DIRECTOR
Martijn Sengers

WRITERS
*Bram de Rooij
Karl Lieberman
Brandon Henderson*

DESIGNERS
*Antonio da Costa
Feike Kloostra
Edwin Nikkels
Jurgen Nedebock*

PRODUCTION COMPANY
Framfab Gothenburg

CREATIVE DIRECTORS
*Sicco Beerda
Jason Holzman*

ANNUAL ID
07038N

URL
*www.prize-entry.com/
volvo_potc/oneshow/
microsites/*

WIRELESS/MOBILE ADVERTISING: BUSINESS TO CONSUMER

NASCAR YOU'VE GOT THERE
Ricky Bobby drives up to the third screen.

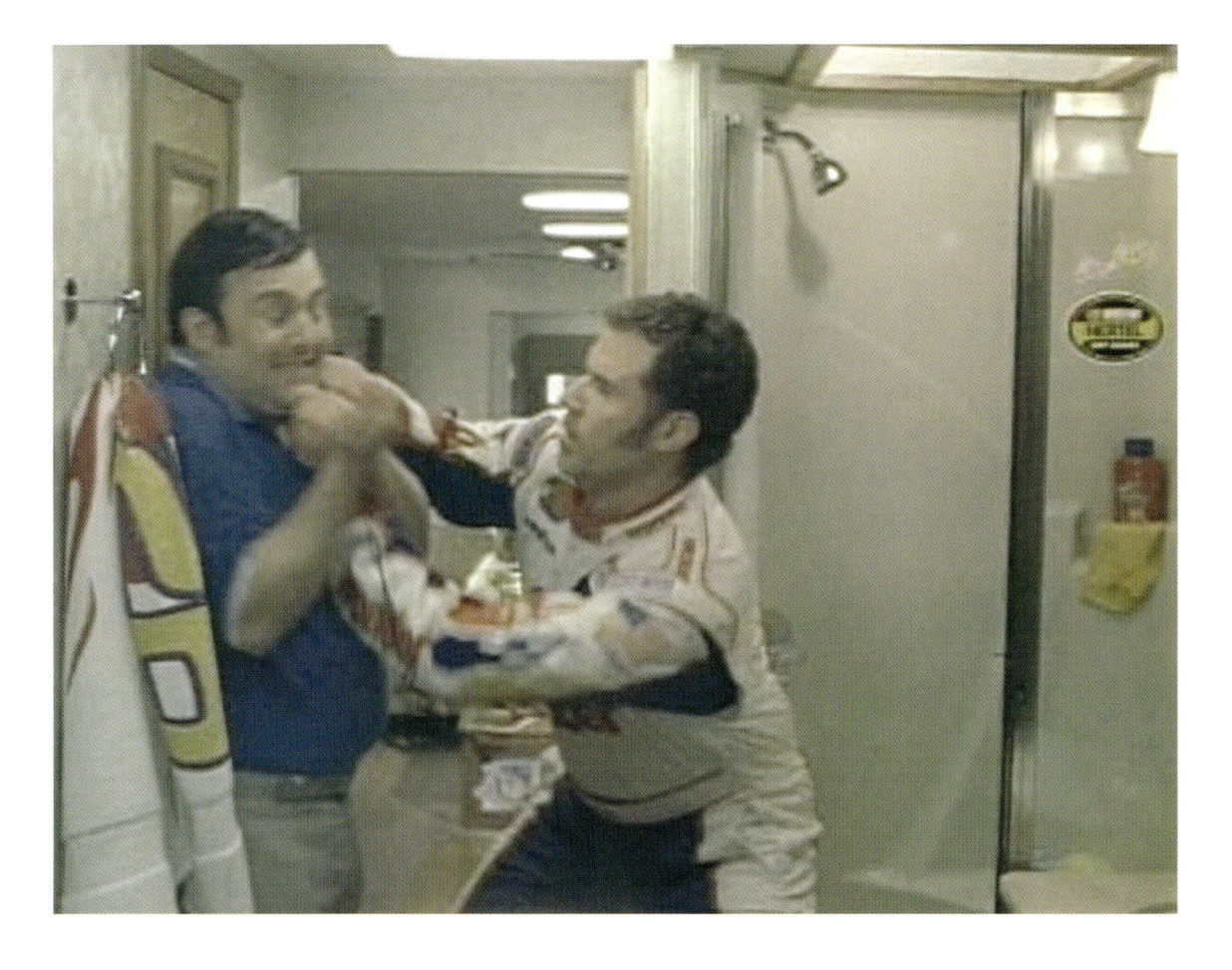

WIRELESS/MOBILE ADVERTISING: BUSINESS TO CONSUMER

GOLD

AGENCY
TBWA\Chiat\Day/
New York

CLIENT
Sprint

ART DIRECTOR
Anthony Sperduti

WRITER
Adam Alshin

AGENCY PRODUCER
Laura Ferguson

PRODUCTION COMPANY
Biscuit Filmworks

DIRECTOR
Tim Godsall

CREATIVE DIRECTORS
Gerry Graf
Adam Alshin
Anthony Sperduti

ANNUAL ID
07039N

In creating that campaign the main thing Anthony and I looked for were ideas that essentially got out of Will's way. You've already got Will Ferrel as a doofus Nascar driver. We're asking him to shamelessly hock Sprint products. It seemed the idea was already there. We figured that if he just remained in character, and played up the bad-acting-athlete/product pitchman thing that we've seen countless times from the commercially saturated world of Nascar, we'd have something interesting.

We went out to shoot one script, but the night before, Anthony, Tim and I knocked out about 10 new ones. On the day of the shoot, we sprung the extra scripts on Will and his agent Jimmy Miller, they liked them all, and we shot them really quickly over the course of about 5 hours. Jimmy Miller and Will were surprised by all the extra work because initially Sprint was hesitant to do anything more than the "approved script." But as we found with Sprint, the less we fed into the black hole that was their bureaucracy, the more we got done. And the client loved the end result. - *Adam Alshin*

WIRELESS/MOBILE ADVERTISING: BUSINESS TO CONSUMER

A BEARD IN THE HAND
Spring Mobile cuts through the mumble jumble.

WIRELESS/MOBILE ADVERTISING: BUSINESS TO CONSUMER

SILVER

AGENCY
Åkestam.Holst/
Stockholm

CLIENT
Spring Mobile

ART DIRECTOR
Paul Collins

WRITER
Filip Laurent

MULTIMEDIA ARTIST
Henrik Berglund

ANNUAL ID
07040N

URL
www.akestamholst.se/
awards/Spring

Our client offers a special technical solution, which optimizes quality of sound in a cell phone. The brief was to illustrate the difference in sound quality between them and the rest of the competitors within the market.

"Talking into your beard" is a well-known Swedish saying when it comes to mumbling or simple communication break-down. We took this one step further by creating an online application that literally illustrates speech quality.

Our solution resulted in a "real-time" voice distorter that works by letting the user interact with the campaign microsite, while listening to the result in the mobile phone at the same time.

This is how it worked:

-We asked the user to fill his/hers mobile number into the banner ad on our client's site. After entering the number and clicking on test, the user's cell phone instantly starts to ring.

-Once he or she answers, they would hear someone mumbling in the phone. Using an interactive slider in the banner ad on our client's site, we asked the user to drag it from bad sound to good sound quality while listening to the telephone call. The mumbling would become clearer and clearer the more you dragged the slider from bad sound quality to good sound quality.

WIRELESS/MOBILE ADVERTISING: BUSINESS TO CONSUMER

GIMME SHELTER
Interactive bus stops makes the wait worthwhile.

For a demo, text a code below to 33992.

NS: for News
SP: for Sports
WR: for Weather
CH: for Chat
TR: for Travel
MV: for Movies
VI: for Video
EM: for Email
SC: for Search
MP: for Maps
SG: for Shopping
CM: for Camera

To see more, visit onTreo.com

WIRELESS/MOBILE ADVERTISING: BUSINESS TO CONSUMER

BRONZE

AGENCY
AKQA/
San Francisco

CLIENT
Palm

ART DIRECTOR
Thiago Zanato

DESIGNERS
Hoj Jomehri
Terry Lee
Jeremy Gray

MULTIMEDIA ARTISTS
Stephen Clements
Caio Lazzuri
Matthew Law

PROGRAMMER
Steve Sherwood

INFORMATION ARCHITECT
Lawrence Yang

CREATIVE DIRECTORS
PJ Pereira
Rei Inamoto
Bob Pullum
Adam Lau

ANNUAL ID
07041N

URL
awards.sf.akqa.com/ontreo/creative/kiosk.html

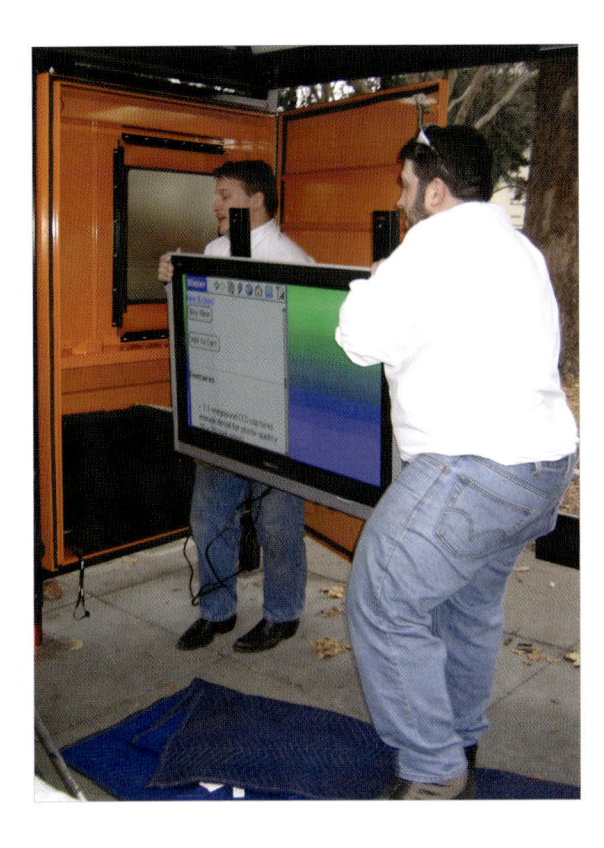

SMS-enabled bus shelters in New York, Los Angeles, and San Francisco (an industry first) were able to give non-Treo owners a taste of what life is like to have a Treo on the go through SMS-triggered flash demos that showed live feeds of weather, news, sports, etc. And local relevant content through the screen of a large Treo.

Bus shelters featured a short code where users who interact receive an SMS with more info about Treo, as well as a link to a WAP site that feature a mini brochure on Treo. Treo owners who went to this link would go to a special web page that featured links to many of the partners featured in the campaign. Some bus shelters were lenticular executions that featured an email functionality of offering multiple email accounts.

WIRELESS/MOBILE ADVERTISING: BUSINESS TO CONSUMER

TURN STYLE
This MINI will take *you* for a spin.

WIRELESS/MOBILE ADVERTISING: BUSINESS TO CONSUMER

BRONZE

AGENCY
Interone Worldwide/ Munich

CLIENT
MINI Brand Management

WRITER
Stephen James

DESIGNER
Silja Schulwitz

PROGRAMMERS
Michael Ploj
Patrick Decaix
Eva Suerek

CREATIVE DIRECTORS
Mike John Otto
Martin Gassner

ANNUAL ID
07042N

URL
www.interone.de/ cms/projects/mini// TYM/index_en.html

MINI stays on the move even when you're not behind the wheel. With this fascinating mobile application in combination with motion-sensitive software, you simply hold your phone in your hand, move it to the left and right—and the image of the MINI follows suit! Or it is the MINI that makes you turn?

EMAIL MARKETING: BUSINESS TO CONSUMER

GET LOST
An illustrated email adventure challenges LOST's captive audience.

EMAIL MARKETING: BUSINESS TO CONSUMER

Our goal was to fire up new viewers and existing LOST fans for the second season of the TV series by creating a viral buzz with an off-beat, storytelling campaign, drawing the target groups into the mysterious story.

To communicate the launch of the second season of the successful series LOST, an integrated campaign surrounding an interactive adventure was developed. The unusual aspect was that it took place in people's email systems. In four episodes, the users experienced directly in emails from the first-person perspective what it feels like to be part of LOST: mastering mazes, overpowering sharks and cracking a secret code with which to take part in a competition on a mysterious website.

In turn, the website functioned in the same way as a conventional computer console which can only be operated using keyboard shortcuts. Users had to be resourceful or to know the right forums and blogs to consult, as the only way to unearth more goodies about the second season of LOST—wallpapers, screensavers, 3D animations of the leading actors and actresses matching the on-air design, thrilling insider information, etc.—was with the help of a handful of correct key strokes.

The campaign attained above-average email opening rates of 58 percent; 22 percent of recipients took part in the competition, and several thousand emails were forwarded to friends. The goodies on the website also went down very well with LOST fans. Over 17 percent of users who visited the website not only registered for the email episodes or took part in the competition, but also took a look at the additional goodies mentioned above.

GOLD

AGENCY
Jung von Matt/
Hamburg

CLIENT
ProSieben Television

ART DIRECTORS
Sven Loskill
Jeannette Bergen

WRITER
Robert Ehlers

DESIGNER
Martin Schlierkamp

MULTIMEDIA ARTISTS
Christoph Maeschig
Ralf Lechner
Holger Jaquet
Leif Abraham
Felix Schulz

PROGRAMMERS
Yasmine Bechmann
Jan-M. Studt

CREATIVE DIRECTOR
Simone Ashoff

ANNUAL ID
07043N

URL
award.jvm.de/
oneshow/lost/

EMAIL MARKETING: BUSINESS TO CONSUMER

CREASE THE PEACE
R/GA welcomes you to the fold.

■ R/GA

WELCOME

GET IDEAS ◇   PREVIEW & SEND ◇

■ R/GA

TO CREATE A CARD, START TYPING. EACH COMPLETE SENTENCE GENERATES A NEW ORIGAMI SHAPE, SO BE SURE TO INCLUDE PROPER PUNCTUATION.

GET IDEAS ◇   PREVIEW & SEND ◇

EMAIL MARKETING: BUSINESS TO CONSUMER

SILVER

AGENCY
R/GA/New York

CLIENT
R/GA/New York

WRITERS
Chapin Clark
Steve Caputo

DESIGNERS
Jeff Baxter
Wade Convay
Jonathan Lee
Heidi Ng
Fura Johannesdottir
Jill Nussbaum
Elena Sakevich
Pablo Gomez
Akane Kodani

PROGRAMMERS
David Bolton
Hector Larios
Chris Hinkle
Patrick Fitzgerald

AGENCY PRODUCER
Emily Olson

MUSIC & SOUND
Dan LaPlaca

ORIGAMI ARTISTS
Joseph Wu
Jun Maekawa

CREATIVE DIRECTOR
Gui Borchert

ANNUAL ID
07044N

Call it a new wrinkle in a venerable art form: R/GA chose origami as the inspiration for its 2006 holiday card, using stop-motion photography and Flash to bring the season's greetings to life through dozens of origami models. Some of the designs are traditional, others are holiday themed, and a few push the boundaries of what might be considered "true" origami. All were created in house by the R/GA team. Recipients can make their own animated cards simply by typing a message. The programming logic then searches for keywords to return thematically relevant origami. Half the fun is trying to figure out how words conjure particular animals or objects.

EMAIL MARKETING: PUBLIC SERVICE/NON-PROFIT/EDUCATIONAL

DEPILATED DISPATCHES
They're bringing hairy back.

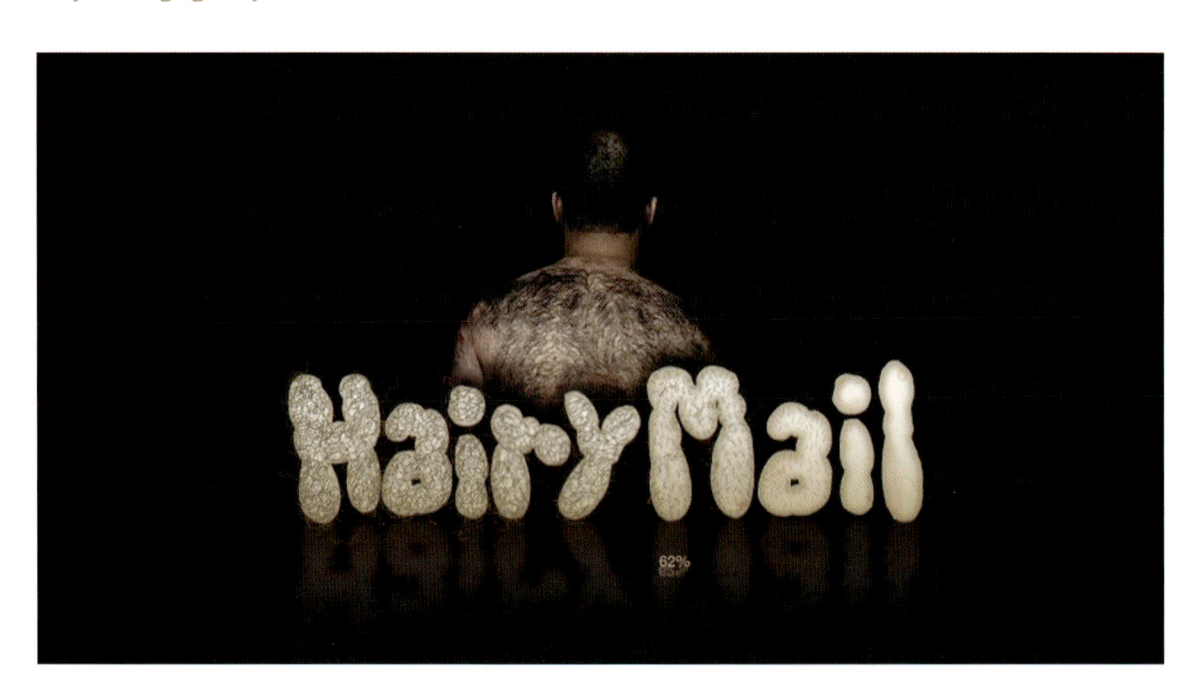

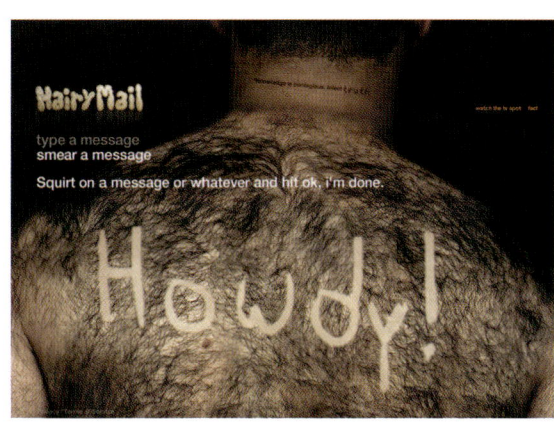

EMAIL MARKETING: PUBLIC SERVICE/NON-PROFIT/EDUCATIONAL

BRONZE

AGENCY
Arnold/Boston

CLIENT
American Legacy Foundation/truth

ART DIRECTORS
Mike Costello
Meghan Siegal

WRITERS
Marc Einhorn
Matt Ledoux

DESIGNERS
Cuban Council
Brad Kayal

PROGRAMMERS
Cuban Council
Ebbey Mathew

CREATIVE DIRECTORS
Pete Favat
Alex Bogusky
John Kearse
Tom Adams
Meghan Siegal

ANNUAL ID
07045N

URL
www.hairy-mail.com

Hairy-mail.com is the world's first web-based back-hair messaging system. On this site, people could send fellow enthusiasts thick, luscious greetings written in the back of a rather hirsute individual. Like in the corresponding TV spot, we point out that one of the chemical ingredients in cigarettes is also an ingredient in hair removal products. A hairy-mail widget was also created, with which users could leave "hairy comments" on friends' MySpace pages or blogs. The benefit of the widget was that new messages could be created directly from a comment, rather than having to return to the truth profile. This upped the pass-along value exponentially, and as of January 2007, over 85,000 hairy-mail "infections" had been sent along. -Marc Einhorn

ONLINE BRANDED CONTENT: BUSINESS TO CONSUMER

TRICKS OF THE TRADE
Beauty is only pixel deep.

ONLINE BRANDED CONTENT: BUSINESS TO CONSUMER

GOLD

AGENCY
Ogilvy & Mather/
Toronto

CLIENT
Unilever/Dove

ART DIRECTORS
Tim Piper
Mike Kirkland

WRITER
Tim Piper

MULTIMEDIA ARTISTS
Edward Cha
Eric Makila
Kevin Gibson
Bob Zagorskis

PRODUCTION COMPANY
Reginald Pike

DIRECTORS
Yael Staav
Tim Piper

MUSIC & SOUND
Vapor Music Group

CREATIVE DIRECTORS
Janet Kestin
Nancy Vonk

ANNUAL ID
07046N

URL
www.youtube.com/
watch?v=iYhCn0jf46U

We needed to raise awareness of the Dove Self-Esteem Fund and the Real Beauty Workshop with almost no media budget.

The solution was to create a viral film (or series) to run on campaignforrealbeauty.ca, encouraging mothers/mentors of young girls to get involved with the Dove Self-Esteem Fund's workshops, online tools and resources. "Evolution" is designed to be an attention-grabber. It uses an artful time-lapse treatment to demonstrate how much work goes into creating the image of a "poster girl."

The workshops sold out across Canada. Globally, mass awareness of the Dove Self-Esteem Fund and its tools and resources was achieved. "Evolution" aired as content on television shows and news programs throughout the world. In fact, Rosie O'Donnell declared on her program *The View* that she was "gonna use Dove from now on just because of that ad." The talent was interviewed on *Entertainment Tonight* and several other high profile shows in the U.S. and Canada.

"Evolution" was uploaded onto YouTube where it attracted much attention. Within a week, "Evolution" became the top-rated, most talked about, most favorite video across several categories. The film has been viewed online by millions, and Unilever estimates a media value equivalent of $150 million.

ONLINE BRANDED CONTENT: BUSINESS TO CONSUMER

ROCKIN' THE MADRAS
Tea Partay defines Prep-Hop.

ONLINE BRANDED CONTENT: BUSINESS TO CONSUMER

SILVER

AGENCY
Bartle Bogle Hegarty/
New York

CLIENT
Smirnoff

ART DIRECTOR
Amee Shah

WRITERS
Matt Ian
Clay Weiner

AGENCY PRODUCER
Lisa Setten

PRODUCTION COMPANY
H.S.I. Productions

DIRECTOR
Julien Christian Lutz

MUSIC & SOUND
Taj Critchlow
J Diggz

CREATIVE DIRECTOR
Kevin Roddy

ANNUAL ID
07047N

URL
www.teapartay.com

It was important for us not to do just another cornball, white guy rap parody. Jamie Kennedy already did Malibu's Most Wanted. Why bother celebrating more rich idiots who fancy themselves gangsta?

We wanted more of a twist with this piece, more of an insight. Fortunately, we are both familiar with prep culture having married a guy from Chestnut Hill, PA (Amee) and having grown up in Greenwich, CT (Matt). This put us in an ideal position to capture the nuances and the subtleties of what it truly means to be prep, right down to Lilly Pulitzer prints, the summer rope bracelets and the Nantucket Lightship Baskets. And that's what we think makes this more than just another dumb rap parody. We actually created a new genre, Prepsta, instead of just doing yet another piss-take on suburban whiteys play-acting like badass pimps.

We'd like to believe that it's this careful attention to detail that people responded to. But maybe they just liked it when Muffy and Buffy shook their asses. It's hard to tell. - *Matt Ian and Amee Shah*

ONLINE BRANDED CONTENT: BUSINESS TO CONSUMER

MORE HOMER BY THE POUND
You know its British when Marge drives on the wrong (right) side.

ONLINE BRANDED CONTENT: BUSINESS TO CONSUMER

BRONZE

AGENCY
devilfish/
London

CLIENT
Sky One

ART DIRECTOR
Nik Stewart

WRITER
Jonny Parker

MULTIMEDIA ARTIST
The Quarry

PRODUCTION COMPANY
Gorgeous

DIRECTOR
Chris Palmer

MUSIC & SOUND
Scramble

CREATIVE DIRECTOR
Richard Holman

ANNUAL ID
07048N

As well as re-affirming the channel as the home of the show, we also were asked to create a loveable and entertaining brand film that would use Sky One's most popular property to enhance viewers' relationship with the channel. This all had to be achieved with great sensitivity to Simpsons fans by being true to the spirit and the detail of the original.

We came up with the disconcertingly simple idea of showing an archetypical British family—who bear an uncanny resemblance to the show's characters—rushing home to watch the show in the way that The Simpsons themselves do in the title sequence. Springfield becomes Sheffield.

An exhaustive casting process, which sought to capture key traits of each of The Simpsons family, as well as intense location scouting, brought us cast and locations which bear a strong resemblance to the original whilst being authentically British.

The resulting film is a captivating union of *The Simpsons* and everyday British life, paying homage to the show's standing in contemporary comedy and the UK viewing public's affection for it.

NEW MEDIA INNOVATION & DEVELOPMENT

RUN DIFFERENT

The very physical and sweaty world of running is now digitally networked.

NEW MEDIA INNOVATION & DEVELOPMENT

Nike+ is reinventing running by revolutionizing how a brand reaches its audience through meaningful personal experiences, invaluable data brought to life online, and brand-enhancing two-way communication. Nike appointed R/GA to design and build the customer experience for Nike+, including the software that supports data transfer from iTunes to the nikeplus.com site. Nikeplus.com bridges two products, a Nike shoe and an iPod nano. A sensor in Nike+ running shoes tracks data and transmits it to a runner's iPod, which is automatically uploaded to nikeplus.com when the iPod is synched. The Nike+ digital platform allows runners to set goals, compare runs, track individual progress, as well as connect with the community through virtual challenges and the global forum.

GOLD

AGENCY
R/GA/New York

CLIENT
Nike

WRITERS
Josh Bletterman
Alison Hess

DESIGNERS
Jeff Baxter
Wade Convay
Gary Van Dzura
Ed Kim
Michael Reger
Elena Sakevich
Claudia Bernett
Joe Tobens

MULTIMEDIA ARTISTS
Mark Voelpel
Kiril Yeretsky

PROGRAMMERS
Nick Coronges
Aaron Ambrose
Noel Billig
Matthias Hader
Asako Kohno
William Lee
Michael Mosley
Michael Piccuirro
Geoffrey Roth
Ben Sosinski
John Tubert
Stan Wiechers
Nauman Hafiz
Michele Roman
August Yang

AGENCY PRODUCERS
Matt Howell
Sean Lyons
Brock Busby
Daniel Jurow
James Kuo
David Ross

CREATIVE DIRECTORS
Nick Law
Kris Kiger
Richard Ting
Gui Borchert
Natalie Lam
Jill Nussbaum
Michael Spiegel

ANNUAL ID
07050N

NEW MEDIA INNOVATION & DEVELOPMENT

THE AIR DYNAMIC
Nike launches another high-tech shoe into thin air.

NEW MEDIA INNOVATION & DEVELOPMENT

SILVER

AGENCY
AKQA/London

CLIENT
Nike

ART DIRECTOR
Masaya Nakade

WRITER
Nick Bailey

MULTIMEDIA ARTISTS
Greg Mullen
Alex Wills

PROGRAMMERS
Richard Leggett
Matthew Elwin
Stephen Smith
Lee Banks

CREATIVE DIRECTOR
Daniel Bonner

ANNUAL ID
07051N

URL
awards.akqa.com/awards2006/nike/festivalofair/interactiveshoes.htm

A spectacular 'Festival of Air' was created at NikeTown London to celebrate the arrival of the Nike Air Max 360, the ultimate evolution of Nike Air technology. The integrated campaign featured interactive exhibits including basketball and running challenge, a virtual shoe, in store data capture, window displays and a website to showcase the heritage and performance benefits of Nike Air Technology.

JUMP HIGHER THAN LEBRON: In the first of two 14-day challenges, shoppers were challenged to equal basketballer LeBron James's vertical leap of 112cm with a hoop set up inside the store.

IMAGE CAPTURE: A ring light and retro-reflective screen allowed us to capture a sequence of still images of each jump attempt with the background already keyed-out. A bespoke application which we designed automatically measured the maximum height of each leap.

REAL-TIME COMPOSITING: Each challenger's image sequence was instantly composited with a stadium shot and combined with their name and jump height to create a unique souvenir image which challengers could access via festivalofair.com, and which also appeared on screens in the window at NikeTown.

RUN AS FAST AS PAULA: For the second two-week challenge, treadmills were set up in store and challengers invited to maintain Paula Radcliffe's record-breaking marathon pace for as long as possible.

LIVE VIDEO CAST: Three competitors at a time were filmed and the footage relayed to giant screens inside the store, together with the time elapsed and a progress bar showing distance covered.

HELIOS PROJECTION: To showcase the brand new Nike Air Max 360 shoe we projected an interactive 3D model of the shoe onto thin air using revolutionary Helio Display technology—a first for a brand in the U.K.

INTERACTIVITY: When touched, the model exploded to reveal the individual components of the shoe, while captions appeared explaining the function of each part.

NEW MEDIA INNOVATION & DEVELOPMENT

LOCAL MOTION
Bus ads that know where you are, even if you don't, but really need that 4am cheeseburger.

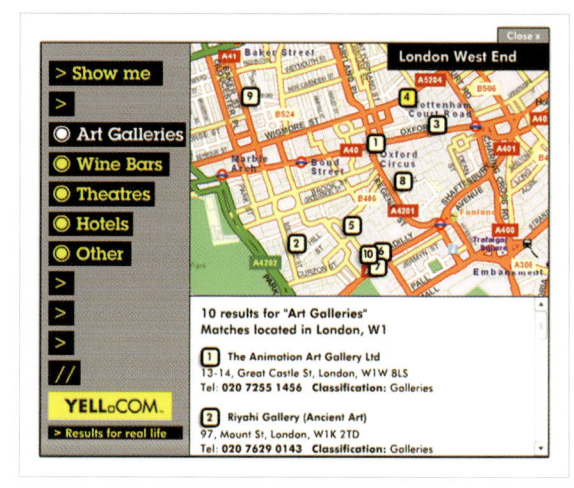

NEW MEDIA INNOVATION & DEVELOPMENT

SILVER

AGENCY
AKQA/London

CLIENT
Yell.com

ART DIRECTOR
James Capp

WRITER
Phil Wilce

DESIGNERS
Dan Wright
Chris Williams

CREATIVE DIRECTOR
Daniel Bonner

ANNUAL ID
07052N

URL
awards.akqa.com/ awards2006/yell/ results/popup3.html

Yell.com asked AKQA to raise awareness of the Yell.com brand by creating a unique, relevant and motivating brand campaign that would increase consumer understanding of Yell.com's offering and benefits. The challenge for AKQA was to use innovative media to create a unique advertising campaign that reached Yell.com's broad target audience through a variety of media touch-points.

Accomplishing an industry-first, these LED Bus Supersides were equipped with GPS tracking technology; displaying geographically targeted ads highlighting local information and the breadth of online directory listings.

AKQA equipped 25 of London's double-decker buses with the technology and targeted messaging, which works to deliver localized ads to commuters showing what can be found in the area depending on the bus' location.

NEW MEDIA INNOVATION & DEVELOPMENT

ACCELER8
Take this sexy beast of a car on a long drive along the coast.

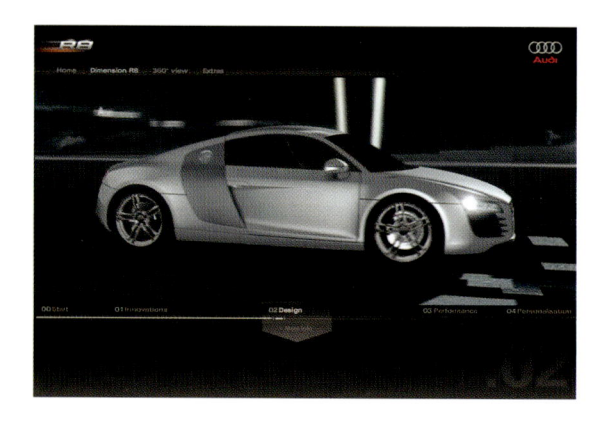

NEW MEDIA INNOVATION & DEVELOPMENT

BRONZE

AGENCY
argonauten G2/
Düsseldorf

CLIENT
Audi

ART DIRECTOR
Oliver Hinrichs

PROGRAMMERS
Sven Gessner
Dorian Roy
Oliver List

INFORMATION ARCHITECT
Wolfgang Schulz

CONTENT STRATEGIST
Wolfgang Schulz

CREATIVE DIRECTOR
Sven Küster

ANNUAL ID
07053N

URL
microsites.audi.com/audir8/

The R8 is associated with the successful Le Mans race cars, and its design is based on the pioneering concept car Le Mans Quattro from 2003. The aim of the microsite was to present the characteristics of athleticism and progressivism in an emotional way, enabling people to experience Audi's expertise in the area of sports cars while establishing the R8 in the relevant set of sports car buyers.

The microsite guides the user into the R8 dimension, an interactive film in which the viewers can experience all facets of the vehicle first-hand. The 3-D rendered film shows the Audi R8 on the racetrack, in the city and on a long drive along the coast. Each of these film sequences is assigned to a specific chapter: Innovation, Design and Performance. The entire film was designed and implemented without a real Audi R8 even having to touch the asphalt. A soundtrack was composed especially for the film to strengthen the emotional impact like in major film productions.

The user is able to navigate within the site by using the video timeline and dive into the different content sections over seamlessly connected video transitions. An intelligent pre-loading mechanism ensures that subsequent scenes are always available. The customizable 360° view of the Audi R8 emerges from the video as an integrated element which lets the user interactively take control of the movie. Every combination of view angle, car color and exterior equipment can be selected while remaining in the movie scenery.

It is by combining state of the art technology, cutting-edge motion graphics and an intuitive navigation that the Audi R8 microsite is able to immerse the user into a unique, innovative and yet content relevant online experience. The interactive movie brings the best of two worlds together: great cinema that sends shivers down the spines of its viewers combined with the interactive possibilities of the Web.

111

NEW MEDIA INNOVATION & DEVELOPMENT

A GIRL NAMED JOHNNIE

Hot digital PA serves information straight-up, the way you like it.

NEW MEDIA INNOVATION & DEVELOPMENT

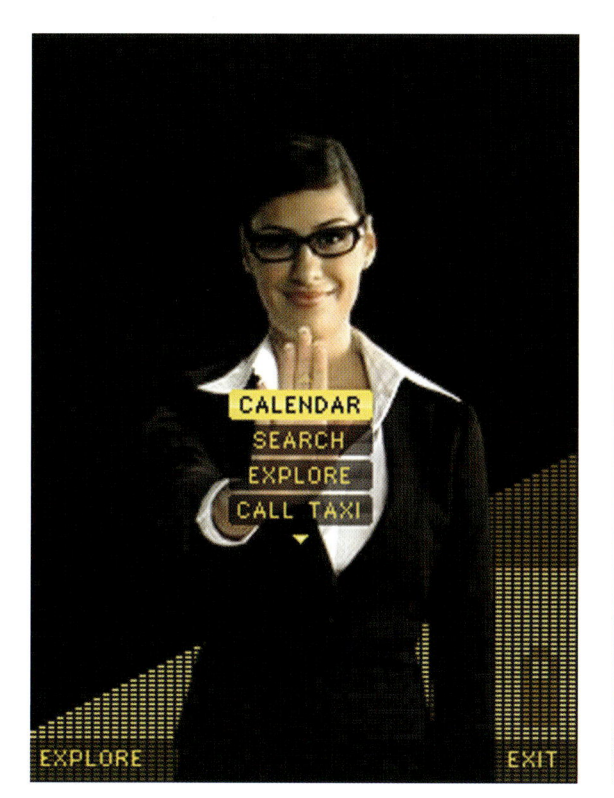

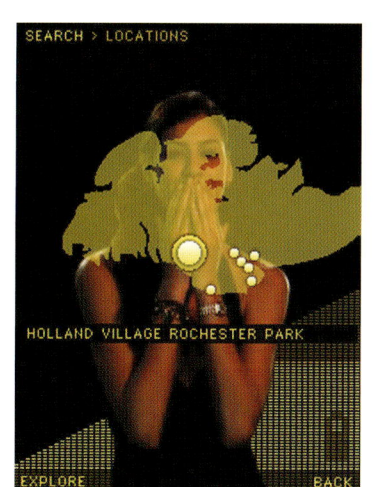

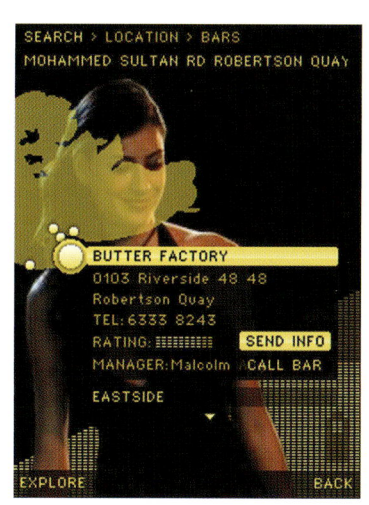

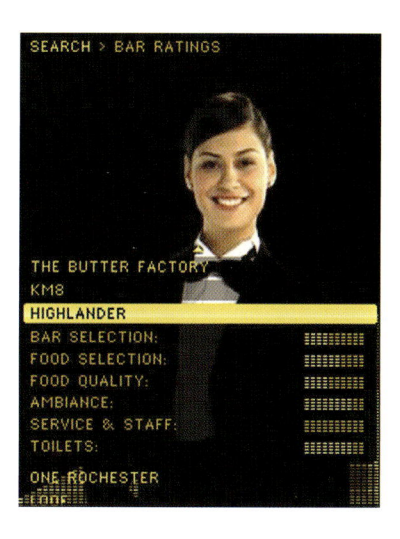

BRONZE

AGENCY
Ogilvy/Singapore

CLIENT
Diageo

ART DIRECTORS
Xavier Teo
Robert Davies
Mark Taylor

WRITERS
Grace Tan
John Scott

PROGRAMMERS
Stefan Wessels
Dave O'Reilly
Shang Liang

PRODUCTION COMPANIES
Pervyn Lim
Kenny Ong
Celica S.

CREATIVE DIRECTOR
Peter Moss

ANNUAL ID
07054N

URL
www.our-work.com/jw/digitalpa/

The brief was to create a groundbreaking way to connect with members of Johnnie Walker's RM program, 24degrees.

Taking digital innovation to new heights, Johnnie Walker launched a world first—a Digital Personal Assistant that can be loaded onto mobile phones. Providing 24/7 access, the Digital PA uses a stylish flash-based video interface to serve up branded content, special offers and invitations to exclusive members-only events. It creates an omni-present, always-connected, location-aware digital window to loyal drinkers, driving consumption and increasing brand equity by developing an intense and unique relationship with them.

NEW MEDIA INNOVATION & DEVELOPMENT

LOST HIGHWAY

Chase MINI down the world weird web.

NEW MEDIA INNOVATION & DEVELOPMENT

BRONZE

AGENCY
Profero/London

CLIENT
MINI

ART DIRECTOR
Scott Clark

DESIGNERS
Johan Arlig
Jamie Long

PROGRAMMER
Chris O'Byrne

CREATIVE DIRECTOR
Matt Powell

ANNUAL ID
07055N

URL
www.profero.com/mini_whiterabbit

The notion behind the "Follow the White Rabbit" campaign blurs the distinction between whether it is a creative idea or media idea, instead it is just an idea that works and at the same time seamlessly fits in with the cheeky and irreverent persona of the MINI brand. Profero was briefed to create a brand-building online campaign to act as a teaser for the launch of the new MINI in November. We wanted to bring the idea of a MINI adventure to life online at the same time not just copy the above the line campaign.

Through our planning and customer insight we found people's online user habits were far from adventurous. We wanted to bring back the adventure of the web, to disrupt the way people surfed the internet by taking them on a MINI adventure to the most obscure, yet brilliant and distinctive British content on the net we never get to see.

Inspired by the *The Matrix* and *Alice in Wonderland*, "Follow the White Rabbit" was born, which in a nutshell took users on an unexpected journey to a series of independent websites and offered an experience like never before.

So not only did we create the executions using 3D Flash animation and CGI, we also had to find and choose real websites where we took users to as part of their journey. We started with an initial list of 456 sites and short listed them down to 12 to make up three separate unique journeys.

The user was taken on one of three possible journeys; each selected randomly and the user will never see the same journey twice. Furthermore it is one of the few true examples of a branding campaign online where the only branding is the car: the ad clearly states "This is not the way to the MINI website," and at the end of the journey we leave them with nowhere to go, encouraging them to find another journey.

OTHER INTERACTIVE DIGITAL MEDIA

SHADOWDANCING IN SHIBUYA
Xbox casts sorcery and spells on Tokyo's vertiginous cityscape.

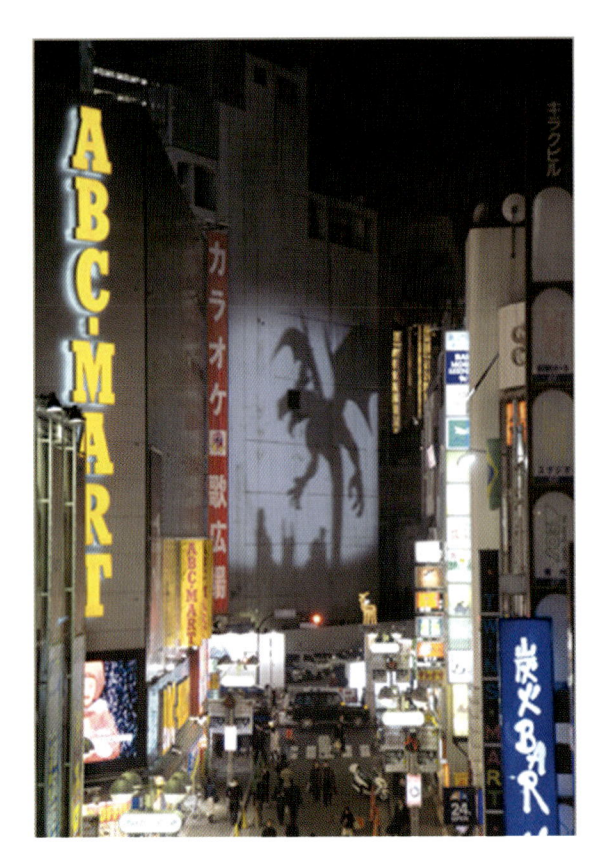

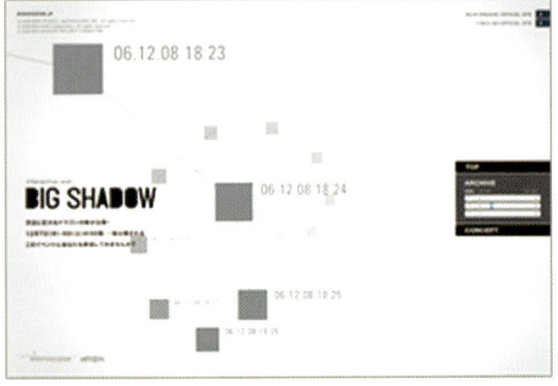

OTHER INTERACTIVE DIGITAL MEDIA

GOLD

AGENCY
GT/Tokyo

CLIENT
Microsoft

ANNAUL ID
07056N

URL
bigshadow.jp/

Blue Dragon is a video game wherein the protagonist's shadow becomes a dragon when he fights. To promote the title, we focused on the primordial human experience of shadow-play. We projected magnified shadows of ordinary people in town and created a system whereby they could play with their own shadows. A person's shadow is projected as a giant shadow image, which can suddenly change into the shape of a dragon. This creates a new and engaging interactive experience. A shadow can also be manipulated via the Web while viewing a webcam image. We wanted to provide a fresh experience that links the city and the Internet as well as people and shadows.

The "shadows" are not real shadows, but rather projections of images captured by a video camera and manipulated with a specially-developed C++ program and then cast onto the wall by four powerful projectors. This combination of technology enables the "shadows" to morph into shapes such as the dragon shadow images. However, our goal was not to show off advanced technology, but rather to see how close we could get to the primordial experience of shadows, which everyone carries in their memory.

Shadows of the participants' movements are projected upon a massive wall of a building, 7-stories high. When participants perform particular actions such as raising their arms over their heads, a giant dragon shadow appears out of the participants' shadows. Via the Internet, another person's "shadow" can be added to the on-site wall-projection in real-time using a webcam that picks up the off-site image. The relayed images are archived and can be viewed as a sequence of still images arranged in a spiral along a time axis.

OTHER INTERACTIVE DIGITAL MEDIA

IMAGINING GREEN
Saturn's return to our planet with a hybrid for everyone.

OTHER INTERACTIVE DIGITAL MEDIA

SILVER

AGENCY
Goodby, Silverstein & Partners/San Francisco

CLIENT
Saturn

ART DIRECTOR
Chris Valencius

WRITER
Toria Emery

CONTENT STRATEGISTS
Mike Geiger
Brit Charlebois
Hilary Bradley

PRODUCTION COMPANIES
Obscura Digital
The Barbarian Group

CREATIVE DIRECTORS
Jeff Goodby
Keith Anderson
Will McGinness

ANNUAL ID
07057N

URL
www.goodbysilverstein.com/awards/one_show_07/nextfest.html

The installation at WIRED NextFest 2006 focused on Saturn's Green Line hybrid vehicles. Because the Green Line is designed to be affordable, Saturn has democratized hybrid technology for the good of the planet and customers' wallets. GSP, Obscura Digital and the Barbarian Group teamed up to create a display that was equally inclusive and inviting.

A 45-foot-wide, high-resolution reactive and interactive wall of animated, stylized grass anchored the 4,000-square-foot space. Via a kiosk, visitors were asked, "What if everyone drove a hybrid?" For each answer, a blade of grass grew on the screen and connected with the user's thought—creating a user-generated, product-relevant art display.

To highlight specific features and hybrid components, super high-definition CAD-based animations were mapped and projected onto the cars. The effect was like pulling back the sheet metal or seeing the car with x-ray vision.

Finally, a motion-sensitive hologram of a life-sized man was on hand to explain the hybrid technology in greater detail using *Minority Report*-style floating graphics.

Nearly everyone who came to the display commented that the interactive/reactive grass wall acted as a beacon, drawing them straight to the installation. Combined with information from the car projections and holograms, visitors discovered something they hadn't known before: Saturn is more forward-thinking than they had realized.

OTHER INTERACTIVE DIGITAL MEDIA

FULL FLAME
A film festival website gets a fiery makeover.

OTHER INTERACTIVE DIGITAL MEDIA

BRONZE

AGENCY
McKinney/Durham

CLIENT
Full Frame Documentary Film Festival

ART DIRECTOR
Ryan O'Hara Theisen

WRITER
Chad Lynch

DESIGNERS
Tim McCracken
Scott Williford

MULTIMEDIA ARTISTS
Larry Olson
Amariah Olson
Obin Olson

PROGRAMMERS
Tarik Laham
Craig Mann
Clive Sweeney
Scott Williford

AGENCY PRODUCERS
Melissa Jenkins
Rich Beck
Anson Burtch

PRODUCTION COPMANIES
McKinney
DV3 Productions

CREATIVE DIRECTOR
David Baldwin

ANNUAL ID
07058N

URL
www.awardshow
submissions.com/
assets/fullframefire

In spring 2004 we launched a new site for the Full Frame Documentary Film Festival. To complement the hands-on nature and minimal funding of documentary filmmaking, an intricate shadowbox design was constructed of cardboard to serve as the homepage. And cardboard, as we all know, is highly flammable.

When Full Frame later requested a site redesign for added functionality, we applied real-world properties of combustion to the online environment. We burned their current site to the ground. This seemingly implausible act established a viable reason, to those on the outside looking in, for a new site to be constructed.

Word of the "tragedy" spread through mass e-mails, viral news clips and a temporary evacuation web page. Over three days, fire progressively consumed the site, eventually burning itself out. On the fourth day, we unveiled the new site.

This blending of reality with fiction—transplanting a disaster from the three-dimensional world to two-dimensional cyberspace—garnered a great deal of attention for what could have otherwise been a common occurrence.

INTEGRATED BRANDING CAMPAIGN

GEEK KING
His Creepiness finds new life with a trio of gaming titles.

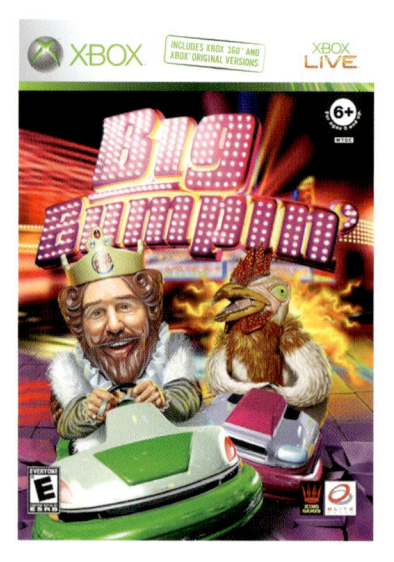

INTEGRATED BRANDING CAMPAIGN

With the success of BK's various advertising campaigns, from Subservient Chicken, to the Whopperettes, Whopper Jr, to the King himself, a dynasty of characters has been created for the fast food chain. What better way to make these BK personalities a bigger part of our customers' lives than to go beyond advertising and include them in engaging, interactive consumer entertainment?

Each game gives you control over a BK character in a number of different game-playing scenarios: pocket-bike racing, bumper cars, and a unique form of stealth adventure where you're able to go behind the mask of the King. The promotion was a huge success, getting millions of consumers to voluntarily interact with the brand and contributing to an incredible 40 percent spike in quarterly profits.

But it didn't end there. The games were also a big success in the video game market as well. Within two months, Burger King stores had sold over 3.2 million games, besting Xbox-favorite, *Gears of War*, for the coveted title of the best-selling video game of the holiday season. If we added it all up—the games have been played over 20 million times for about 1,302 years worth of gameplay/time spent with the King. This promotional effort not only cut through the clutter, engaging customers in a way that TV or print campaigns can never do, but it became a piece of cultural entertainment that people actively sought out and paid money to interact with. Truly a customer experience worthy of the King.

GOLD

AGENCIES
Crispin Porter + Bogusky/Miami
Equity Marketing/Miami

CLIENT
Burger King

ART DIRECTORS
Aramis Israel
Mark Taylor

WRITERS
Ryan Kutscher
Jeff Gillette
Aramis Israel
Bob Cianfrone
Jake Mikosh
Rob Thompson

DESIGNERS
Mike Del Marmol
Alvaro Ilizarbe
Pres Rodriguez
Carlos Lange
Conor McCann
Joe Miranda
Jiwon Lee
Logan

AGENCY PRODUCERS
Rupert Samuel
Eric Rasco
Brian Rekasis
Jessica Reznick
Sheri Radel
Bill Meadows
Jurgen Dold

PRODUCTION COMPANIES
Blitz Games
Evolution Engine
Plus Productions

DIRECTORS
Aramis Israel
Dan Ruth
Eric Rasco

CREATAIVE DIRECTORS
Alex Bogusky
Rob Reilly
Jeff Benjamin
Kim Thompson
Jon Banks

ANNUAL ID
07059N

URL
www.cpbgroup.com/
awards/bkxboxgames
integrated.html

INTEGRATED BRANDING CAMPAIGN

"DON'T BE SUCKING"
GTI untricks cars with the help of Wolfgang and Helga, straight auto Deutschland.

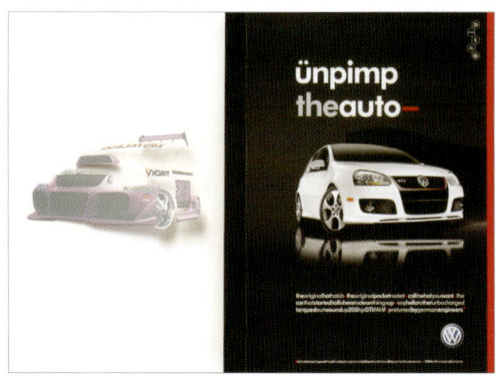

INTEGRATED BRANDING CAMPAIGN

GOLD

AGENCY
Crispin Porter + Bogusky/Miami

CLIENT
Volkswagen

ART DIRECTORS
Tiffany Kosel
Mike Ferrare
Rahul Panchal
Aramis Israel
Tom Zukoski

WRITERS
Scott Linnen
Mike Howard
Jeff Gillette
Ryan Kutscher

DESIGNERS
Conor McCann
Chean Wei Law

AGENCY PRODUCERS
Rupert Samuel
Matt Bonin
Winston Binch
Dan Ruth
Paul Sutton
Jessica Hoffman
Bill Meadows

PRODUCTION COMPANIES
IQ Interactive
RSA
Motive

DIRECTORS
Matt Walsh
Jonas Akerlund

CREATIVE DIRECTORS
Alex Bogusky
Andrew Keller
Jeff Benjamin
Rob Strasberg
Tony Calcao
Scott Linnen

ANNUAL ID
07060N

URL
www.cpbgroup.com/awards/vwgtiintegrated.html

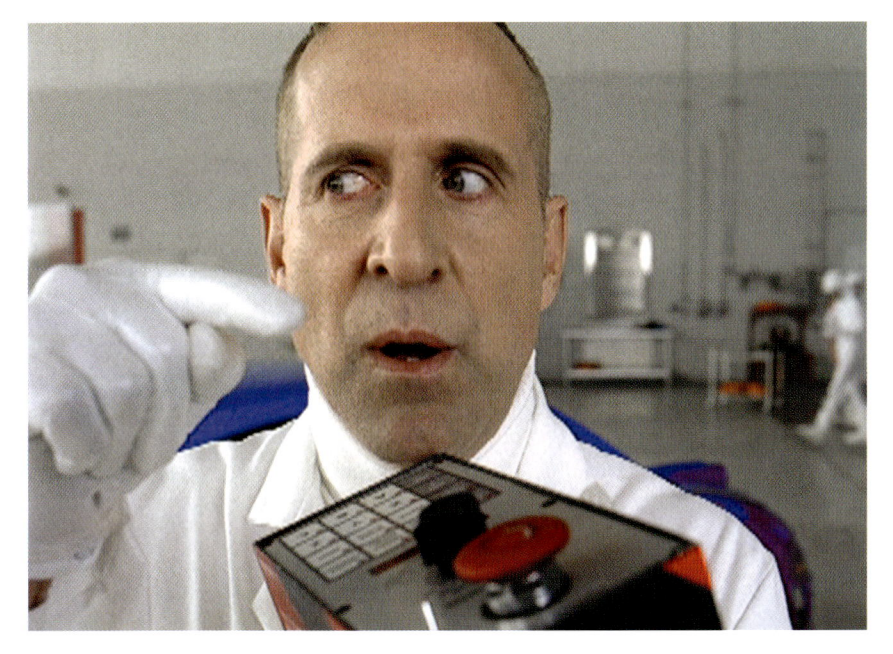

Twenty years ago Volkswagen created a monster. In 1984, VW introduced the GTI, giving birth to Hot Hatch culture, and along with it came a new breed of car owner: the tuner. Fast forward to present day, where in any parking lot in America you can find one of these tuner's "pimped" rides: a tacky economy car adorned with ostentatious racing decorations applied with little regard for taste or performance.

With the Un-pimp campaign Volkswagen sought to get tuner culture back on track, and reassert the dominance of German Engineering, as represented in all it's glory by the 200 HP VW GTI. Videos on YouTube showed German Engineers ruthlessly "un-pimping" tuner mobiles, and teaching their owners about the new GTI. At VWFeatures.com we created a GTI Configurator that let visitors customize their GTI's with all the available features, after which they could take their pre-tuned whip on a virtual joyride with the beautiful German Engineer, Helga.

We also brought Helga to life by creating a MySpace page for her, featuring a profile, a soundboard, ring tones, a question and answer section, and pictures of her on vacation. As of the present date she has over 8,400 friends. Another key component of the campaign was the creation of the "V-Dub" hand signal. This sign has become a cultural phenomenon of its own among the Volkswagen family and across eBay and enthusiaest sites like VWVortex.com. Banners brought the car and its features to life and put the german pre-tuned car into the hands of users.

INTEGRATED BRANDING CAMPAIGN

KNIGHTS IN WHITE SPANDEX

Nike plays with costume and messes with cultural stereotypes.

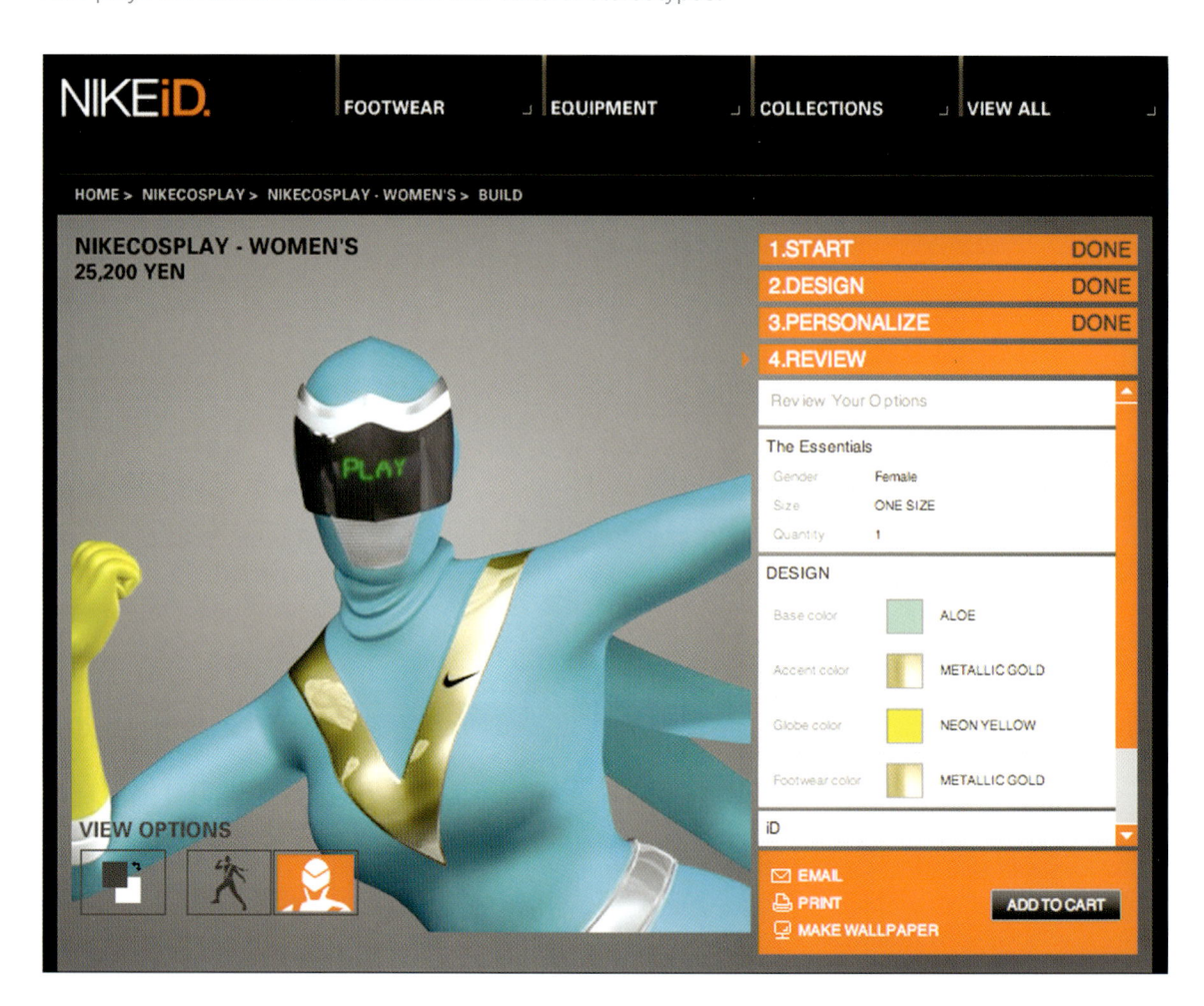

Night Club

Famous Running Club

INTEGRATED BRANDING CAMPAIGN

Club World Cup Final

Fashion Boutique

Poster (Point of Sales)

SILVER

AGENCY
ADK/Tokyo

CLIENT
Nike

ART DIRECTOR
Naoki Ito

WRITER
Naoki Ito

DESIGNERS
Saiko Kamikanda
Toshinori Matsuura

MULTIMEDIA ARTIST
Kenichi Iida

AGENCY PRODUCERS
Yasutoshi Hosoike
Shunsuke Kakinami
Takeshi Fukuda
Mits Minowa

PRODUCTION COMPANIES
TYO Productions
Root Communications

DIRECTORS
Kan Eguchi
Toru Terashima
Yasuhiro Yamanaka
Toshihiro Tomioka

CREATIVE DIRECTORS
Naoki Ito
Tatsuro Sato

ANNUAL ID
07061N

URL
akibaman.jp/
nikecosplay/

"Colorlessness" is an evil that has spread throughout Japan. The Japanese lack color in their lives, and they must break out of their shells. NIKEiD is an innovative online service where you can customize Nike shoes with infinite colors and materials. This colorful self-expression will deal a massive blow to the "colorlessness" of the Japanese.

This viral promotion campaign, taking place in Akihabara under the concept of "the Net meets the real world," originated from a commercial spot that was first released exclusively on YouTube. One month after the movie was unveiled, the Cosplay website went online (in the guise of a costume merchandising site), as did the "grey suit" protagonist's blog in connection to guerilla-like appearances in real places. Special ringtones for cell phones, and videocasts were realized as well, and this set of different measures eventually created a buzz, both on the Internet and beyond. Within two months after it first appeared on YouTube, the video was viewed more than 500,000 times, and special features were published in magazines, on TV and net news programs. "Akibaman" ranked seventh in the list of the most popular keywords entered in Internet search engines. The "Just a Joke" experience then relaunched the viral promotion.

INTEGRATED BRANDING CAMPAIGN

TERRAIN OR SHINE

Polaris challenges the other guys to an ATV bust-up. It's a CEO-down!

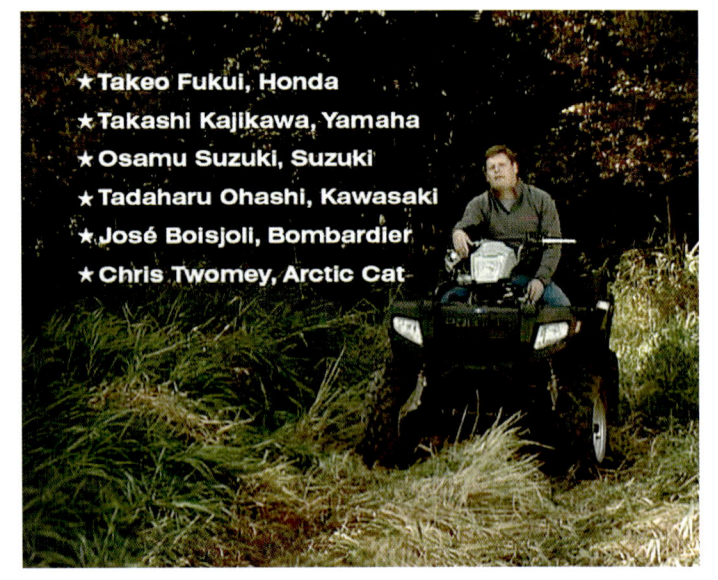

128

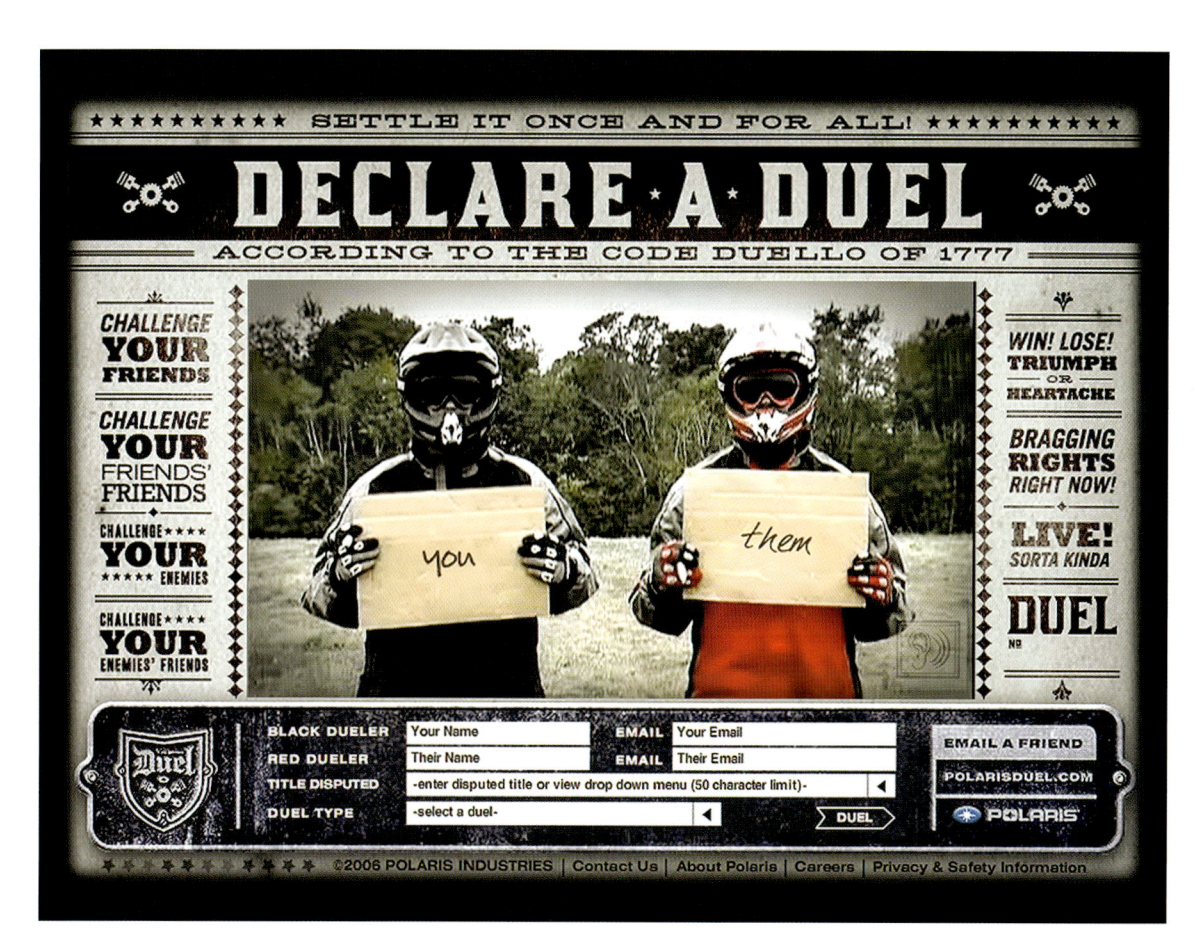

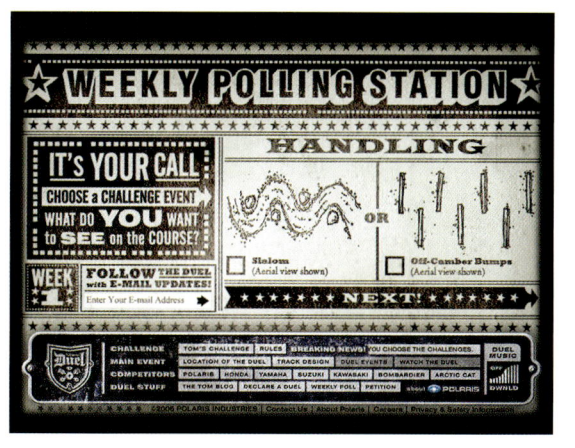

INTEGRATED BRANDING CAMPAIGN

SILVER

AGENCY
McKinney/Durham

CLIENT
Polaris Industries

ART DIRECTORS
David Hermanas
Scott Pridgen
Micah Whitson
Jennifer Matthews

WRITERS
Keith Greenstein
Mona Hasan
John Guynn
Brian Murray

DESIGNERS
Scott Pridgen
Tim McCracken

PROGRAMMERS
Clive Sweeney
Brad Patterson
John Haughie

AGENCY PRODUCERS
Nora Mishriky
Cathy Wilson
Suzanne Moore

CONTENT STRATEGIST
Adam Blumenthal

DIRECTORS
Keith Greenstein
David Hermanas
Steve Van Osdale

CREATIVE DIRECTORS
David Baldwin
Liz Paradise
Keith Greenstein
David Hermanas

ANNUAL ID
07062N

URL
www.awardshow
submissions.com/
DUEL_integrated.html

It was actually very easy to convince the CEO of Polaris to pick a fight with his competitors. Sure, our budget was 1/20th that of our competitors. And yeah, the Polaris board of directors wanted to fire their own CEO over initiating The Duel. But other than that, it was all smooth sailing.

INTEGRATED BRANDING CAMPAIGN

SHOCK AND AUTO
TV spots' serious message lightens up online with improbable car-crushing scenarios.

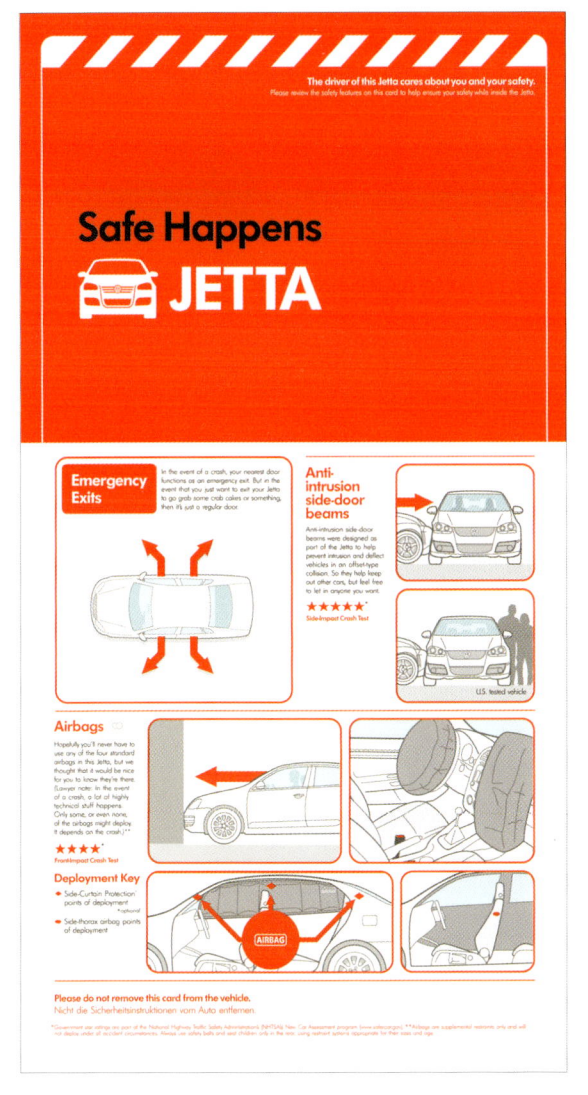

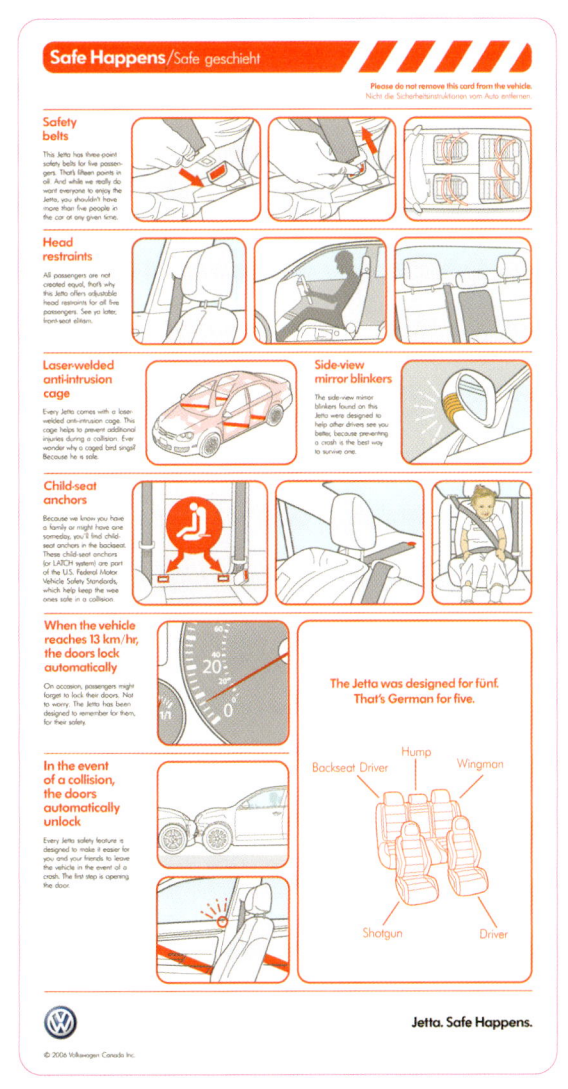

INTEGRATED BRANDING CAMPAIGN

BRONZE

AGENCY
Crispin Porter + Bogusky/Miami

CLIENT
Volkswagen

ART DIRECTORS
Dave Clemens
Dawn Yemma
Kevin Koller
Mike Ferrare

WRITERS
Tim Roper
Yutaka Tsujino
Carl Corbitt
Jason Wolske

DESIGNERS
Conor McCann
Thomas Rodgers
James Martis

MULTIMEDIA ARTIST
Dayoung Ewart

AGENCY PRODUCERS
Rupert Samuel
Winston Binch
Letitia Jacobs
Cheri Anderson
Dan Ruth
Jessica Hoffman
Meghan DeBruler
Paul Sutton
Darren Himebrook
Neil D'Amico
Rebekah Mateu
David Niblick
Barrie Bamberg
Bill Meadows

PRODUCTION COMPANIES
Hanson Dodge
Epoch Films
Domani Studios
Motive

DIRECTORS
Scott Prindle
Matt Walsh
Phil Morrison
Matt Aselton

CREATIVE DIRECTORS
Alex Bogusky
Andrew Keller
Rob Strasberg
Tony Calcao
Jeff Benjamin

ANNUAL ID
07063N

URL
www.cpbgroup.com/awards/vwfeaturesjetta.html

A once beloved brand had lost its relevance and suffered five consecutive years of sales decline. But there was a bright spot within it all, both Jetta and Passat happened to include a rather impressive laundry list of German engineered safety features. Most automobile safety ads relied on the same old formula: controlled collisions in controlled environments with simulated human beings. This was the inspiration for "Safe Happens."

At VWFeatures.com, shoppers lovingly customized their very own Jettas, before using a menu to lovingly pulverize it. "Safe Happens" ignited one of the most robust conversations of the year, on showroom floors across the country, the conversation had turned to safe.

INTEGRATED BRANDING CAMPAIGN

BLUE TRUTH
Happy passengers are your best advertisements.

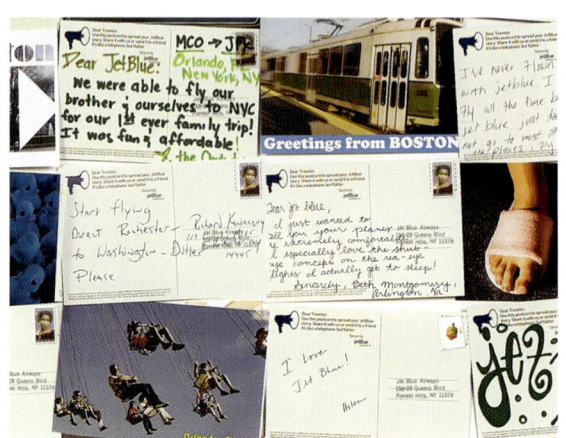

132

INTEGRATED BRANDING CAMPAIGN

BRONZE

AGENCY
JWT/New York

CLIENT
JetBlue

ART DIRECTOR
Robert Rasmussen

WRITERS
Andrew Ault
Lisa Topol
Daniel Gonzalez

DESIGNERS
MESH Architects
MAS Design

MULTIMEDIA ARTISTS
Local Projects
Ian Lamont-Havers
Ryan McKenna
Seth Pomerantz

AGENCY PRODUCERS
Anthony Garetti
Philip Schneider
Robin Pelleck
Zu Al-Kadiri

PRODUCTION COMPANY
JWTwo

CREATIVE DIRECTORS
Peter Nicholson
Jeremy Postaer
Robert Rasmussen
Andrew Ault
Ty Montague
Jeremy Hollister
Judy Wellfare

ANNUAL ID
07064N

JetBlue Airways is a brand built on word of mouth. Our goal was to capture and amplify this consumer voice. A 12' x 18' interactive mobile kiosk was fabricated and sent on a 12-city tour, recording consumer stories. The collected video was given to artists to animate, thus creating TV commercials, website content, web films and in-flight videos. Some fans went as far as to recreate these spots, posting their own viral video versions on YouTube. Passenger photographs were made into postcards. Customers hand-wrote stories on them and sent them in. These became posters, print ads, and direct mail. To further show the customer love, we created radio by recording actual customer calls.

SELF-PROMOTION: WEB SITES

EYE SHUFFLE
mono makes some funny faces.

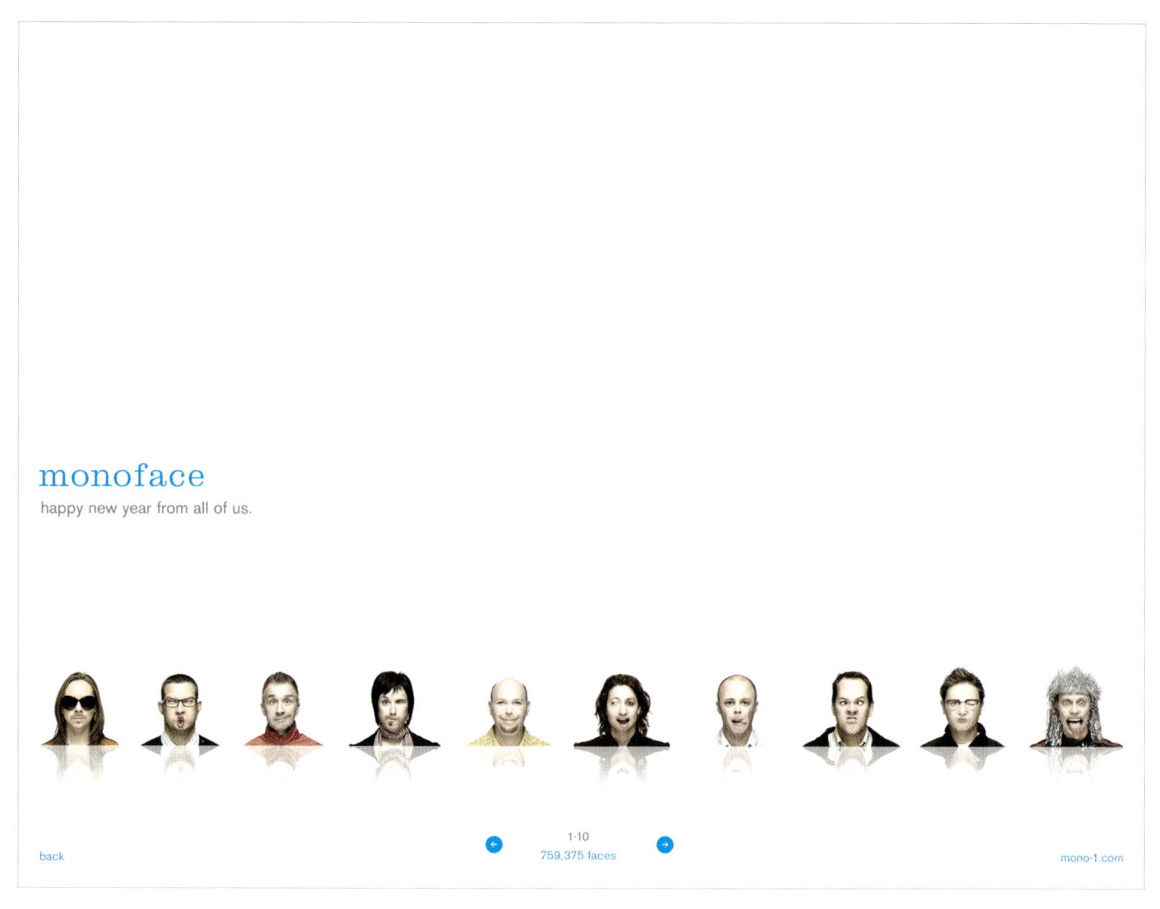

SELF-PROMOTION: WEB SITES

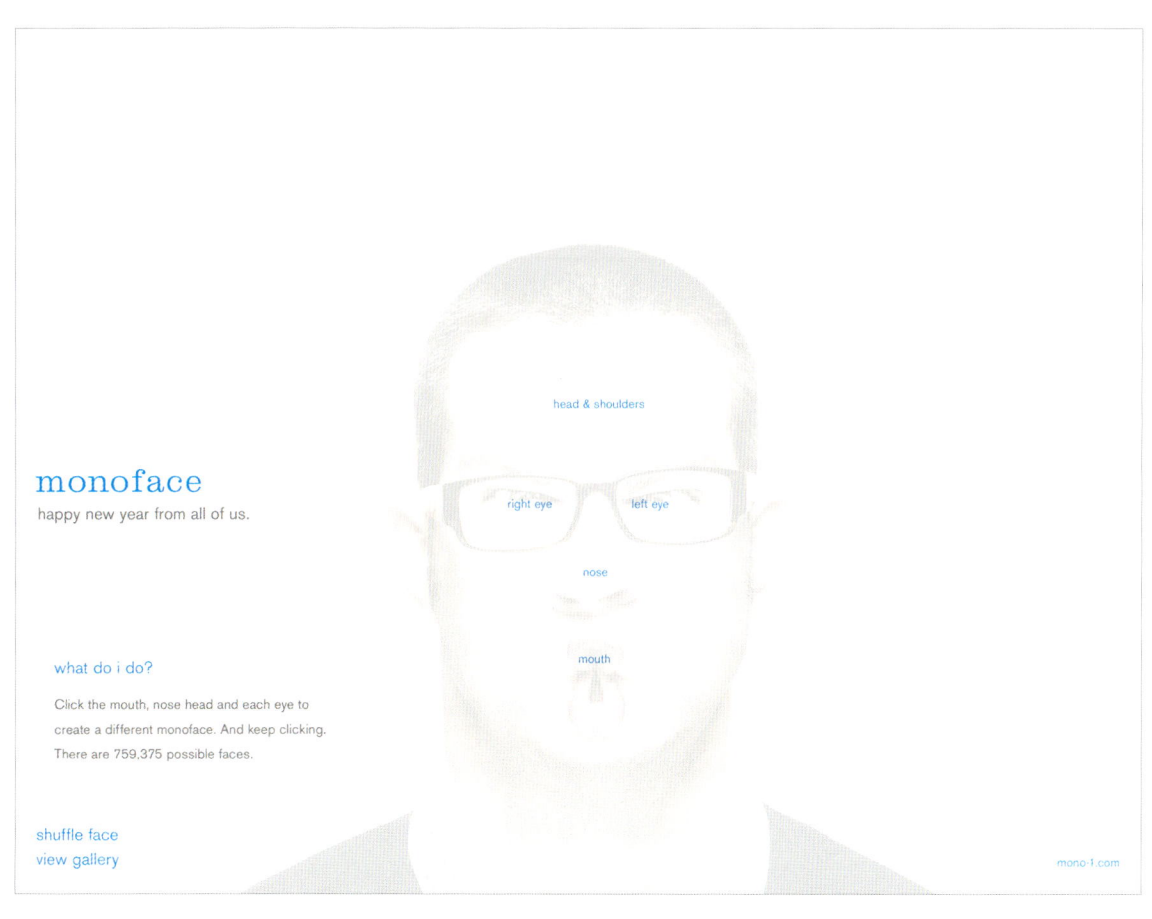

GOLD

AGENCY
mono/Minneapolis

CLIENT
mono

PHOTOGRAPHER
Stephanie Rau

PROGRAMMER
Jim Park

CREATIVE DIRECTOR
mono

ANNUAL ID
07065N

URL
www.mono-1.com/monoface

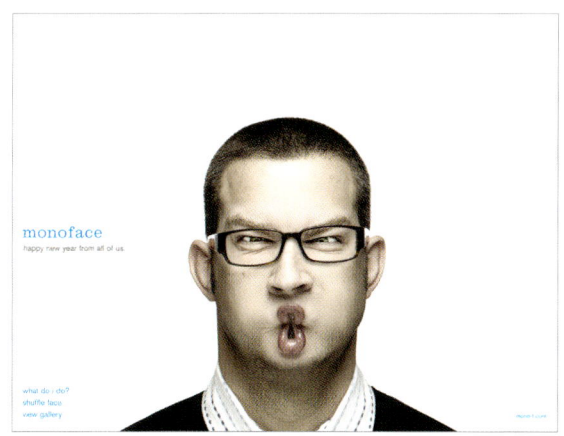

monoface is a simple Flash site that allows viewers to seamlessly create over 750,000 different faces made up from the facial features of mono employees.

The message: Happy New Year from all of us.

135

SELF-PROMOTION: WEB SITES

CULTURAL EVOLUTION
Jonathan Yuen traces tradition with a light hand.

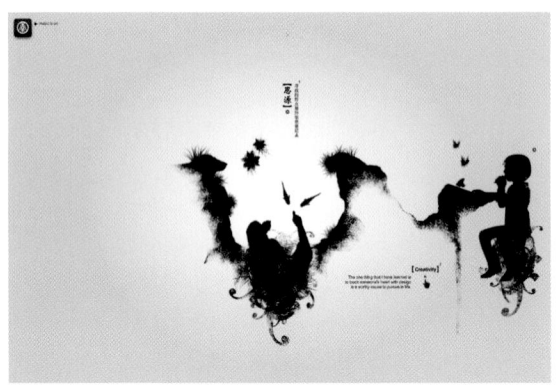

SELF-PROMOTION: WEB SITES

SILVER

AGENCY
*Jonathan Yuen/
Singapore*

ART DIRECTOR
Jonathan Yuen

WRITER
Jonathan Yuen

ANNUAL ID
07066N

URL
www.jonathanyuen.com

The challenge in designing a self-promotion web presentation is not only to engage potential employers/clients with good work in the portfolio, but also to give the viewer insight into the designer's personality, belief and goals.

With that challenge in mind, jonathanyuen.com was designed as an interactive design narrative journey, which slowly unfolds itself in a series of segments as the viewer explores the site. Each segment uses illustrated metaphors to conceptually signify attributes and information about myself. These metaphorical segmentation engages the viewer to relate to the philosophical concepts behind the visuals with the contents, e.g. I see the design process is akin to the evolution of butterfly metamorphosis, with emphasis on my belief that great works come from trust and honesty, like a child.

My cultural roots has a profound influence on my visual design as well. I have always appreciated the aesthetics of traditional Chinese painting, which I have based my illustration style on. The classical style says much about my aesthetic base, and my goal is to have this cultural graphical approach lend a unique visual narrative experience to the site. - *Jonathan Yuen*

SELF-PROMOTION: WEB SITES

LISTEN TO THE BLINK
An online hangout for Malaysia's scenesters.

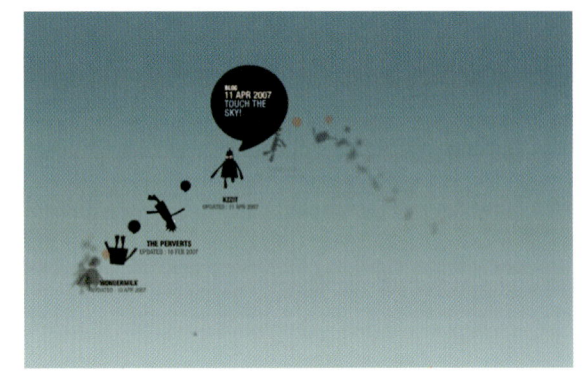

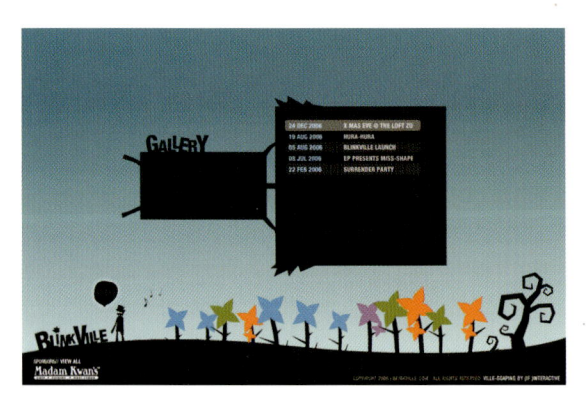

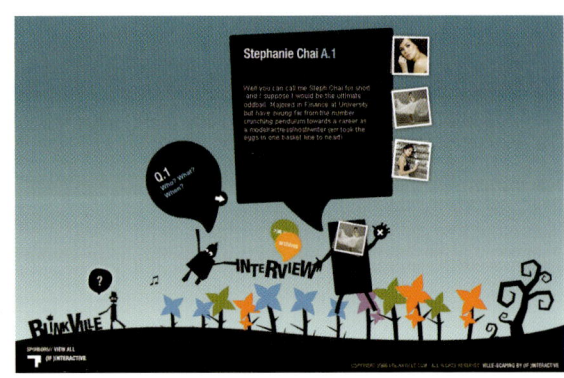

138

SELF-PROMOTION: WEB SITES

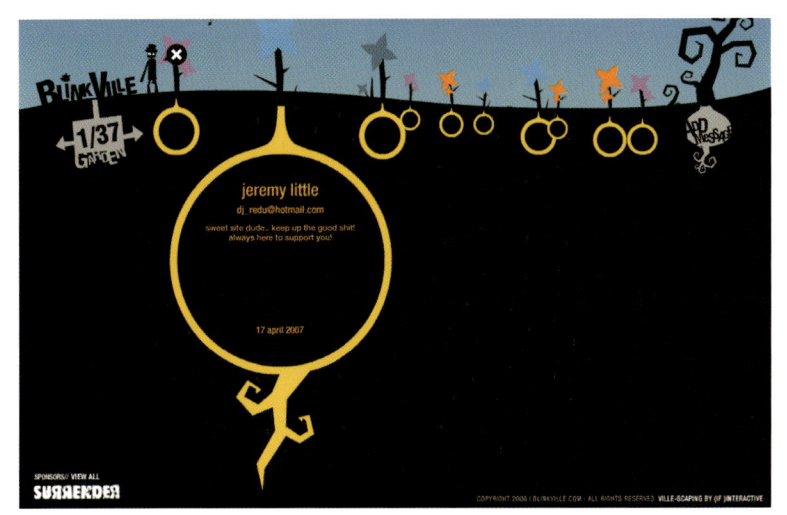

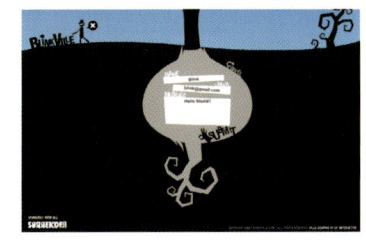

BRONZE

AGENCY
(if) Interactive/
Kuala Lumpur

CLIENT
DJ Blink

WRITER
Blink

DESIGNER
Birdie Ting

PROGRAMMER
LeeSeng

CREATIVE DIRECTOR
Sanyen Liew

ANNUAL ID
07067N

URL
if.net.my/awards/
index.htm#blinkville

Blinkville is a personal and collaborative website designed for local music and design related industries. It was developed for DJ Blink who is an active and popular club deejay in Malaysia.

This site allows DJ Blink and his friends with similar interests to express and share their thoughts about music and design issues in Malaysia. Visitors are able to view blog messages, interviews, galleries and news posted by DJ Blink and his network. Visitors are also able to "plant" messages into the site that creatively symbolize public voices in support of the Blinkville foundation. More attractively, this site features a dynamic landing page where bloggers' icons "dance" to the beat of the background music.

MERIT WINNERS
PG: 141-233

BANNERS – FIXED SPACE: BUSINESS TO CONSUMER – SINGLE

MERIT

AGENCY
AgênciaClick/
São Paulo

CLIENT
The Coca-Cola Company

ART DIRECTOR
Vicente da Silva e Silva

DESIGNER
Pedro Burneikov

PROGRAMMERS
Andre Brunetta
Andre Cardozo

CREATIVE DIRECTOR
Ricardo Figueira

ANNUAL ID
07068N

URL
www.arehumba.
net/2006/cocacola/
partitura/en

MERIT

AGENCY
AgênciaClick/
São Paulo

CLIENT
Caixa Economica Federal

ART DIRECTORS
Daniel Cabral
Mateus Braga
Rafael Augusto
Ricardo Makoto
Rodrigo Hiram

WRITER
Soraya Coelho

PROGRAMMERS
Carolina Albuquerque
Helio Miranda
Marcelo Macedo

CREATIVE DIRECTORS
Raphael Vasconcellos
Ricardo Figueira

ANNUAL ID
07069N

URL
www.arehumba.
net/2006/caixa/
cadeiraderodas/en

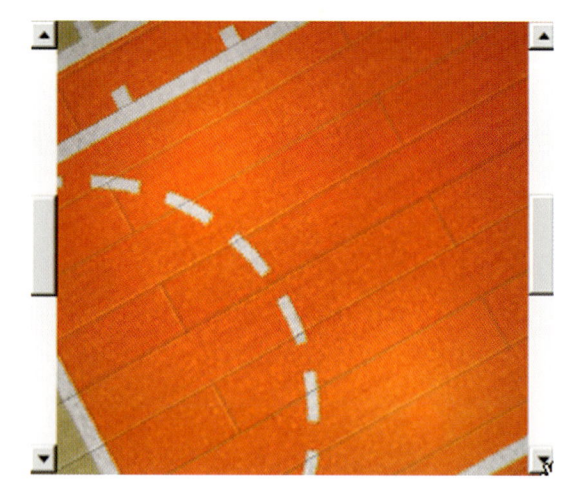

142

BANNERS – FIXED SPACE: BUSINESS TO CONSUMER – SINGLE

MERIT

AGENCY
Crispin Porter +
Bogusky/Miami

CLIENT
Volkswagen

ART DIRECTORS
James Martis
Thomas Rodgers

WRITER
Mike Howard

PRODUCTION COMPANY
Domani Studios

CREATIVE DIRECTORS
Alex Bogusky
Andrew Keller
Jeff Benjamin
Rob Strasberg
Tony Calcao

ANNUAL ID
07070N

URL
www.cpbintegrated.
com/staging/
awards/paddle/
paddleshifter.html

MERIT

AGENCY
Crispin Porter +
Bogusky/Miami

CLIENT
Volkswagen

ART DIRECTOR
Conor McCann

WRITER
Jeff Gillette

PROGRAMMER
Jordi Ortega

PRODUCTION COMPANY
Zugara

CREATIVE DIRECTORS
Alex Bogusky
Andrew Keller
Tony Calcao
Rob Strasberg
Jeff Benjamin

ANNUAL ID
07071N

URL
www.cpbgroup.com/
awards/vdubs
jambanner.html

143

BANNERS – FIXED SPACE: BUSINESS TO CONSUMER – SINGLE

MERIT

AGENCY
Crispin Porter + Bogusky/Miami

CLIENT
Slim Jim

ART DIRECTORS
Conor McCann
Keith Scott

WRITER
Guy Rooke

PRODUCTION COMPANY
Squarewave

CREATIVE DIRECTORS
Alex Bogusky
Tom Adams
Jeff Benjamin

ANNUAL ID
07072N

URL
www.cpbgroup.com/awards/sjtrapbanner.html

MERIT

AGENCY
Crispin Porter + Bogusky/Miami

CLIENT
Volkswagen

ART DIRECTORS
Kevin Koller
John Antoniello

CREATIVE DIRECTORS
Alex Bogusky
Andrew Keller
Rob Strasberg
Tony Calcao
Scott Linnen
Jeff Benjamin

ANNUAL ID
07073N

URL
www.cpbgroup.com/awards/blanklikearabbit.html

BANNERS – FIXED SPACE: BUSINESS TO CONSUMER – SINGLE

MERIT

AGENCY
Crispin Porter +
Bogusky/Miami

CLIENT
Burger King

ART DIRECTORS
John Antoniello
Dave Swartz

WRITER
Dave Banta

PRODUCTION COMPANY
Squarewave

CREATIVE DIRECTORS
Alex Bogusky
Andrew Keller
Rob Reilly
James Dawson-Hollis
Jeff Benjamin

ANNUAL ID
07074N

URL
www.cpbgroup.com/
awards/bkuk
angusbanner.html

MERIT

AGENCY
Del Campo Nazca
Saatchi & Saatchi/
Martinez

CLIENT
Answer Seguro
On Line

ART DIRECTORS
Pablo Tajer

WRITER
Daniel Sacroisky

PROGRAMMER
Three Melons

CREATIVE DIRECTORS
Gastón Bigio
Jonathan Gurvit

ANNUAL ID
07075N

URL
www.threemelons.
com/demos/
answer_en3.aspx

145

BANNERS – FIXED SPACE: BUSINESS TO CONSUMER – SINGLE

MERIT

AGENCY
Nordpol+/Hamburg

CLIENT
Renault

ART DIRECTOR
Dominik Anweiler

MULTIMEDIA ARTIST
Mark Hoefler

CREATIVE DIRECTOR
Ingo Fritz

ANNUAL ID
07076N

URL
www.nordpol.com/
2006/renault/
cliorace/en/start.php

MERIT

AGENCY
Ogilvy/ San Francisco

CLIENT
Yahoo!

ART DIRECTORS
Robert Wakeland
Kate Shay

WRITER
Ryan Cochrane

PROGRAMMER
Scott Johnson

CREATIVE DIRECTORS
Arthur Ceria
Fabio Costa

ANNUAL ID
07077N

URL
sfawards.com/yahoo/
getyourfreakon

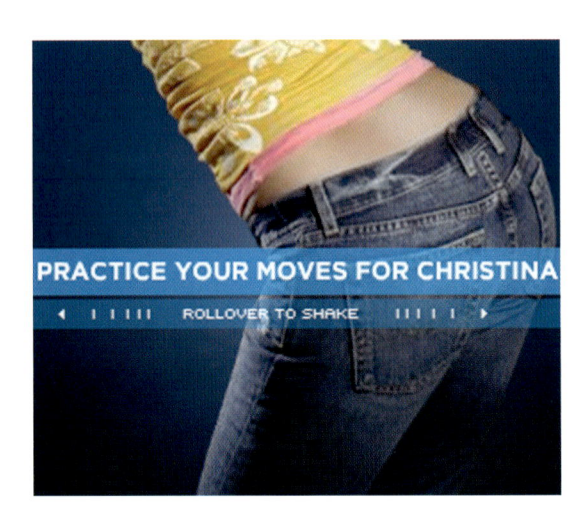

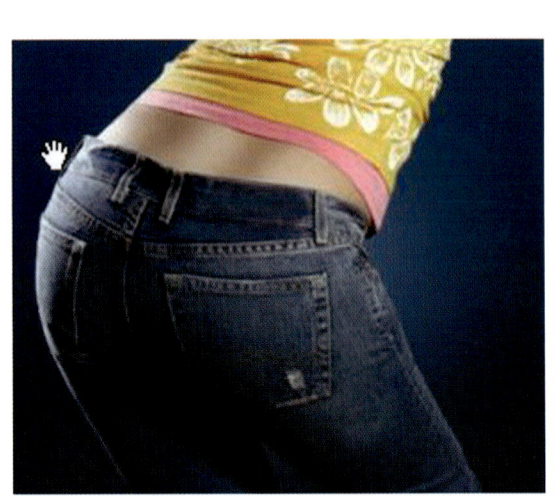

146

BANNERS – FIXED SPACE: BUSINESS TO CONSUMER – SINGLE

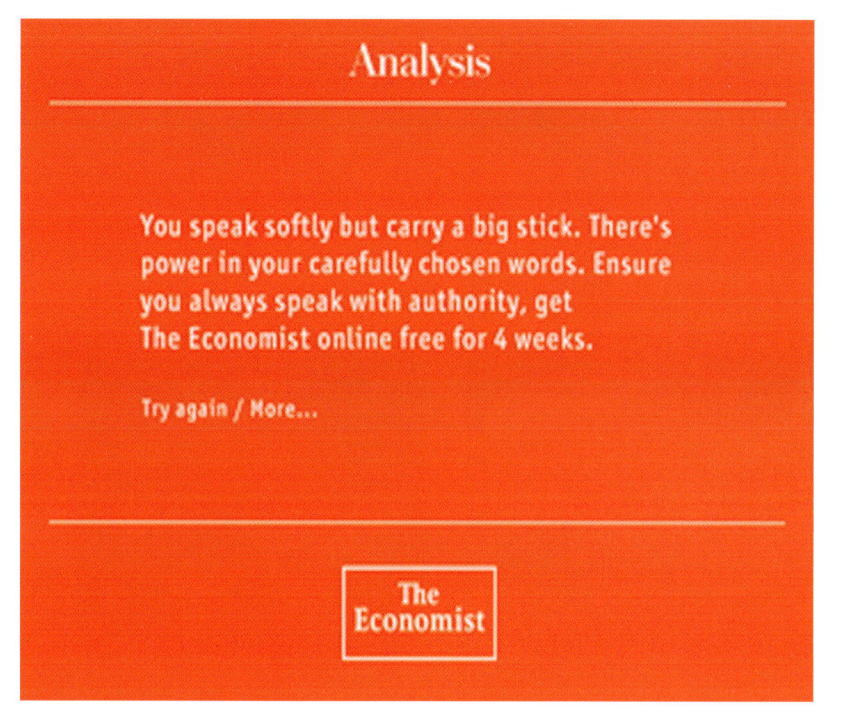

MERIT

AGENCY
OgilvyOne Worldwide/
Hong Kong

CLIENT
The Economist

ART DIRECTOR
Thibault Kim

WRITER
Houston Wong

DESIGNER
Carrie Leung

CONTENT STRATEGISTS
Jennifer Chan
Fiona Yeung
Greg Carton

CREATIVE DIRECTOR
Tony Peck

ANNUAL ID
07078N

URL
210.0.187.184/
Awards2007/one
show2007/Economist/
Voice/index.htm

MERIT

AGENCY
Wunderman/
São Paulo

CLIENT
Land Rover

ART DIRECTOR
Eco Moliterno

WRITER
Eco Moliterno

MULTIMEDIA ARTIST
Ricardo Martins

CREATIVE DIRECTOR
Eco Moliterno

ANNUAL ID
07079N

URL
www.theinternuts.
com/2006/landrover/
alarm/en

147

BANNERS – FIXED SPACE: BUSINESS TO CONSUMER – CAMPAIGN

MERIT

AGENCY
AKQA/San Francisco

CLIENT
The Coca-Cola Company

ART DIRECTOR
Karishma Mehta

WRITER
Dominick Walker

MULTIMEDIA ARTISTS
Michelle Murata
Guillermo Torres

PROGRAMMER
Steven Sherwood

CREATIVE DIRECTOR
PJ Pereira

ANNUAL ID
07080N

URL
awards.sf.akqa.com/creative/sprite/sublymonal/

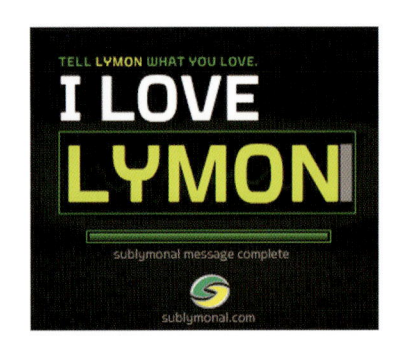

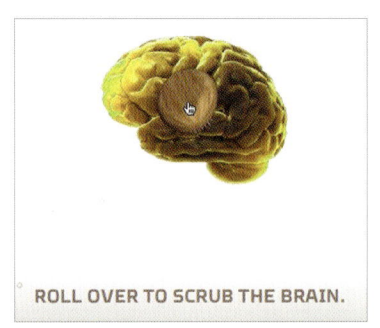

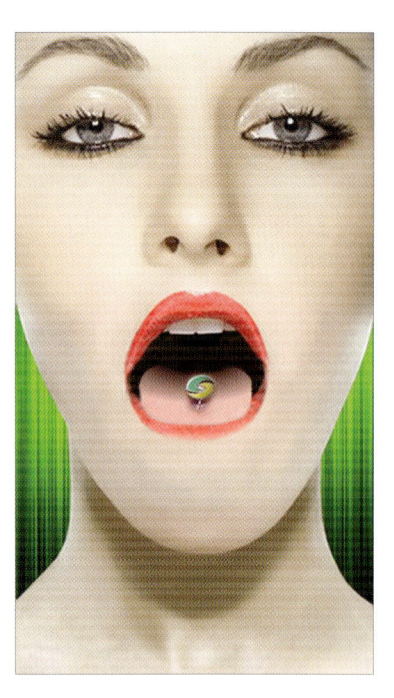

MERIT

AGENCY
Goodby, Silverstein & Partners/
San Francisco

CLIENT
Comcast

ART DIRECTOR
Michael Coyne

WRITER
Nat Lawlor

CONTENT STRATEGISTS
Mike Geiger
Peter Albrycht
Dora Lee

PRODUCTION COMPANIES
Templar
Unit-9

CREATIVE DIRECTOR
Will McGinness

ANNUAL ID
07081N

URL
www.goodbysilverstein.com/awards/one_show_07/comcast_power_boost.html

BANNERS – FIXED SPACE: BUSINESS TO CONSUMER – CAMPAIGN

MERIT

AGENCY
Goodby, Silverstein & Partners/San Francisco

CLIENT
Comcast

ART DIRECTOR
Aaron Dietz

WRITER
Mandy Dietz

CONTENT STRATEGISTS
Mike Geiger
James Taylor
Amanda Kelso

PRODUCTION COMPANY
Natzke Design

CREATIVE DIRECTORS
Jamie Barrett
Will McGinness

ANNUAL ID
07082N

URL
www.goodbysilverstein.com/awards/one_show_07/comcast_faster

BANNERS – FIXED SPACE: BUSINESS TO BUSINESS – SINGLE

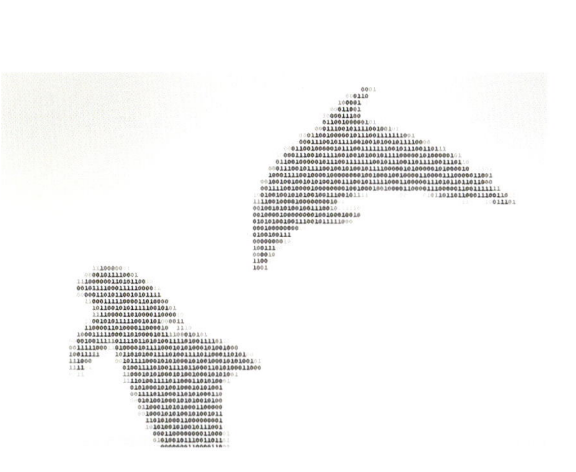

MERIT

AGENCY
OgilvyInteractive/Madrid

CLIENT
Telefonica

ART DIRECTOR
Ramiro Alda

WRITER
Mari Carmen Blanco

PROGRAMMERS
Enrique Gonzalo
Oscar Garcia

CREATIVE DIRECTOR
Jess Rasines

ANNUAL ID
07083N

URL
www.essolotrabajo.com/metamorphosis1c/

149

BANNERS – FIXED SPACE: BUSINESS TO BUSINESS – CAMPAIGN

MERIT

AGENCY
OgilvyInteractive/
Madrid

CLIENT
IAB

ART DIRECTORS
Diego Gonzalez
José María García

WRITERS
Jose Escuadra
Mari Carmen Blanco
Angela Medina

PROGRAMMERS
Enrique Gonzalo
Oscar García

CREATIVE DIRECTOR
Jesús Rasines

ANNUAL ID
07084N

URL
www.essolotrabajo.com/
touch1d/

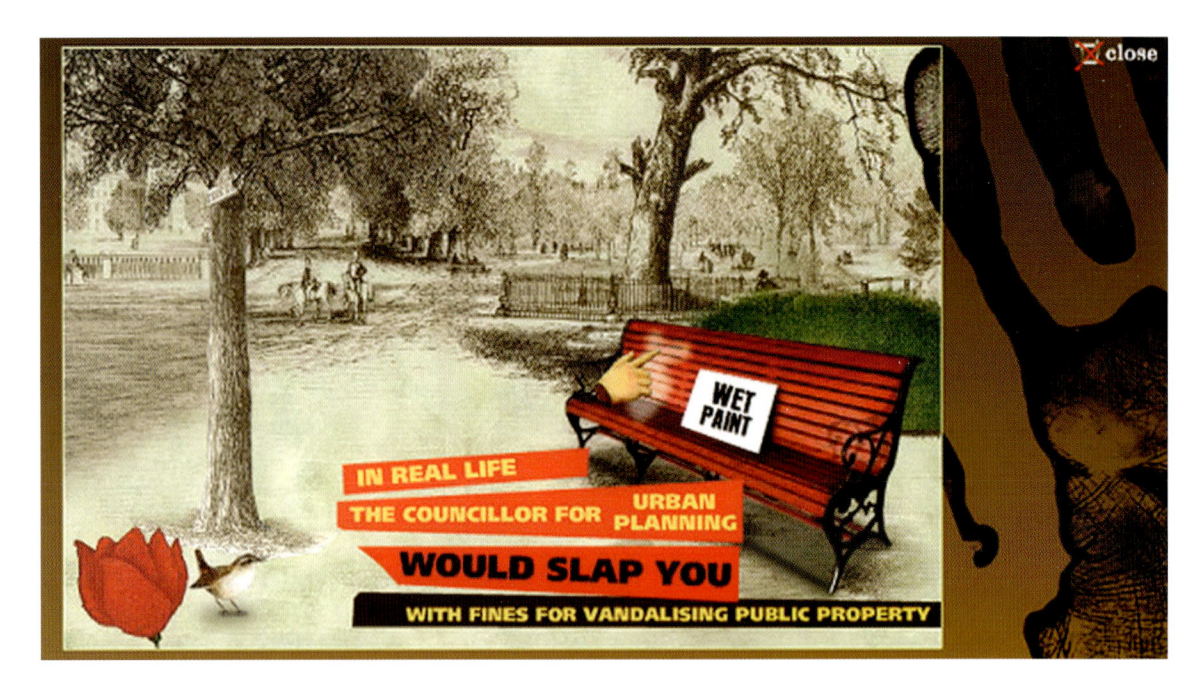

BANNERS – FIXED SPACE: PUBLIC SERVICE/NON-PROFIT/EDUCATIONAL – SINGLE

MERIT

AGENCY
Clemmow Hornby Inge/
London

CLIENT
The Roy Castle Foundation

ART DIRECTOR
Thiago De Moraes

WRITER
Ewan Paterson

CREATIVE DIRECTOR
Ewan Paterson

ANNUAL ID
07085N

URL
www.avealook.com/
rc/baby.html

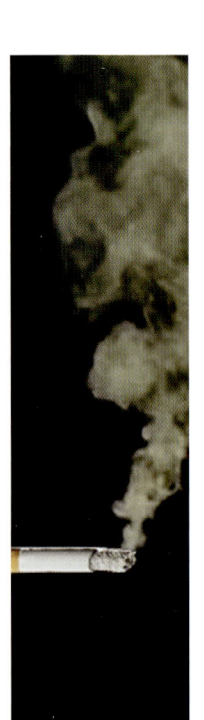

BANNERS – FIXED SPACE: PUBLIC SERVICE/NON-PROFIT/EDUCATIONAL – SINGLE

MERIT

AGENCY
Leo Burnett/Sydney

CLIENT
World Wildlife Fund

ART DIRECTORS
Kieran Ots
Michael Spirkovski

WRITERS
Vicky Burrough
Grant McAloon

CREATIVE DIRECTOR
Mark Collis

ANNUAL ID
07086N

URL
www.leoburnett.com.
au/awards/work/
digital/wallaby.html

MERIT

AGENCY
Saatchi & Saatchi/
Singapore

CLIENT
AWARE

ART DIRECTORS
Jae Soh
Robin Tan

WRITERS
Justine Lee
Roger Makak

DESIGNER
Robin Tan

PROGRAMMER
Robin Tan

CREATIVE DIRECTOR
Andy Greenaway

ANNUAL ID
07087N

URL
www.the-ideas.com/
2006/aware/

151

BANNERS – FIXED SPACE: PUBLIC SERVICE/NON-PROFIT/EDUCATIONAL – SINGLE

MERIT

AGENCY
Saatchi & Saatchi/
Frankfurt

CLIENT
Schirn Kunsthalle

ART DIRECTOR
Martin Anderle

WRITER
Dominik Bauer

CONTENT STRATEGIST
Sandra Schamber

CREATIVE DIRECTORS
Sebastian Schier
Peter Huschka

ANNUAL ID
07088N

URL
www.saatchi-interactive.
de/awards/schirn/
en/index.html

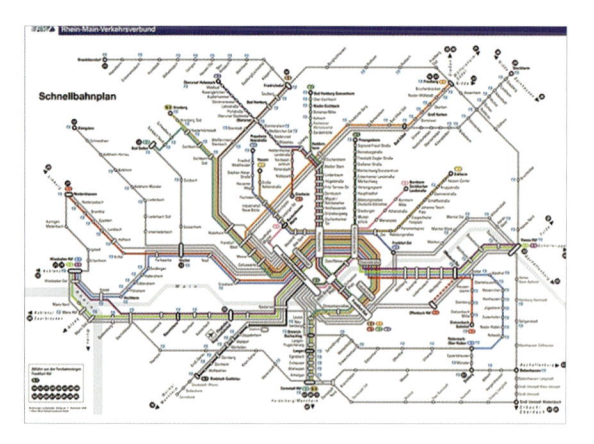

BANNERS – DYNAMIC: BUSINESS TO CONSUMER – SINGLE

MERIT

AGENCY
AKQA/London

CLIENT
Yell.com

ART DIRECTOR
James Capp

WRITER
Phil Wilce

DESIGNERS
Dan Wright
Chris Williams

CREATIVE DIRECTOR
Daniel Bonner

ANNUAL ID
07089N

URL
awards.akqa.com/
awards2006/yell/
digital/richmedia.html

BANNERS – DYNAMIC: BUSINESS TO CONSUMER – SINGLE

MERIT

AGENCY
AKQA/San Francisco

CLIENT
Xbox

ART DIRECTOR
David Lee

WRITER
Justin Kramm

DESIGNER
Liz Balin

CREATIVE DIRECTORS
Rei Inamoto
PJ Pereira

ANNUAL ID
07090N

URL
awards.sf.akqa.com/
creative/2006/
xbox_fsx/take
control/index.html

MERIT

AGENCY
Butler, Shine, Stern & Partners/Sausalito

CLIENT
MINI

ART DIRECTOR
Andreas Tagger

WRITER
Chris Hancock

PRODUCTION COMPANY
Klipmart

CREATIVE DIRECTORS
John Butler
Mike Shine
Nei Sobral Caetano da Silva

ANNUAL ID
07091N

URL
staging.bssp.com/
oneshow07/mini_
parking_garage/

153

BANNERS – DYNAMIC: BUSINESS TO CONSUMER – SINGLE

MERIT

AGENCY
Butler, Shine, Stern & Partners/Sausalito

CLIENT
MINI

ART DIRECTOR
Andreas Tagger

WRITER
Chris Hancock

PRODUCTION COMPANY
Klipmart

CREATIVE DIRECTORS
John Butler
Mike Shine
Nei Sobral Caetano da Silva

ANNUAL ID
07092N

URL
staging.bssp.com/oneshow07/mini_parking_mantra/

MERIT

AGENCY
Crispin Porter + Bogusky/Miami

CLIENT
Volkswagen

ART DIRECTOR
DaYoung Ewart

WRITER
Mike Howard

PRODUCTION COMPANY
Domani Studios

CREATIVE DIRECTORS
Alex Bogusky
Andrew Keller
Jeff Benjamin
Rob Strasberg
Tony Calcao

ANNUAL ID
07093N

URL
www.cpbintegrated.com/staging/awards/pinball/pinball.html

BANNERS – DYNAMIC: BUSINESS TO CONSUMER – SINGLE

MERIT

AGENCY
Crispin Porter +
Bogusky/Miami

CLIENT
Volkswagen

ART DIRECTOR
James Martis

WRITER
Mike Howard

PRODUCTION COMPANY
Zugara

CREATIVE DIRECTORS
Alex Bogusky
Andrew Keller
Jeff Benjamin
Tony Calcao
Rob Strasberg

ANNUAL ID
07094N

URL
www.cpbintegrated.
com/staging/awards/
smoke/smoke.html

MERIT

AGENCY
Daddy/Gothenburg

CLIENT
Red Bull

ART DIRECTOR
Jonas Hedeback

WRITER
Johan Kruse

MULTIMEDIA ARTISTS
Oskar Joelson
Erik Sterner

PROGRAMMERS
Oskar Joelson
Per Rundgren

CONTENT STRATEGIST
Robert German

PRODUCTION COMPANY
Mad Cat studios

ANNUAL ID
07095N

URL
www.daddy.se/
comp/2007/one
show/redbull/

BANNERS – DYNAMIC: BUSINESS TO CONSUMER – SINGLE

MERIT

AGENCY
Dentsu/Tokyo

CLIENT
TOTO

WRITERS
Satoshi Nakajima
Mikiko Nishihara

MULTIMEDIA ARTISTS
see index

INFORMATION ARCHITECT
see index

CONTENT STRATEGISTS
see index

PRODUCTION COMPANIES
see index

CREATIVE DIRECTORS
Masahiko Yasuda
Yuki Abe

ANNUAL ID
07096N

URL
www.interactive-salaryman.com/pieces/fspov_e/

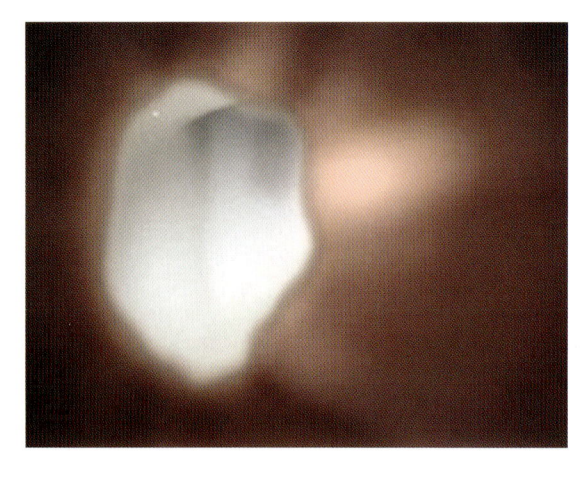

MERIT

AGENCY
F/Nazca Saatchi & Saatchi/São Paulo

CLIENT
Neo Quimica

ART DIRECTOR
Lucio Rufo

WRITER
Cristiane Gribel

DESIGNER
William Queen

PROGRAMMER
Paulo Pacheco

INFORMATION ARCHITECTS
Alexandre Bessa
Paula Obata

CREATIVE DIRECTORS
Fabio Fernandes
Fabio Simoes

ANNUAL ID
07098N

URL
www.adversiting.net/2006/48

BANNERS – DYNAMIC: BUSINESS TO CONSUMER – SINGLE

MERIT

AGENCY
glue/London

CLIENT
Virgin Money

ART DIRECTORS
Simon Lloyd
Christine Turner

WRITERS
Simon Lloyd
Christine Turner

DESIGNER
Nitin Mistry

MULTIMEDIA ARTISTS
see index

PROGRAMMER
Billy Vine

PRODUCTION COMPANY
Upset TV

CREATIVE DIRECTOR
Seb Royce

ANNUAL ID
07099N

URL
www.bestofg.com/one
show/vm_ballerina.php

MERIT

AGENCY
glue/London

CLIENT
adidas

ART DIRECTOR
Adam King

WRITER
Lewis Raven

DESIGNERS
Leon Ostle
Matt Verity

MULTIMEDIA ARTIST
Simon Cam

CONTENT STRATEGIST
Miranda Ross

CREATIVE DIRECTOR
Seb Royce

ANNUAL ID
07100N

URL
bestofg.com/oneshow/
adidas_throwme.php

157

BANNERS – DYNAMIC: BUSINESS TO CONSUMER – SINGLE

MERIT

AGENCY
Marketel/Montreal

CLIENT
Infopresse

ART DIRECTORS
Robert Lee
Stéphane Gaulin

WRITERS
Linda Dawe
Nicolas Baudry

MULTIMEDIA ARTISTS
Marie-Michèle Cloutier
Stéphanie Vallée

PROGRAMMERS
Bob Mainguy
Dominique Gauthier

CREATIVE DIRECTOR
Normand Miron

ANNUAL ID
07101N

URL
www.vote4usorwewillboil
yourrabbitinspaghetti
sauce.com/one/bush-
game/bush_game.html

MERIT

AGENCY
OgilvyOne Worldwide/
Bangkok

CLIENT
Lamton

ART DIRECTOR
Anuwat Nitipanont

PROGRAMMER
Seksun Duangsong

CREATIVE DIRECTOR
Saharath Sawadatikom

ANNUAL ID
07102N

URL
zyberhub.com/
ca/bright/

BANNERS – DYNAMIC: BUSINESS TO CONSUMER – SINGLE

MERIT

AGENCY
OgilvyOne Worldwide/
Bangkok

CLIENT
Bond

ART DIRECTOR
Ekalak Vorranartpankul

WRITER
Vichai Thanasilpisan

CREATIVE DIRECTOR
Saharath Sawadatikom

ANNUAL ID
07103N

URL
zyberhub.com/ca/fly/

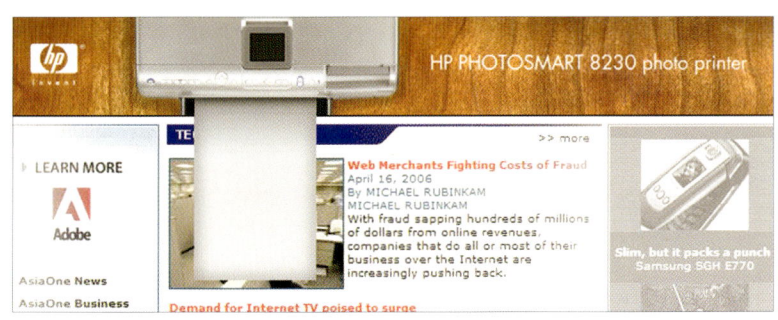

MERIT

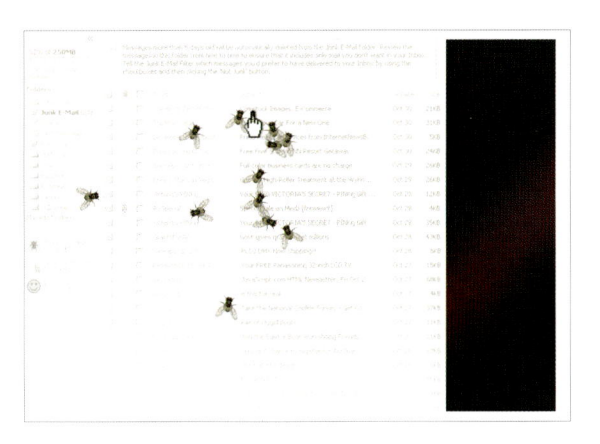

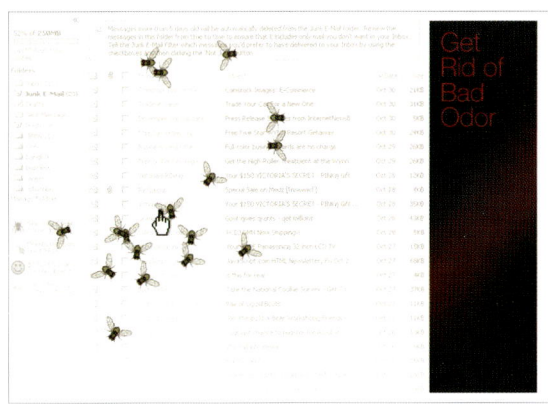

AGENCY
Saatchi & Saatchi/
Singapore

CLIENT
Hewlett Packard

ART DIRECTORS
Robin Tan
Jae Soh

WRITERS
Justine Lee
Roger Makak

PROGRAMMER
Robin Tan

CREATIVE DIRECTORS
Andy Greenaway
Bruce Watt

ANNUAL ID
07104N

URL
www.the-ideas.
com/2006/hp/

159

BANNERS – DYNAMIC: BUSINESS TO CONSUMER – SINGLE

MERIT

AGENCY
Saatchi & Saatchi/
Frankfurt

CLIENT
T-Mobile

ART DIRECTORS
Georg Cockburn
Christian Bartsch

MULTIMEDIA ARTIST
Christian Bartsch

CONTENT STRATEGIST
Ines Horn

CREATIVE DIRECTORS
Sebastian Schier
Peter Huschka

ANNUAL ID
07105N

URL
saatchi-interactive.
de/awards/t-mobile/
t-shirt/en/index.html

MERIT

AGENCY
Syzygy UK/London

CLIENT
Mazda

ART DIRECTOR
Scott Bedford

WRITER
Mark Hillman

DESIGNERS
Boyd Russel
Justin Perryer

CREATIVE DIRECTOR
Scott Bedford

ANNUAL ID
07106N

URL
awards.syzygy.net/
oneshow/cones/

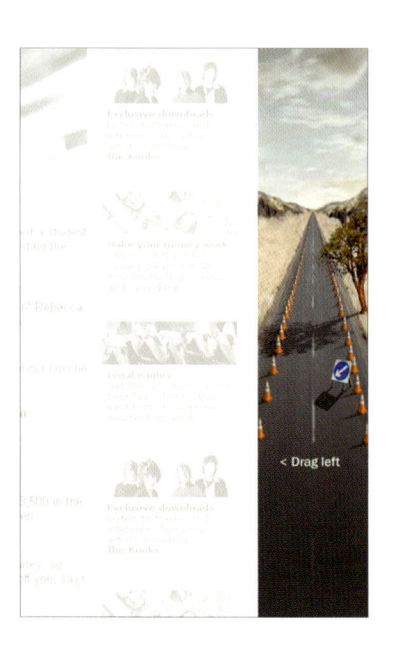

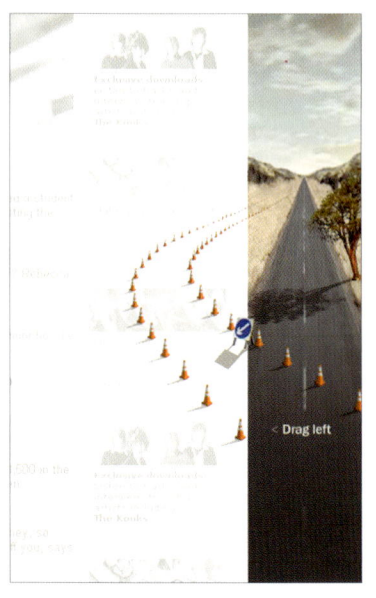

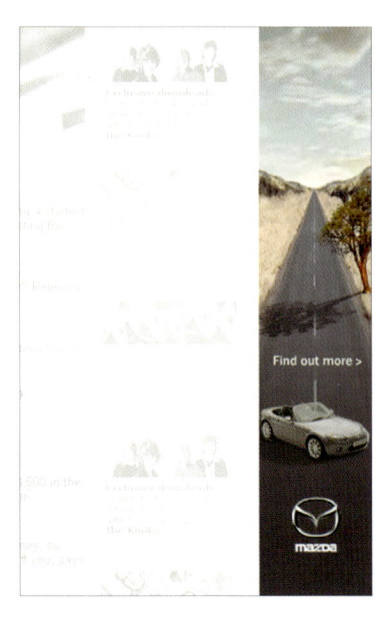

BANNERS – DYNAMIC: BUSINESS TO CONSUMER – SINGLE

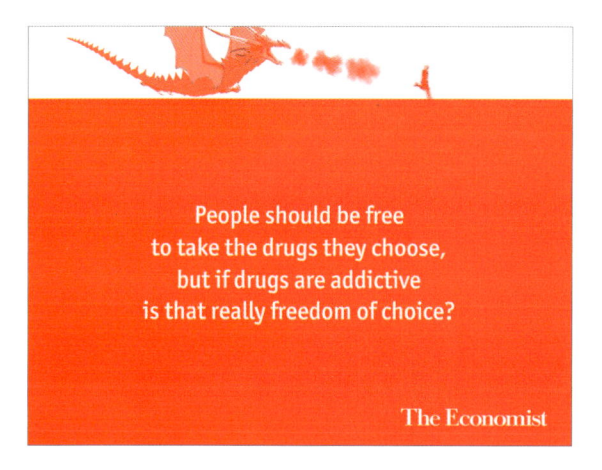

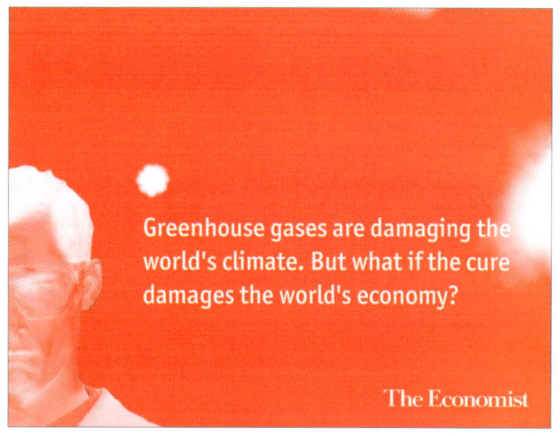

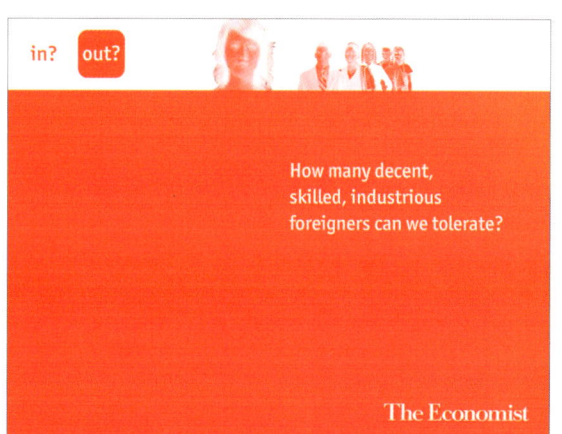

MERIT

AGENCY
Lean Mean Fighting Machine/London

CLIENT
The Economist

DESIGNER
Mark Beacock

PROGRAMMER
Dave Cox

CREATIVE DIRECTORS
Sam Ball
Dave Bedwood

ANNUAL ID
07107N

URL
www.leanmean
fightingmachine.
co.uk/oneshow/
economist/

BANNERS - DYNAMIC: PUBLIC SERVICE/NON-PROFIT/EDUCATIONAL - SINGLE

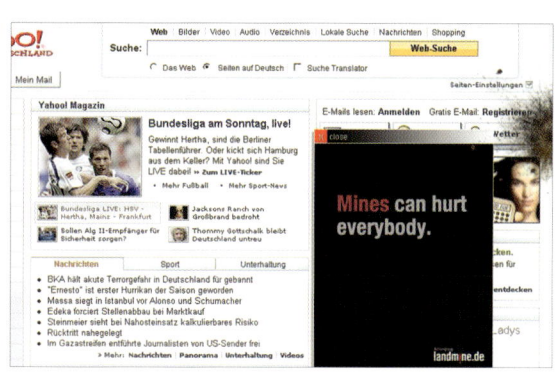

MERIT

AGENCY
Plan.Net Concept/
Munich

CLIENT
Aktionsbündnis
Landmine.de

ART DIRECTOR
Christian Sommer

WRITER
Christian Sommer

DESIGNER
Fite Kiemann

CONTENT STRATEGIST
Patrick Strehle

CREATIVE DIRECTORS
Sabine Brugge
Bernd Huesmann

ANNUAL ID
07108N

URL
awards.plan-net.de/
2007/one_show/landmine

161

BANNERS – DYNAMIC: PUBLIC SERVICE/NON-PROFIT/EDUCATIONAL – SINGLE

MERIT

AGENCY
Savaglio\TBWA/Buenos Aires

CLIENT
Greenpeace International

ART DIRECTOR
Nicolás Suárez

WRITER
Francisco Amorin

PROGRAMMER
Denken

CREATIVE DIRECTORS
Mariano Serkin
Maxi Itzkoff
Ernesto Savaglio

ANNUAL ID
07109N

URL
www.dnkn.com/GP/final_eng1.html

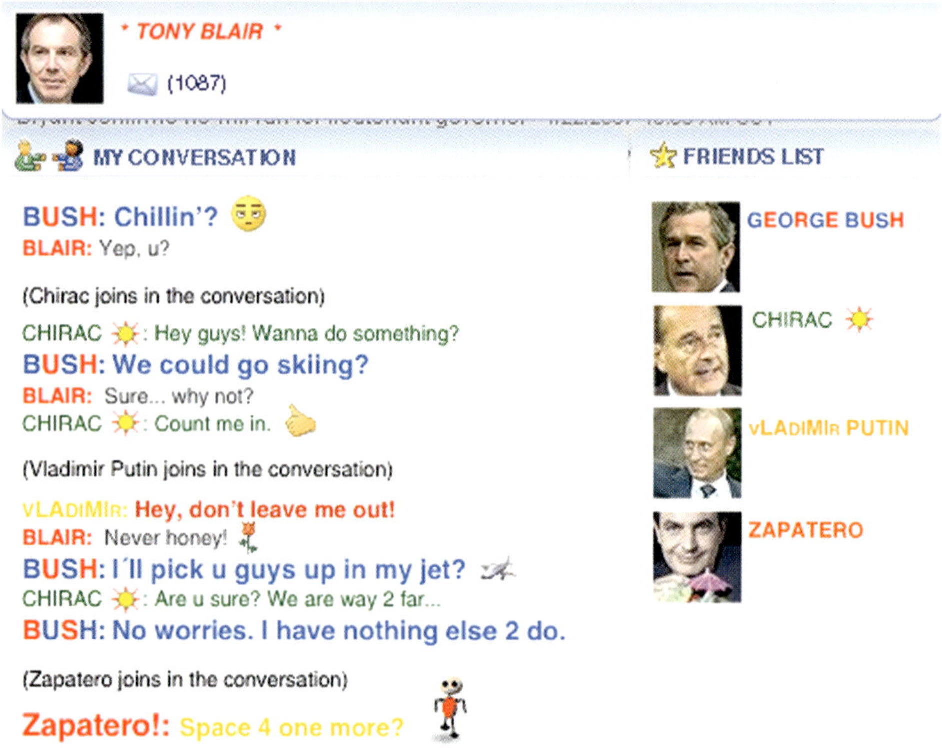

MERIT

AGENCY
Tribal DDB/Mumbai

CLIENT
MTV

ART DIRECTOR
Anis Budye

WRITER
Chaitali Dasgupta

DESIGNER
Deepu Sasikumar

PROGRAMMER
Karthik CK

CREATIVE DIRECTORS
Karl Gnomes
Meera Chandra

ANNUAL ID
07110N

URL
www.tribalddbindia.com/work/2006/worldaidsday.html

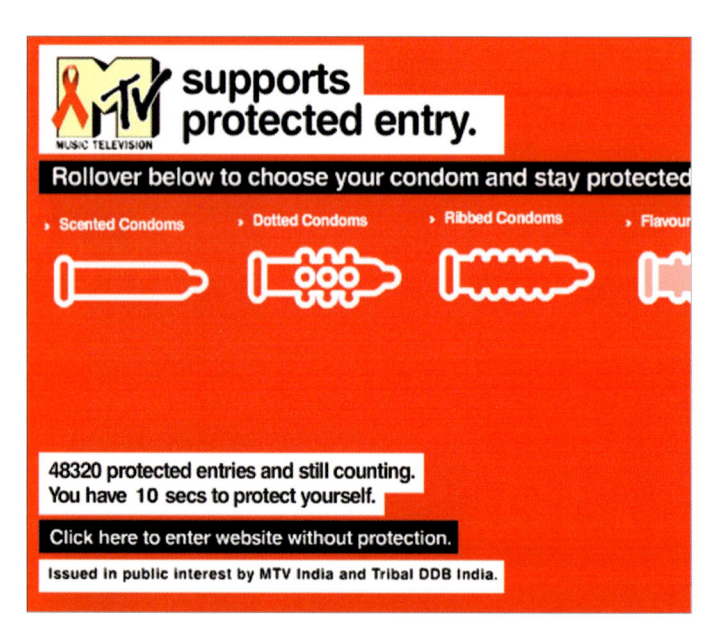

162

MICROSITES: BUSINESS TO CONSUMER

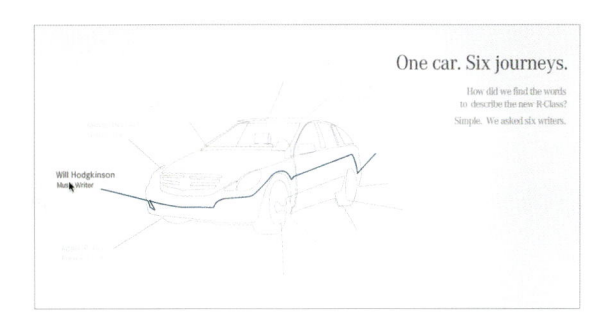

MERIT

AGENCY
Agency Republic/
London

CLIENT
Mercedes-Benz

ART DIRECTOR
Jim Stump

WRITER
Ben Harris

MULTIMEDIA ARTIST
Odin Church

PROGRAMMER
Adam Robertson

CREATIVE DIRECTORS
Gavin Gordon-Rodgers
Gemma Butler

ANNUAL ID
07111N

URL
www.agencyrepublic.
net/awards/one_
show/rclass_micro
site/home.php

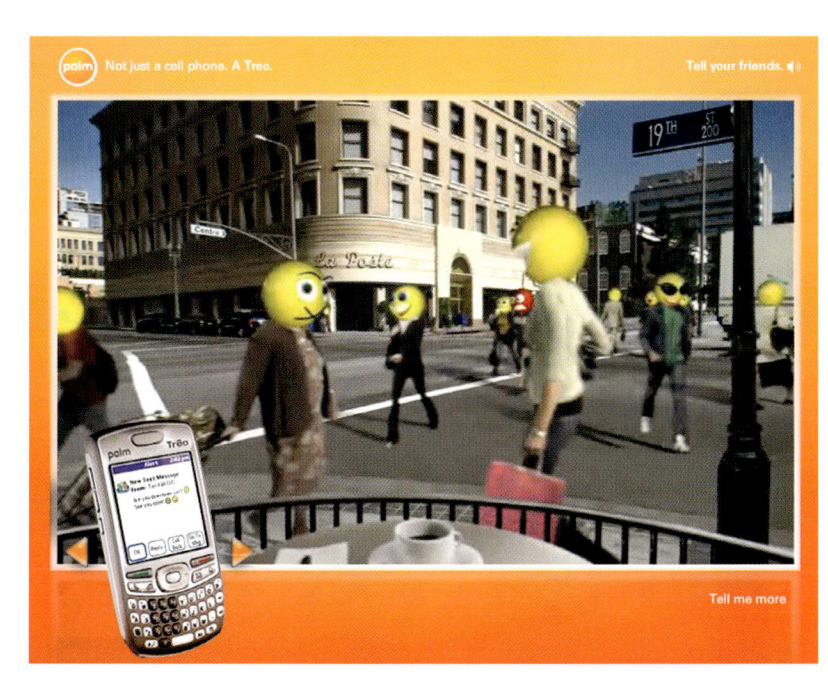

MERIT

AGENCY
AKQA/San Francisco

CLIENT
Palm

ART DIRECTOR
Thiago Zanato

WRITER
Joe Sayaman

MULTIMEDIA ARTISTS
see index

PROGRAMMER
Steve Sherwood

INFORMATION ARCHITECTS
see index

CREATIVE DIRECTORS
PJ Pereira
Rei Inamoto
Bob Pullum
Adam Lau

ANNUAL ID
07112N

URL
awards.sf.akqa.com/
ontreo/creative/web/

MICROSITES: BUSINESS TO CONSUMER

MERIT

AGENCY
AKQA/San Francisco

CLIENT
Nike

WRITER
Bob Hall

DESIGNER
Kevin Hsieh

MULTIMEDIA ARTIST
Caio Lazzuri

PROGRAMMERS
Terry Lee
Mike Knott
Charles Duncan
Paul Liszewski

CREATIVE DIRECTORS
PJ Pereira
Rei Inamoto
Neil Robinson
David Lee

ANNUAL ID
07113N

URL
awards.sf.akqa.com/
creative/nike_lebronIV

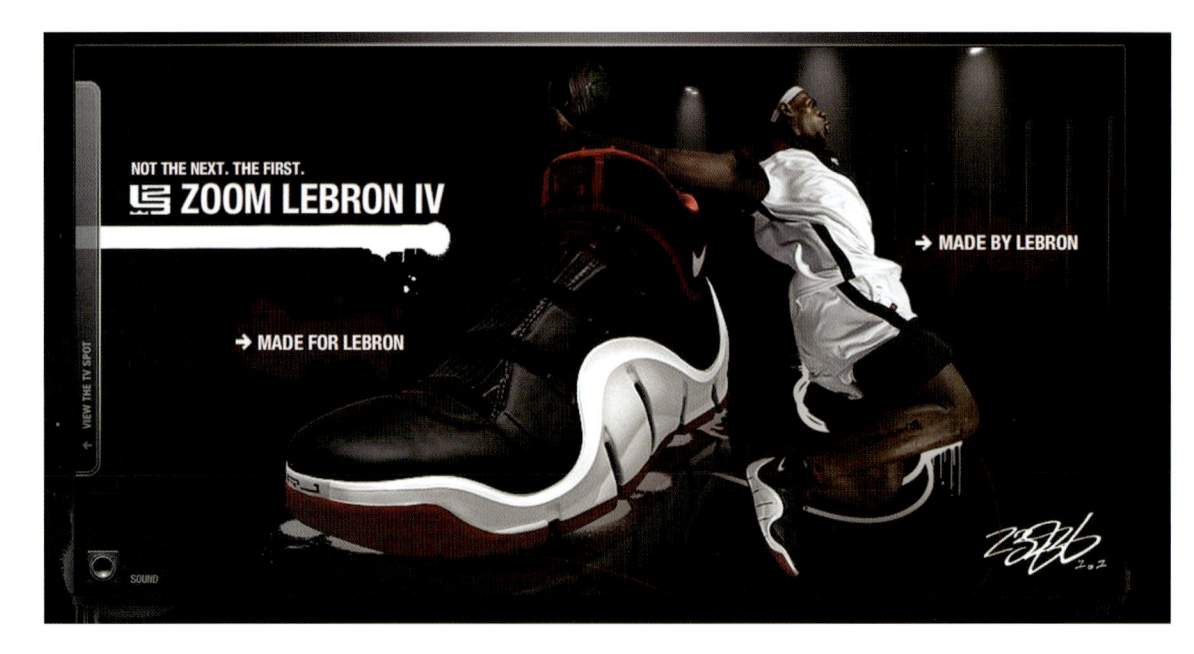

MERIT

AGENCY
AKQA/Washington

CLIENT
ESPN

DESIGNER
Dustin Blouse

MULTIMEDIA ARTIST
Jon Reiling

CREATIVE DIRECTOR
Brendan Dibona

ANNUAL ID
07114N

URL
work.dc.akqa.com/
espn/xgames/

MICROSITES: BUSINESS TO CONSUMER

MERIT

AGENCY
Bartle Bogle Hegarty/
New York

CLIENT
Unilever/Axe

ART DIRECTOR
Jon Randazzo

WRITERS
Amir Farhang
Clay Weiner

DESIGNERS
Emil Lanne
Chris Berger

CREATIVE DIRECTOR
William Gelner

ANNUAL ID
07115N

URL
www.gamekillers.com/
obituary/obituary.html

MERIT

AGENCY
BLITZ/Los Angeles

CLIENT
Adobe

DESIGNERS
Ivan Todorov
Mark Cohn
Adrian Luna
Andru Phoenix
Matt Goshman
Mark Carolin

INFORMATION ARCHITECT
Christine Kavanugh

CREATIVE DIRECTOR
Ken Martin

ANNUAL ID
07116N

URL
www.adobe.com/
go/flashtimeline

165

MICROSITES: BUSINESS TO CONSUMER

MERIT

AGENCY
BLOC/London

CLIENT
EMI Records

PROGRAMMERS
Iain Lobb
Steve Hayes
Xavier Monvoisin

PRODUCTION COMPANY
Rick Palmer

CREATIVE DIRECTOR
John Denton

CONTENT STRATEGIST
Eric Winbolt

ANNUAL ID
07117N

URL
www.in-colour.net

MERIT

AGENCY
Butler, Shine, Stern & Partners/Sausalito

CLIENT
MINI

ART DIRECTORS
Brian Lambert
Mike Caguin
Mike Hughes

WRITERS
Nick Mathisen
Eric Husband

MULTIMEDIA ARTIST
Erik Hunter

CREATIVE DIRECTORS
John Butler
Mike Shine
Nei Sobral Caetano da Silva

ANNUAL ID
07118N

URL
staging.bssp.com/oneshow07/mini_motoring_school_site/

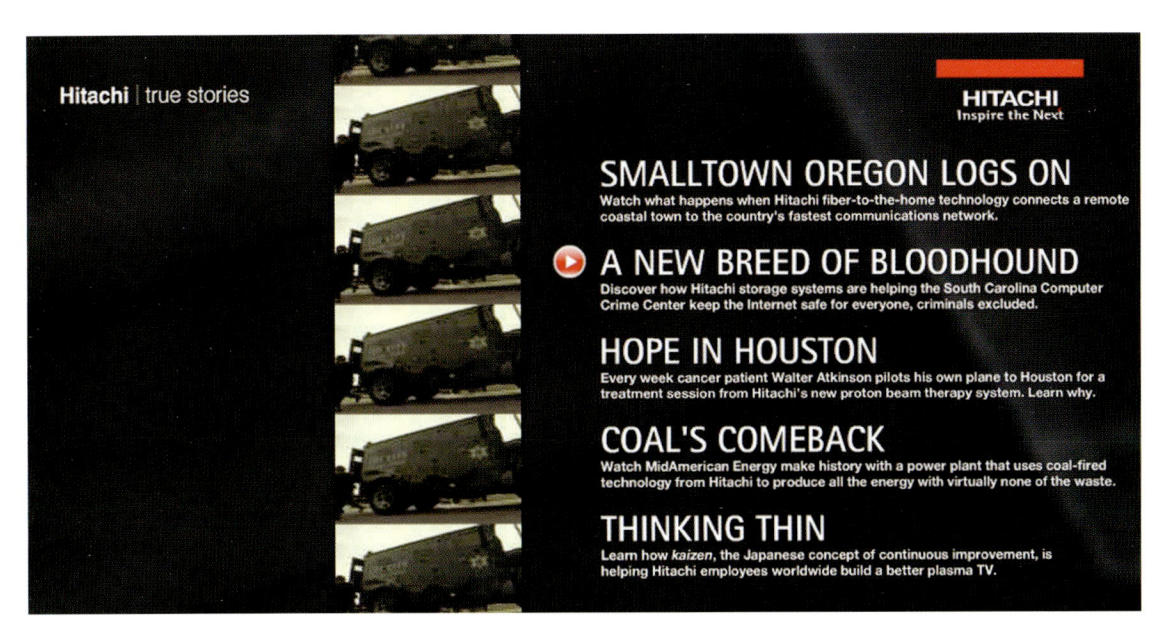

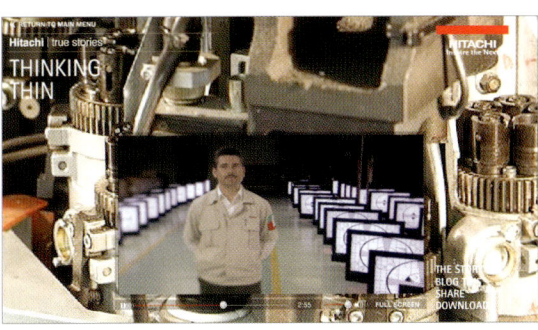

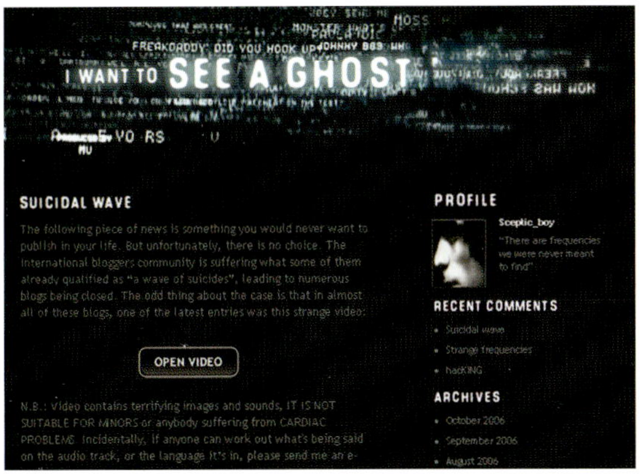

MICROSITES: BUSINESS TO CONSUMER

MERIT

AGENCIES
McCann Worldgroup/
Code and Theory/
New York

CLIENT
Hitachi

ART DIRECTORS
Dylan Dibona
Brandon Ralph

WRITER
Peter Rudy

DESIGNERS
Jeremy Davis
Andrew Wendling

PROGRAMMER
Chris Delia

CREATIVE DIRECTORS
Brandon Ralph
Rob Bagot
John McNeil
Dylan Dibona
Peter Rudy

ANNUAL ID
07119N

URL
www.hitachi.us/
truestories/

MERIT

AGENCY
CP PROXIMITY/
Barcelona

CLIENT
DEA PLANETA

ART DIRECTORS
Jaume Leis
Jordi Ramón

WRITER
Hugo Olivera

PROGRAMMERS
Dani Rocasalbas
Juan Carlos Moscardó

CONTENT STRATEGIST
Iciar Zafra

CREATIVE DIRECTOR
Enric Nel-lo

ANNUAL ID
07120N

URL
thisismywork.com/
oneshow/pulse

167

MICROSITES: BUSINESS TO CONSUMER

MERIT

AGENCY
Crispin Porter +
Bogusky/Miami

CLIENT
Haggar

ART DIRECTORS
Patrick Horn
Kevin Koller

WRITER
Ryan Kutscher

PROGRAMMERS
Matt Walsh
Scott Prindle

PRODUCTION COMPANY
North Kingdom

CREATIVE DIRECTORS
Alex Bogusky
Rob Reilly
Evan Fry
Jeff Benjamin

ANNUAL ID
07121N

URL
www.cpbgroup.com/
awards/gentlemans
disagreement.html

MERIT

AGENCY
Crispin Porter +
Bogusky/Miami

CLIENT
Volkswagen

ART DIRECTORS
Mike Ferrare
Doug Pedersen

WRITERS
Carl Corbitt
Tom Adams

PROGRAMMERS
see index

PRODUCTION COMPANY
Mindflood

CREATIVE DIRECTORS
Alex Bogusky
Andrew Keller
Rob Strasberg
Tony Calcao
Jeff Benjamin

ANNUAL ID
07122N

URL
www.cpbgroup.com/
awards/jettareport.html

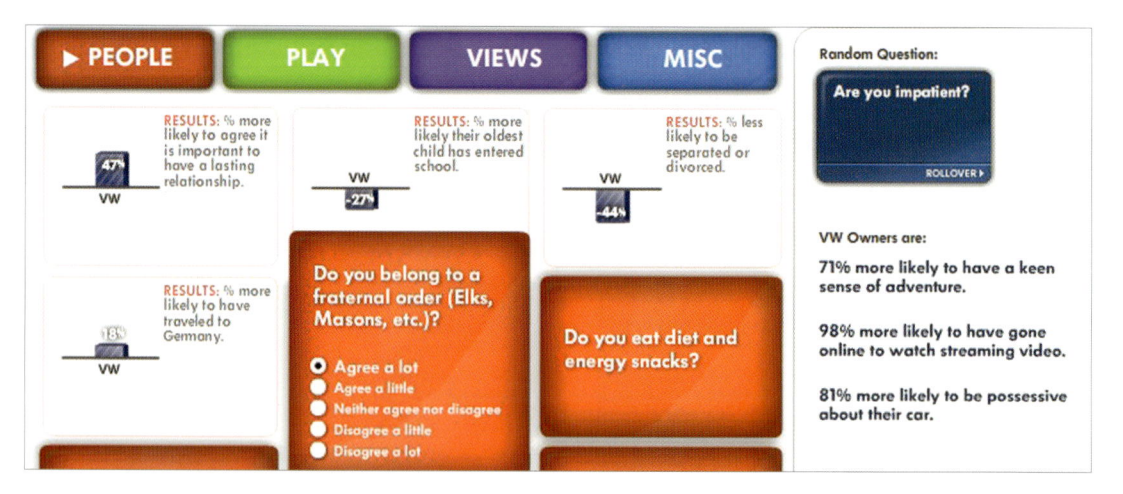

MICROSITES: BUSINESS TO CONSUMER

MERIT

AGENCY
Crispin Porter +
Bogusky/Miami

CLIENT
Volkswagen

ART DIRECTORS
Kat Morris
Conor McCann

WRITER
Rob Thompson

PROGRAMMERS
Scott Prindle
Jordi Ortega
Larry Gordon
Matt Walsh

INFORMATION ARCHITECT
Adam Heathcott

CREATIVE DIRECTORS
Alex Bogusky
Rob Strasberg
Tony Calcao
Jeff Benjamin

ANNUAL ID
07123N

URL
www.cpbgroup.com/
awards/gypsycab.html

MERIT

AGENCY
Crispin Porter +
Bogusky/Miami

CLIENT
Volkswagen

ART DIRECTORS
Tiffany Kosel
Mike Ferrare
Rahul Panchal
Aramis Israel
Tom Zukoski

WRITERS
Scott Linnen
Mike Howard
Jeff Gillette
Ryan Kutscher

DESIGNERS
see index

PRODUCTION COMPANIES
see index

CREATIVE DIRECTORS
see index

ANNUAL ID
07124N

URL
www.cpbgroup.com/
awards/vwfeatures.html

169

MICROSITES: BUSINESS TO CONSUMER

MERIT

AGENCY
Crispin Porter +
Bogusky/Miami

CLIENT
Miller Lite

ART DIRECTORS
Rahul Panchal
Geordie Stephens
Franklin Tipton

PROGRAMMERS
see index

MULTIMEDIA ARTISTS
see index

PRODUCTION COMPANY
Villains

CREATIVE DIRECTORS
Alex Bogusky
Paul Keister
Bill Wright
Jeff Benjamin

ANNUAL ID
07125N

URL
www.cpbgroup.com/
awards/manlaws.html

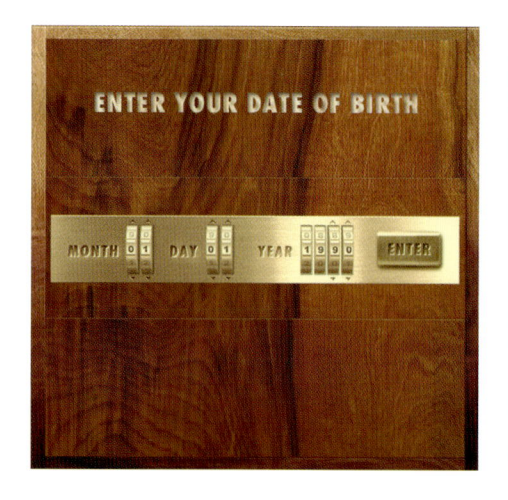

MERIT

AGENCY
Daddy/Gothenburg

CLIENT
Carlsberg

ART DIRECTOR
Mats Tellving

WRITERS
Mikael Andersson
Johan Kruse
Maria Åsman

DESIGNER
Malin Ekman

MULTIMEDIA ARTIST
Erik Sterner

PROGRAMMERS
see index

CONTENT STRATEGISTS
see index

CREATIVE DIRECTOR
Björn Höglund

ANNUAL ID
07126N

URL
www.daddy.secomp/
2007/oneshow/dmc/

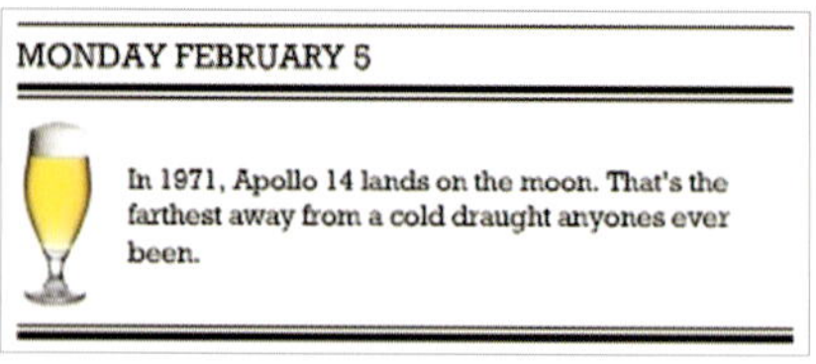

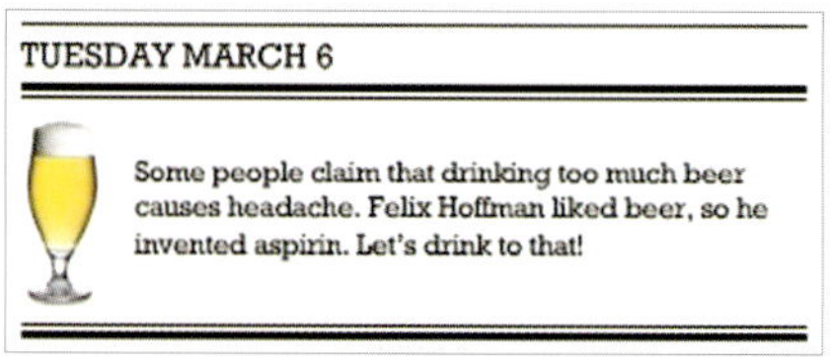

170

MICROSITES: BUSINESS TO CONSUMER

MERIT

AGENCY
Domani Studios/
Brooklyn

CLIENT
Anheuser-Busch

MULTIMEDIA ARTIST
Domani Studios

CREATIVE DIRECTOR
DDB Chicago

ANNUAL ID
07127N

URL
www.tedferguson.com

MERIT

AGENCY
EVB/San Francisco

CLIENT
Orbit White

ART DIRECTORS
Jose Luis Martinez
Liz Balin
Joe Cole
Paul Roy

WRITER
Alexandra Tyler

DESIGNER
Kevin Hsieh

PROGRAMMER
Justin Peterson

PRODUCTION COMPANIES
Rock Fight
Keytoon

CREATIVE DIRECTOR
Jason Zada

ANNUAL ID
07129N

URL
www.evb.com/enter_
2007/friendsofbright.html

171

MICROSITES: BUSINESS TO CONSUMER

MERIT

AGENCY
Fallon/Minneapolis

CLIENT
Georgia Pacific/
Brawny

ART DIRECTORS
Lovisa Almgren
Andy Amadeo
Kris Wixom
Andy Gugel

WRITERS
Alisa Sengel Wixom
Eric Frost
Chris Wolffe

DESIGNERS
see index

PROGRAMMERS
see index

CREATIVE DIRECTORS
see index

ANNUAL ID
07130N

URL
awards.iti.
fallon.com/06/
brawnyacademy

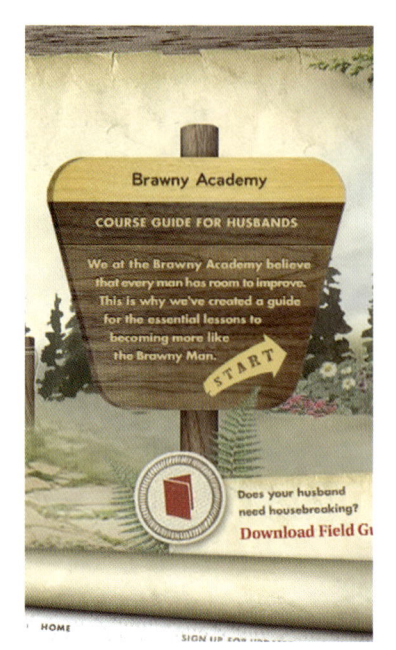

MERIT

AGENCY
Farfar/Stockholm

CLIENT
Nokia Nseries

ART DIRECTOR
Daniel Wall

WRITER
Henrik Berglof

DESIGNERS
Per Hansson
Anders Gustavsson
Bjorn Johansson
Bo Gustavsson

CONTENT STRATEGISTS
Anna Frick

PRODUCTION COMPANIES
Colony
Freecloud
Harakiri

CREATIVE DIRECTOR
Nicke Bergstrom

ANNUAL ID
07131N

URL
www.farfar.se/awards/
oneshow2007/pjotro/

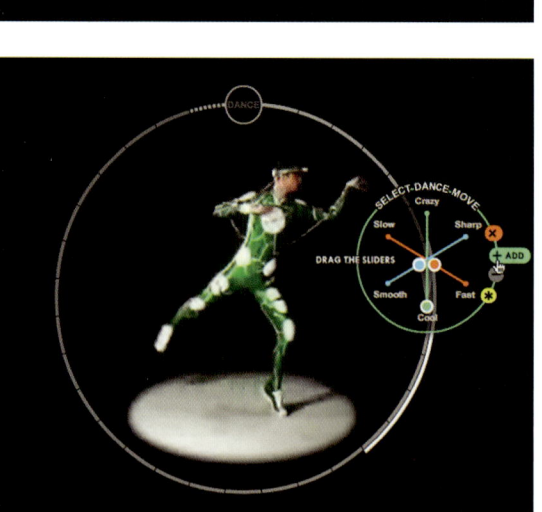

172

MICROSITES: BUSINESS TO CONSUMER

MERIT

AGENCY
Farfar/Stockholm

CLIENT
Nokia Nseries

ART DIRECTOR
Daniel Wall

WRITER
Jeff Salomonsson

DESIGNERS
Per Hansson
Simon Martelius
Erik Norin
Liv Franzen
Bo Gustavsson

PRODUCTION COMPANIES
Colony
Freecloud

CREATIVE DIRECTOR
Nicke Bergstrom

ANNUAL ID
07132N

URL
www.farfar.se/
awards/oneshow
2007/greatpockets/

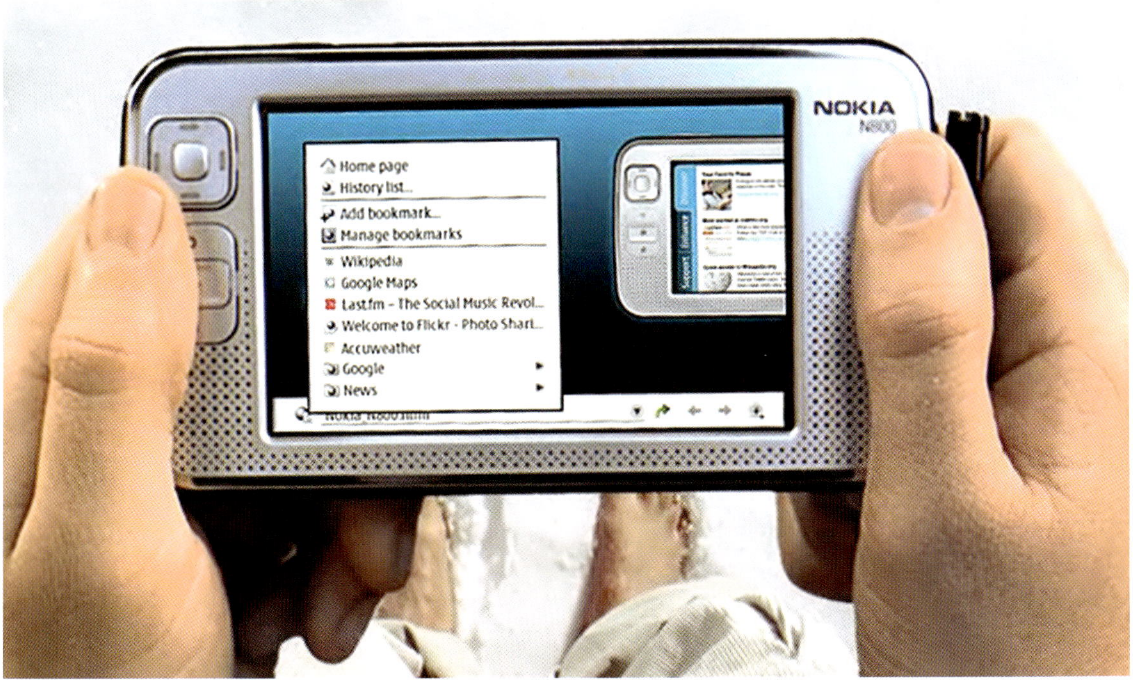

MERIT

AGENCY
Farfar/Stockholm

CLIENT
Nokia Nseries

ART DIRECTOR
Ake Brattberg

WRITER
Jeff Salomonsson

DESIGNER
Rickard Lundberg
Bo Gustavsson
Erik Norin

CONTENT STRATEGIST
Marten Forslund

PRODUCTION COMPANY
Visual Art

CREATIVE DIRECTOR
Nicke Bergstrom

ANNUAL ID
07133N

URL
www.farfar.se/
awards/oneshow
2007/internetwalk/

173

MICROSITES: BUSINESS TO CONSUMER

MERIT

AGENCY
Farfar/Stockholm

CLIENT
Visit Sweden

ART DIRECTOR
Johan Ohrn

WRITER
Tom Eriksen

DESIGNER
Per Hansson

PROGRAMMER
Bo Gustavsson

CONTENT STRATEGIST
Marten Forslund

PRODUCTION COMPANIES
Colony
Harakiri

CREATIVE DIRECTOR
Nicke Bergstrom

ANNUAL ID
07134N

URL
www.farfar.se/awards/
oneshow2007stockholm/

MERIT

AGENCY
Forsman & Bodenfors/
Gothenburg

CLIENT
IKEA

ART DIRECTORS
Andreas Malm
Anders Eklind
Karin Frisell
Mathias Appelblad

WRITERS
Fredrik Jansson
Anders Hegerfors

DESIGNERS
Mikko Timonen
Nina Andersson

PRODUCTION COMPANIES
Sammarco Productions
Kokokaka Entertainment

ANNUAL ID
07135N

URL
demo.fb.se/e/ikea/
comeintothecloset/

MICROSITES: BUSINESS TO CONSUMER

MERIT

AGENCY
Forsman & Bodenfors/
Gothenburg

CLIENT
Volvo

ART DIRECTORS
Marthias Appelblad
Johan Eghammer
Mikko Timonen
Anders Eklind

WRITERS
Jacob Nelson
Filip Nilsson

DESIGNER
Lars Jansson

PRODUCTION COMPANIES
Kokokaka
MFX

ANNUAL ID
07136N

URL
demo.fb.se/e/volvo/c30

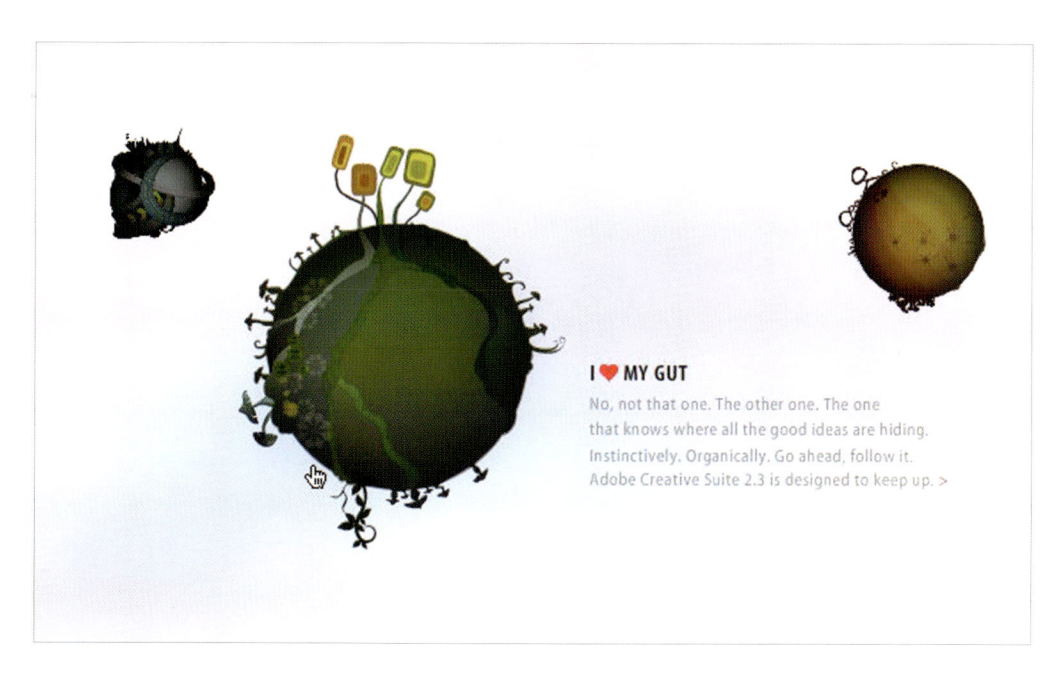

MERIT

AGENCY
Goodby, Silverstein &
Partners/San Francisco

CLIENT
Adobe

ART DIRECTOR
Mark Sikes

WRITER
Spencer Riviera

CONTENT STRATEGISTS
Mike Geiger
Kenna Takahashi

PRODUCTION COMPANY
Unit-9

CREATIVE DIRECTOR
Keith Anderson

ANNUAL ID
07137N

URL
www.goodbysilverstein.
com/creative_mind/

175

MICROSITES: BUSINESS TO CONSUMER

MERIT

AGENCY
Goodby, Silverstein & Partners/San Francisco

CLIENT
Comcast

ART DIRECTORS
Devin Sharkey
Stefan Copiz

WRITER
Dan Rollman

CONTENT STRATEGISTS
Mike Geiger
Brit Charlebois

PRODUCTION COMPANIES
The Barbarian Group
Number-9

CREATIVE DIRECTORS
Will McGinness
Jamie Barrett
Mark Wenneker

ANNUAL ID
07138N

URL
www.comcastic.com/mr_t/index.html

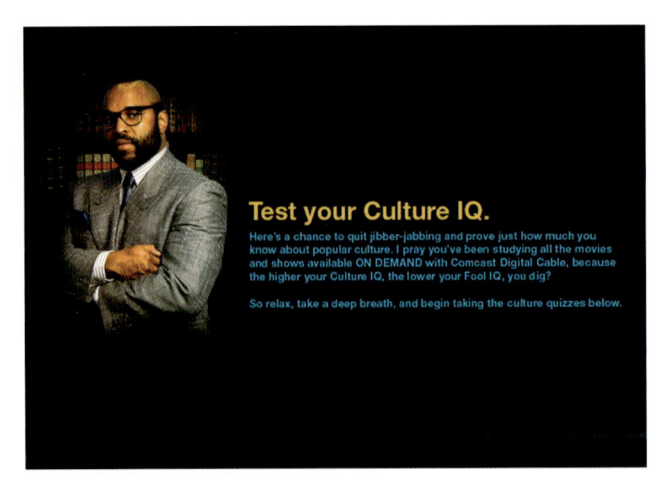

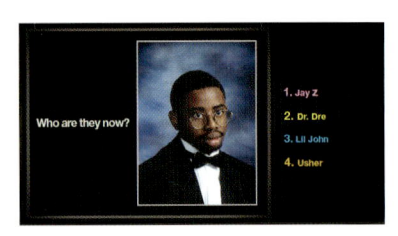

MERIT

AGENCY
Goodby, Silverstein & Partners/San Francisco

CLIENT
California Milk Board

ART DIRECTORS
Robert Lindstrom
Feh Tarty

WRITERS
Nat Lawlor
Pat McKay
Ronny Northrop
Paul Charney

PROGRAMMERS
see index

CONTENT STRATEGISTS
see index

PRODUCTION COMPANY
North Kingdom

CREATIVE DIRECTORS
Jeff Goodby
Will McGinness

ANNUAL ID
07139N

URL
www.cowabduction.com

176

MICROSITES: BUSINESS TO CONSUMER

MERIT

AGENCY
Goodby, Silverstein & Partners/San Francisco

CLIENT
Foster Farms

ART DIRECTOR
Jason Warne

WRITER
Mike Sweeney

CONTENT STRATEGISTS
Mike Geiger
Jonathan Percy

PRODUCTION COMPANY
Unit-9

CREATIVE DIRECTORS
Rich Silverstein
Keith Anderson

ANNUAL ID
07140N

URL
www.thefosterimposters.com

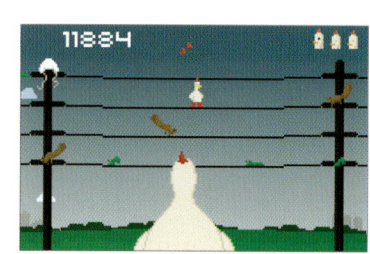

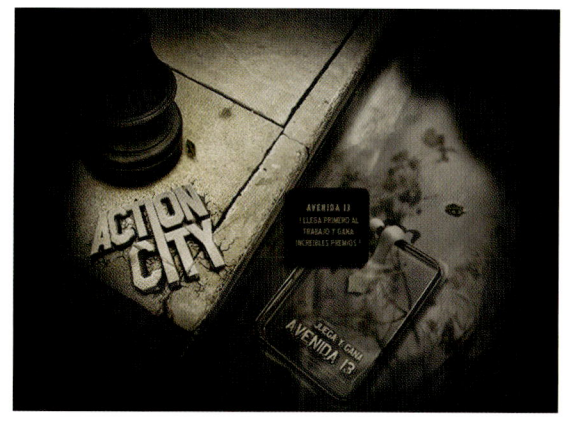

MERIT

AGENCY
Grupo W/Saltillo

CLIENT
Unilever/Rexona

ART DIRECTOR
Miguel Calderon

WRITER
Ivan Gonzalez

DESIGNERS
Miguel Calderon
Jezreel Gutierrez

MULTIMEDIA ARTISTS
Daniel Bates
Sebastian Mariscal
Ulises Valencia

PROGRAMMERS
Raul Uranga
Edgar Ortiz

CREATIVE DIRECTOR
Miguel Calderon

ANNUAL ID
07141N

URL
www.grupowprojects.com/rexona/actioncity

177

MICROSITES: BUSINESS TO CONSUMER

MERIT

AGENCY
Kinetic/Singapore

CLIENT
Flowers Feed The Soul

ART DIRECTOR
Sean Lam

WRITER
Eugene Tan

PROGRAMMERS
Sean Lam
Jason Chan

CREATIVE DIRECTOR
Sean Lam

ANNUAL ID
07142N

URL
www.errortypeone.com/awards/flowersfeedthesoul

MERIT

AGENCY
Lowe Brindfors/Stockholm

CLIENT
Stella Artois/InBev

ART DIRECTORS
Patrik Westerdahl
Johan Tesch

WRITERS
Martin Bartholf
Ryan Spelliscy

MULTIMEDIA ARTIST
Daniel Isaksson

PRODUCTION COMPANY
Against All Odds

CREATIVE DIRECTOR
Matthew Bull

ANNUAL ID
07143N

URL
www.lowebrindfors.se/showroom/stellaartois/ledefi

178

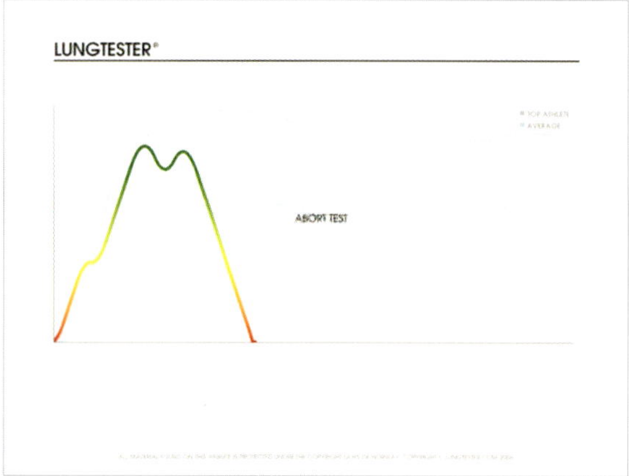

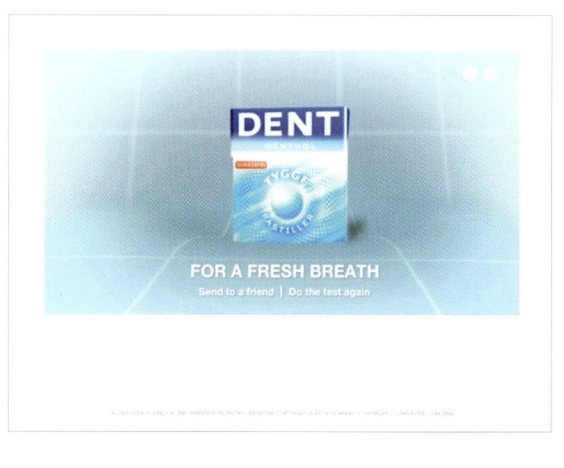

MICROSITES: BUSINESS TO CONSUMER

MERIT

AGENCY
McCann Norway/Oslo

CLIENT
Brynild

ART DIRECTORS
Daniel Wahlgren
Jakob Nielsen

WRITERS
Daniel Wahlgren
Jakob Nielsen

DESIGNER
Kathrine Slapgård

PROGRAMMERS
David Wahlgren
Andre Orefjerd

CONTENT STRATEGISTS
Marius Zachariasen
Anne Gro Carlsson
Anniken Schjøtt

ANNUAL ID
07144N

URL
interaktiv.mccann.no/oneshow/dent/

MERIT

AGENCY
McCann Worldgroup/San Francisco

CLIENT
Microsoft/Windows Vista

ART DIRECTOR
Troy Cooper

WRITERS
Rob Bagot
Demetri Martin
Tommy Means

MULTIMEDIA ARTIST
Michael Gillette

PRODUCTION COMPANY
Mekanism

CREATIVE DIRECTORS
Rob Bagot
Tommy Means
John McNeil

ANNUAL ID
07145N

URL
www.clearification.com

179

MICROSITES: BUSINESS TO CONSUMER

MERIT

AGENCY
North Kingdom/Skellefteå

CLIENT
Toyota

WRITER
Anders Lidzell

DESIGNERS
Staffan Lamm
Bjarne Melin
Andreas Hellström

MULTIMEDIA ARTISTS
see index

INFORMATION ARCHITECTS
see index

CONTENT STRATEGISTS
see index

PRODUCTION COMPANY
Anton Eriksson

ANNUAL ID
07146N

URL
demo.northkingdom.
com/ihuvudetpatoyota/
index_en.html

MERIT

AGENCY
Projector/Tokyo

CLIENT
UNIQLO

ART DIRECTOR
Yoshihiro Toda

PRODUCTION COMPANIES
Monster Films
Projector
Paragraph

CREATIVE DIRECTORS
Yoshiaki Nagasaki
Koichiro Tanaka

ANNUAL ID
07147N

URL
unimix.sonicjam.
co.jp/awards/
mixplayweb.html

MICROSITES: BUSINESS TO CONSUMER

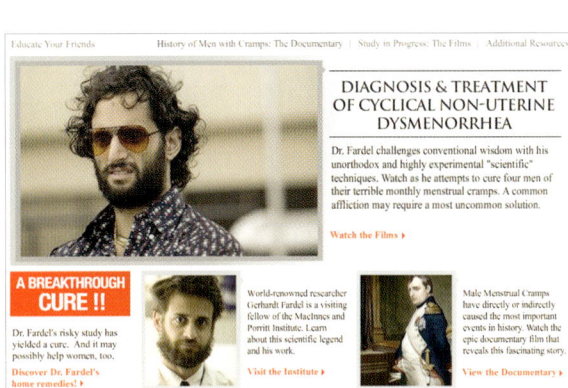

MERIT

AGENCY
Publicis/New York

CLIENT
P&G/Thermacare Menstrual

ART DIRECTOR
Scott Gursky

WRITERS
Scott Sherman
Ed Herbstman
Steven Russell
Kirt Gunn

PRODUCTION COMPANY
Dandelion

CREATIVE DIRECTORS
Karen Ingram
Kirt Gunn

ANNUAL ID
07148N

URL
www.menwithcramps.com

MERIT

AGENCY
SID LEE/Montreal

CLIENT
Arcadia Festival

WRITER
Guillaume Bergeron

PROGRAMMER
Robert Gosselin

PRODUCTION COMPANIES
La Fabrique d'Image
John Barber
Jean-François Éthier
Claudia Roy

MUSIC & SOUND
Studio La Majeure
Studio Apollo

CREATIVE DIRECTOR
Kristian Manchester

ANNUAL ID
07149N

URL
www.showmeto.com/arcadia

181

MICROSITES: BUSINESS TO CONSUMER

MERIT

AGENCY
TAXI/Montreal

CLIENT
Dermtek Reversa

ART DIRECTORS
Patrick Chaubet
Roberto Baibich

WRITERS
Brian Gill
Elyse Noel de Tilly

PRODUCTION COMPANIES
Mecano
La Fabrique d'Image

CREATIVE DIRECTORS
Stephane Charier
Dominique Trudeau

ANNUAL ID
07150N

URL
www.seemore
sideeffects.ca

MERIT

AGENCY
TAXI/Toronto

CLIENT
Amp'd Mobile

ART DIRECTOR
Nuno Ferreira

WRITER
Madeleine Di Gangi

PROGRAMMER
pixelpusher.ca

MULTIMEDIA ARTIST
Meld Media

CREATIVE DIRECTORS
Steve Mykolyn
Jason McCann
Wayne Best

ANNUAL ID
07151N

URL
www.neverinneutral.
com/pinata

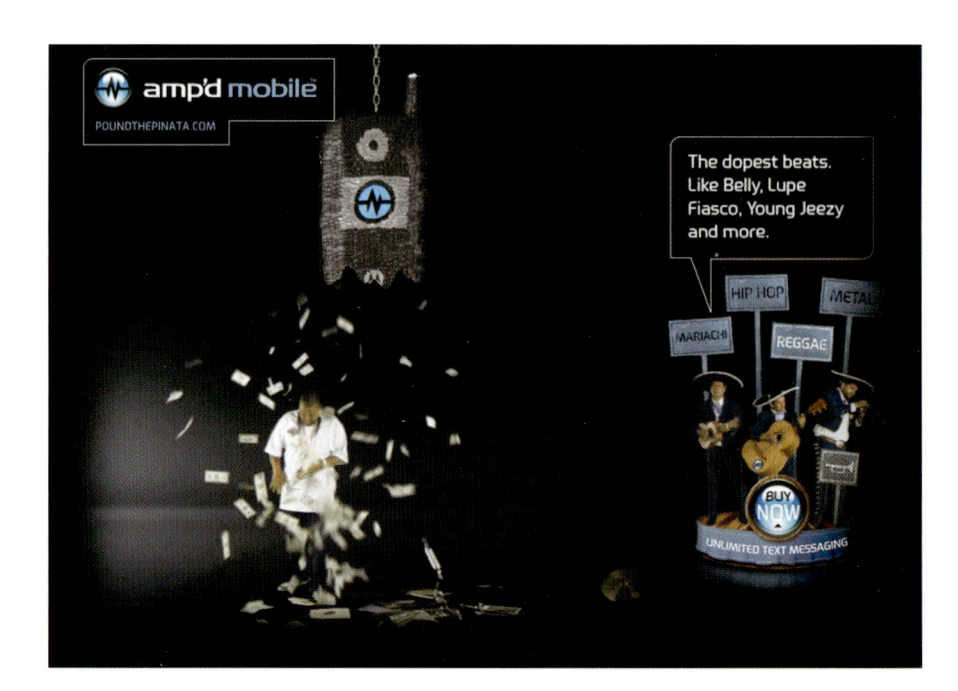

182

MICROSITES: BUSINESS TO BUSINESS

MERIT

AGENCY
Tequila/Los Angeles

CLIENT
Sony PlayStation

ART DIRECTORS
Garman Yip
David Hays

WRITERS
Glenn Sanders
Nick Davidge
Ken Youngleib
John Witting

PROGRAMMERS
Andrew Keegan
Jim Darling

PRODUCTION COMPANY
Tequila Creative

CREATIVE DIRECTORS
Nick Davidge
Doug Speidel

ANNUAL ID
07152N

URL
showcase.tequila.com/
sites/playb3yondSites/

MERIT

AGENCY
Dare/London

CLIENT
Vodafone

DESIGNERS
Dennis Christensen
Will Rose

MULTIMEDIA ARTISTS
David McNulty
Kooch Chung

CREATIVE DIRECTORS
Flo Heiss
James Cooper

ANNUAL ID
07153N

URL
www.daredigital.com/
oneshow07/
microsites/desks

183

MICROSITES: BUSINESS TO BUSINESS

MERIT

AGENCY
Vodafone Group/
Newbury

CLIENT
Vodafone Group

ART DIRECTOR
Robert Lindstroem

PRODUCTION COMPANY
North Kingdom

CREATIVE DIRECTORS
Gabriele Dangel
David Eriksson

ANNUAL ID
07154N

URL
www.vodafone
journey.com

MICROSITES: PUBLIC SERVICE/NON-PROFIT/EDUCATIONAL

MERIT

AGENCY
DDB/São Paulo

CLIENT
Masp Museum

ART DIRECTOR
Pedro Gravena

WRITER
Keke Toledo

PROGRAMMERS
Mauricio Massaia
Wagner Nunes

CREATIVE DIRECTORS
Sergio Valente
Mauricio Mazzariol

ANNUAL ID
07155N

URL
www.judgehere.com/
asone/index.html

184

MICROSITES: PUBLIC SERVICE/NON-PROFIT/EDUCATIONAL

MERIT

AGENCY
Poke/London

CLIENT
Everyman Institute of Cancer Research

ART DIRECTOR
Simon Cook

WRITER
Nathan Cooper

DESIGNER
Simon Cook

PROGRAMMER
Andrew Knott

CREATIVE DIRECTORS
Peter Beech
Iain Tait

ANNUAL ID
07156N

URL
www.cock-a-doodle.co.uk

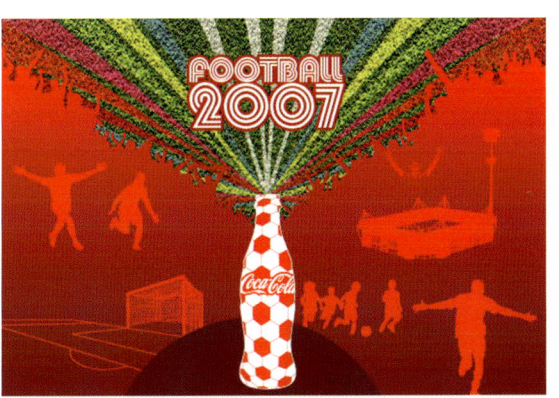

WEB SITES: BUSINESS TO CONSUMER

MERIT

AGENCY
AKQA/New York

CLIENT
The Coca-Cola Company

ANNUAL ID
07157N

URL
www.coke.com

185

WEB SITES: BUSINESS TO CONSUMER

MERIT

AGENCY
Bartle Bogle Hegarty/
New York

CLIENT
Unilever/Axe

ART DIRECTOR
Jon Randazzo

WRITER
Amir Farhang

DESIGNERS
Emil Lanne
Chris Berger

PROGRAMMER
Volume One

CREATIVE DIRECTOR
William Gelner

ANNUAL ID
07159N

URL
www.gamekillers.com

MERIT

AGENCY
Crispin Porter +
Bogusky/Miami

CLIENT
Volkswagen

ART DIRECTORS
see index

WRITERS
see index

DESIGNERS
Conor McCann
Chean Wei Law

MULTIMEDIA ARTISTS
Thomas Rodgers
James Martis

PRODUCTION COMPANIES
see index

CREATIVE DIRECTORS
see index

ANNUAL ID
07160N

URL
www.cpbgroup.com/
awards/vwfeaturesall.
html

WEB SITES: BUSINESS TO CONSUMER

MERIT

AGENCY
DoubleYou/Barcelona

CLIENT
Cacique Rum

ART DIRECTORS
Blanca Piera
Ana Delgado

WRITERS
Emma Pueyo
Paco Conde

DESIGNERS
Lisi Badía
Raül Hernández
Daniel Guillén

PROGRAMMERS
Jose Rubio
Álvaro Sandoval

CREATIVE DIRECTORS
see index

ANNUAL ID
07161N

URL
www.doubleyourpenissize.com/2007/caciquelallamada/oneshow.html

MERIT

AGENCY
DraftFCB/Toronto

CLIENT
Motorola/Motofone

ART DIRECTORS
Graham Ameron
Steve Di Lorenzo

WRITER
David Horovitch

MULTIMEDIA ARTISTS
Dan Purdy
Dov Atlin

CONTENT STRATEGISTS
Paula Swirla
Alan Macdonald
Brinda Khanna
John Swartz

CREATIVE DIRECTOR
Steve Di Lorenzo

ANNUAL ID
07163N

URL
www.fcbpreview.ca/motofone/

WEB SITES: BUSINESS TO CONSUMER

MERIT

AGENCY
DraftFCB/Toronto

CLIENT
Hewlett-Packard

ART DIRECTORS
Anthony del Rizzo
Steve Di Lorenzo

WRITER
Sarah Jane Bowler

MULTIMEDIA ARTISTS
Dan Purdy
Henry Chi
Jason Doherty

CONTETN STRATEGISTS
Alan Macdonald
Kim Leidich

CREATIVE DIRECTORS
Steve Di Lorenzo
Sue Boivin
Nick Chapman

ANNUAL ID
07164N

URL
www.fcbpreview.ca/hp/unity_tree/daily/index.html

MERIT

AGENCY
Forsman & Bodenfors/Gothenburg

CLIENT
Stadium

ART DIRECTORS
Andreas Malm
Paul Jespersen
Paul Eneroth
Mathias Appelblad

WRITERS
Rebecka Osvald
Jorgen Gjaerum

DESIGNERS
Jerry Wass
Mikko Timonen

PRODUCTION COMPANY
B-Reel

ANNUAL ID
07166N

URL
demo.fb.se/e/stadium/thecityisyourstadium/campaign/

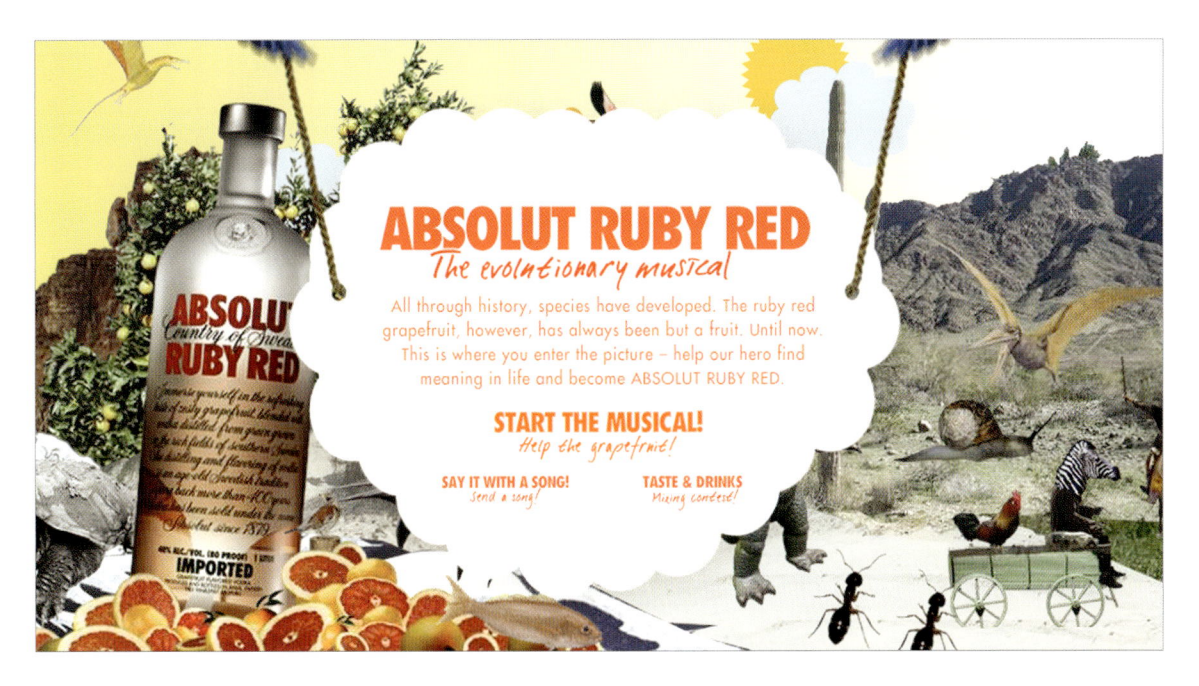

WEB SITES: BUSINESS TO CONSUMER

MERIT

AGENCY
Great Works/
Stockholm

CLIENT
V&S Absolut Spirits

ART DIRECTORS
Jacob Åström
Megan Williams

PROGRAMMER
Jocke Wissing

CREATIVE DIRECTORS
Ted Persson
Rob Smiley

ANNUAL ID
07167N

URL
absolut.com/rubyred

MERIT

AGENCY
Great Works/
Stockholm

CLIENT
V&S Absolut Spirits

ART DIRECTOR
Jesper Versfeld

PROGRAMMERS
Martin Ström
illianced

CREATIVE DIRECTORS
Ted Persson
Sebastien Vacherot

ANNUAL ID
07168N

URL
absolut.com/lomo

189

WEB SITES: BUSINESS TO CONSUMER

MERIT

AGENCY
Great Works/
Stockholm

CLIENT
V&S Absolut Spirits

ART DIRECTOR
Jimmy Poopuu

PROGRAMMER
Jocke Wissing

CREATIVE DIRECTORS
Ted Persson
Sebastien Vacherot

ANNUAL ID
07169N

URL
absolut.com/search

MERIT

AGENCY
IMG SRC/Tokyo

CLIENT
Levi Strauss Japan K.K.

ART DIRECTOR
Atsushi Fujimaki

DESIGNERS
Atsushi Fujimaki
Takeshi Yoshimori

CREATIVE DIRECTORS
Takeharu Ito (The VOICE Production)
Hiroshi Koike

ANNUAL ID
07170N

URL
levi.com/japan/
_product/2006fw/

WEB SITES: BUSINESS TO CONSUMER

MERIT

AGENCY
JWT/New York

CLIENT
Ford

ART DIRECTORS
Doug Wojciewski
Dan Przekop

WRITER
Jonny Leahan

DESIGNERS
see index

PROGRAMMERS
see index

INFORMATION ARCHITECT
Matthew Dull

CONTENT STRATEGIST
Brian Clark

CREATIVE DIRECTORS
Ty Montague
Toby Barlow

ANNUAL ID
07171N

URL
www.fordboldmoves.com

MERIT

AGENCY
NEUE DIGITALE/
Frankfurt

CLIENT
adidas

ART DIRECTOR
Bejadin Selimi

DESIGNER
André Bourguignon

PROGRAMMERS
Heiko Schweickhardt
Thomas Junk

PRODUCTION COMPANY
Effekt-Etage Berlin

CREATIVE DIRECTOR
Elke Klinkhammer

ANNUAL ID
07172N

URL
www.neue-digitale.de/
projects/y-3_fw2006

191

WEB SITES: BUSINESS TO CONSUMER

MERIT

AGENCY
Pyramid Film/Tokyo

CLIENT
Casio

ANNUAL ID
07173N

URL
www.pyramidfilm.co.jp/interactive/awards2007/gzone/en/index.html

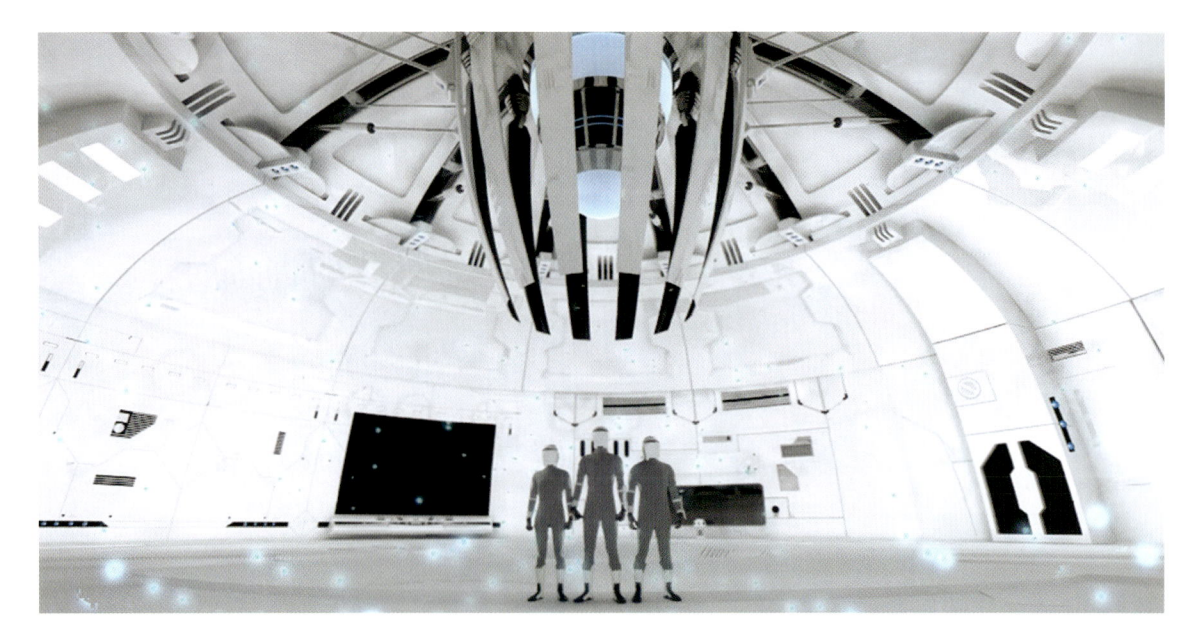

MERIT

AGENCY
R/GA/New York

CLIENT
Nike

DESIGNERS
Yu-Ming Wu
ShuZheng Li

MULTIMEDIA ARTIST
Can Misirlioglu

PROGRAMMERS
Carrie Kengle
Michele Roman
Sunny Nan
Michael Piccuirro

AGENCY PRODUCERS
see index

CREATIVE DIRECTORS
Richard Ting
Joseph Cartman
Steve Caputo

ANNUAL ID
07174N

URL
www.rga.com/award/bball.html

WEB SITES: BUSINESS TO CONSUMER

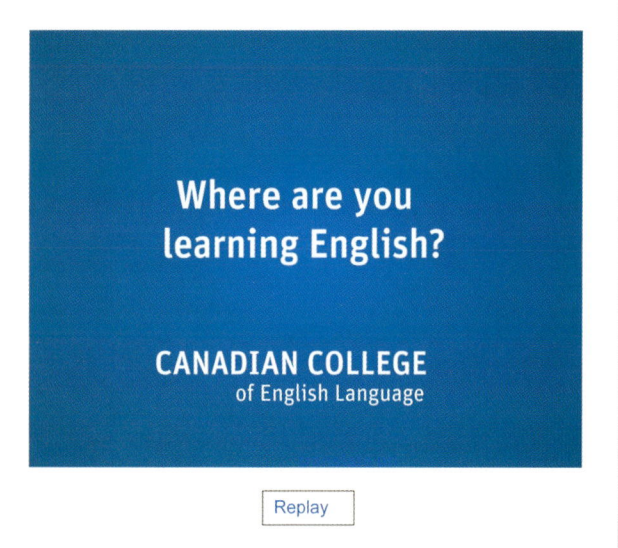

MERIT

AGENCY
Rethink/
Vancouver

CLIENT
Canadian College of
English Language

ART DIRECTOR
Bart Batchelor

WRITER
Michael Milardo

CREATIVE DIRECTORS
Chris Staples
Ian Grais

ANNUAL ID
07175N

URL
www.poptranslator.com

MERIT

AGENCY
Saatchi & Saatchi/
Torrance

CLIENT
Toyota

ART DIRECTOR
Kelly Kliebe

WRITER
Anthony Wells

PRODUCTION COMPANY
Hello Design

CONTENT STRATEGIST
Shannon Duffy

CREATIVE DIRECTORS
Johann Conforme
Peter Kang

ANNUAL ID
07176N

URL
www.saatchila.com/yaris

193

WEB SITES: BUSINESS TO CONSUMER

MERIT

AGENCY
Wieden + Kennedy/
Portland

CLIENT
Old Spice

ART DIRECTOR
Nik Daum

WRITER
Val Klump

PRODUCTION COMPANY
Domani Studios

CREATIVE DIRECTORS
Mark Fitzloff
Monica Taylor

ANNUAL ID
07177N

URL
www.experience
oldspice.com

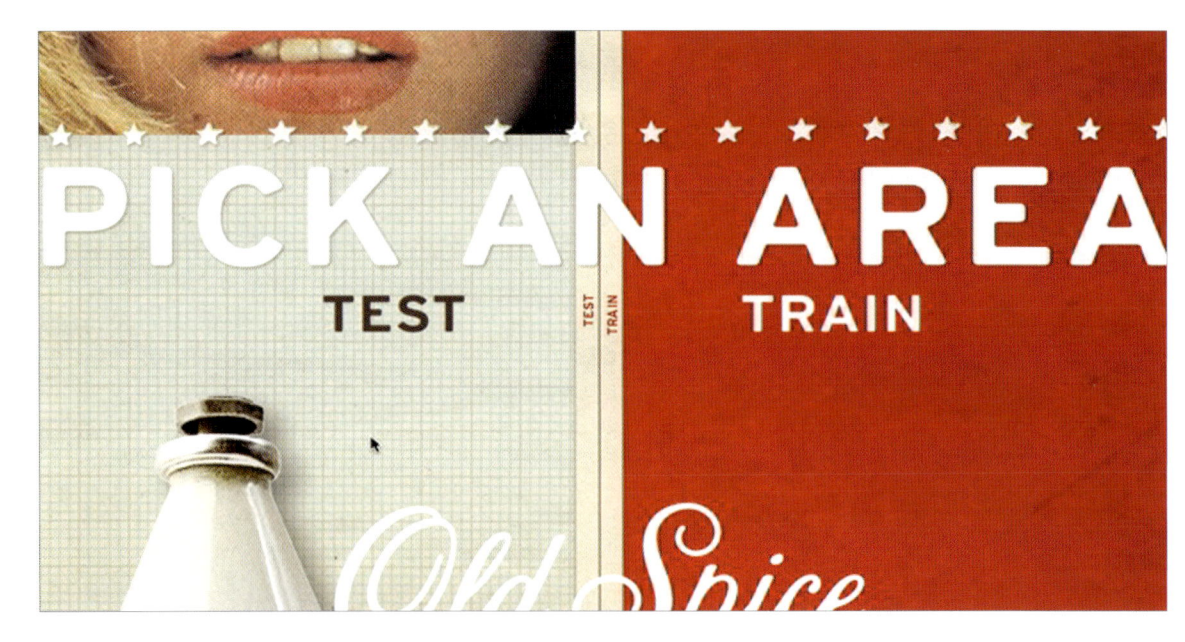

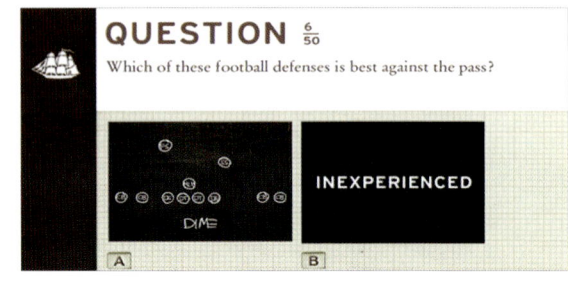

MERIT

AGENCY
Wysiwyg Comunicación
Interactiva/Madrid

CLIENT
Diesel

ART DIRECTORS
Kike Besada
Pablo García
Javier Jiménez
Conchi Novoa

WRITERS
Daniel Molinillo
Elena Baños

PROGRAMMERS
Carlos Martínez
Ricardo Sánchez
Juan Carlos Fernández

INFORMATION ARCHITECTS
Luis M. Corbacho
Ignacio Alvarez-Borrás

CREATIVE DIRECTORS
Marga Castaño
Nuria Martínez

ANNUAL ID
07178N

URL
www.wysiwyg.net/fest07/
oneshow/diesel/

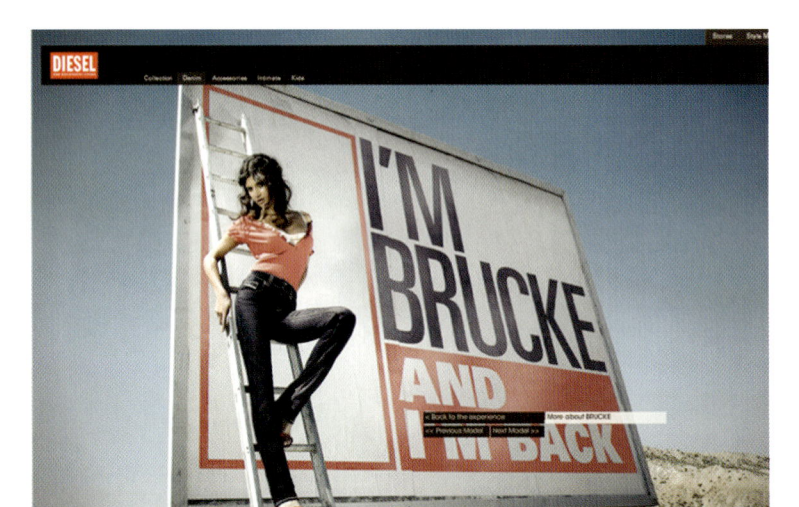

WEB SITES: BUSINESS TO BUSINESS

MERIT

AGENCY
Lowe/New York

CLIENT
Advertising Women of New York

ART DIRECTORS
John Morton
Maggi Machado

WRITER
Stephanie Price

CREATIVE DIRECTORS
Fernanda Romano
Mark Wnek

ANNUAL ID
07180N

URL
www.pigsanonymous.com

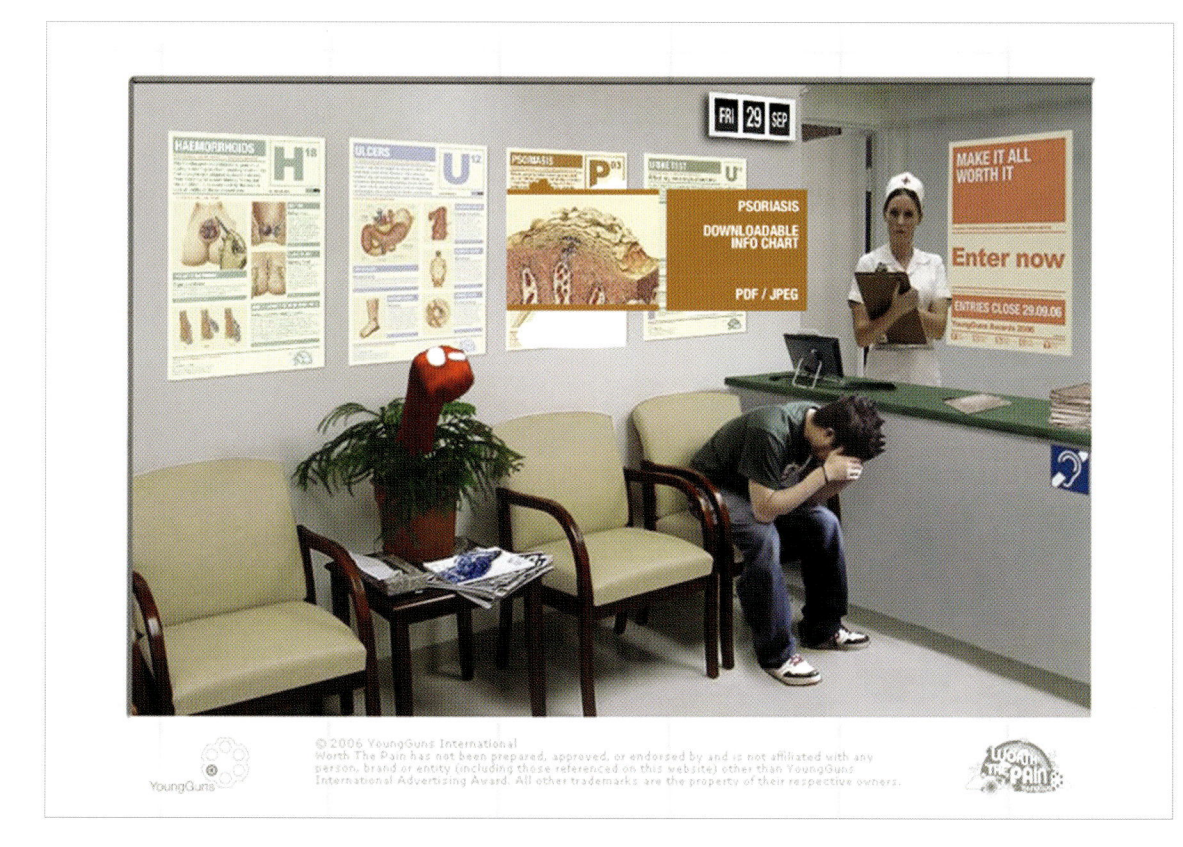

MERIT

AGENCY
Saatchi & Saatchi/Auckland

CLIENT
Young Guns

ART DIRECTORS
Matty Burton
Dave Bowman
Steve Back
Andy DiLallo
Brian Merrifield
Chris Jones
Matt Swinburne
Jay Ng
Cameron Harris

WRITERS
see index

DESIGNER
Daniel Liao

CREATIVE DIRECTORS
Mike O'Sullivan
Toby Talbot

ANNUAL ID
07181N

URL
www.oursites.co.nz/youngguns

195

WEB SITES: E-COMMERCE

MERIT

AGENCY
Rich Creative/Richmond

CLIENT
T2

ART DIRECTOR
Bryce Ford

DESIGNER
Andy Thomas

PROGRAMMERS
Andy Gargan
Marcus Van Malsen
Cam Manderson

MULTIMEDIA ARTIST
Sacha Jerrems

INFORMATION ARCHITECT
Danielle Stephens

CONTENT STRATEGIST
Chris Rooke

ANNUAL ID
07182N

URL
www.t2tea.com

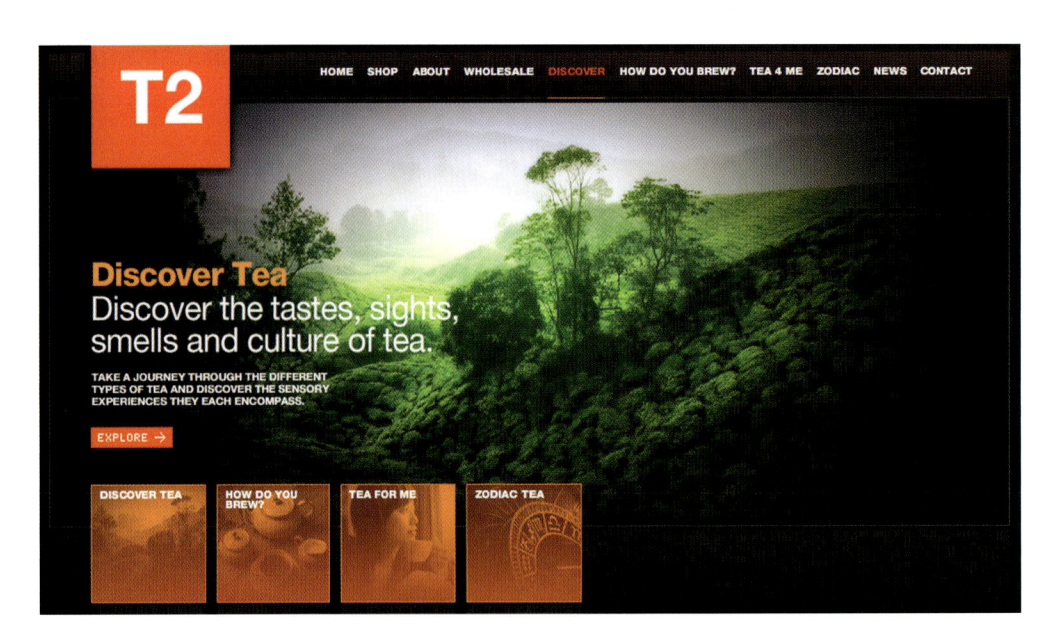

WEB SITES: PUBLIC SERVICE/NON-PROFIT/EDUCATIONAL

MERIT

AGENCY
AKQA/Washington

CLIENT
The Global Fund to Fight AIDS, TB and Malaria

ART DIRECTOR
Virginia Golden

PROGRAMMER
Alex Nguyen

CONTENT STRATEGIST
Jon Lee

ANNUAL ID
07183N

URL
work.dc.akqa.com/globalfund/

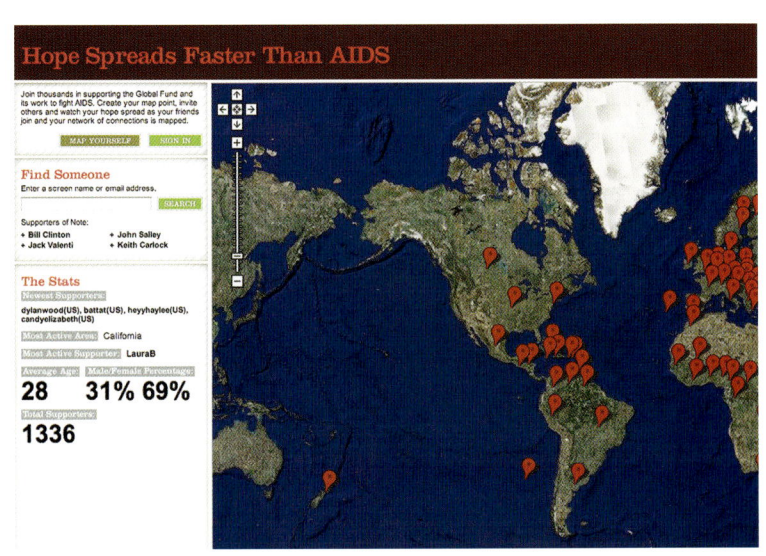

196

WEB SITES: PUBLIC SERVICE/NON-PROFIT/EDUCATIONAL

MERIT

AGENCY
ARC Worldwide/Leo Burnett/Singapore

CLIENT
Samaritans of Singapore

ART DIRECTORS
Alan Leong
Ho WeePeng

WRITER
Mak Kyeli

DESIGNER
Christine Thamrin

MULTIMEDIA ARTIST
Arai Lanju

PROGRAMMER
Aaron Khoo

CREATIVE DIRECTOR
Valerie Cheng

ANNUAL ID
07184N

URL
sos.arcww.com.sg

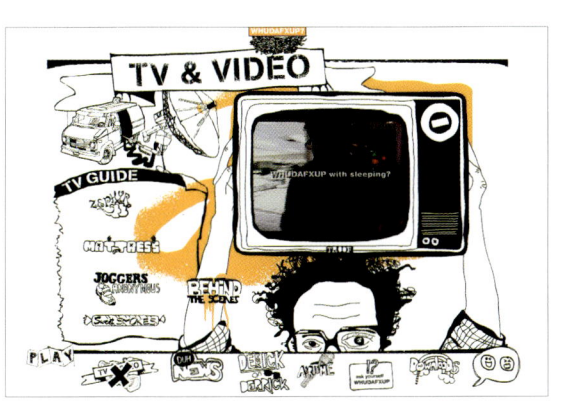

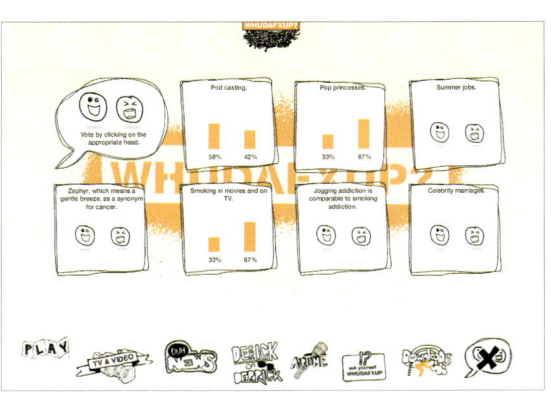

MERIT

AGENCY
Arnold/Boston

CLIENT
American Legacy Foundation/truth

ART DIRECTOR
Meghan Siegal

WRITER
Marc Einhorn

DESIGNERS
see index

MULTIMEDIA ARTISTS
Neal Bessen
Chris Teso
Eben Chaffee

PROGRAMMERS
Ebbey Mathew
Chris Teso

CREATIVE DIRECTORS
see index

ANNUAL ID
07185N

URL
www.whudafxup.com

197

WEB SITES: PUBLIC SERVICE/NON-PROFIT/EDUCATIONAL

MERIT

AGENCY
Cactus Marketing Communications/
Denver

CLIENT
Colorado State Tobacco Education and Prevention Partnership, STEPP

PRODUCTION COMPANY
Agency Net

ANNUAL ID
07186N

URL
www.ownyourc.com

MERIT

AGENCY
Firstborn/New York

CLIENT
Edison Innovation Foundation

ART DIRECTOR
Victor Brunetti

MULTIMEDIA ARTIST
Josef Kjaergaard

PROGRAMMER
Gicheol Lee

CONTENT STRATEGIST
Dan LaCivita

ANNUAL ID
07187N

URL
thomasedison.org/

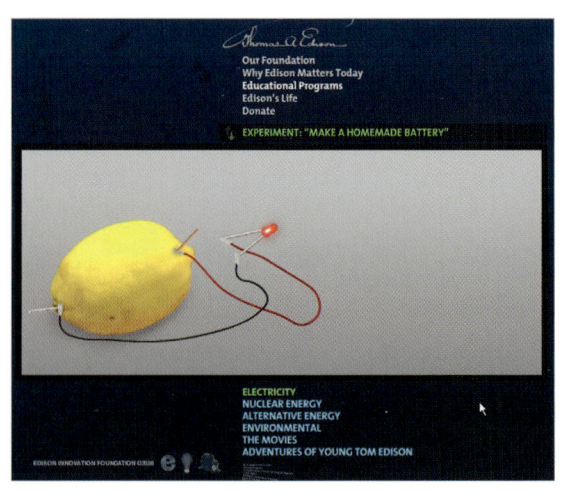

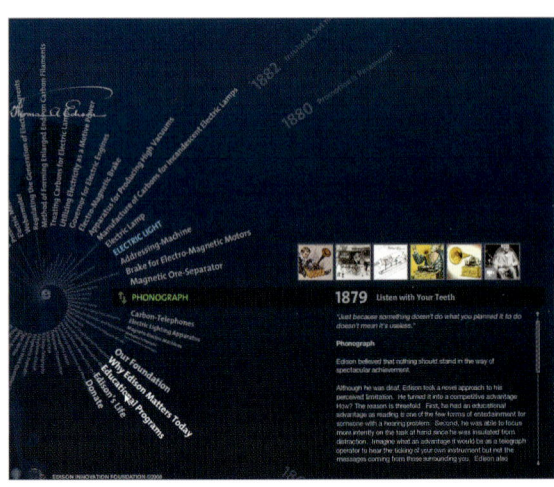

WEB SITES: PUBLIC SERVICE/NON-PROFIT/EDUCATIONAL

MERIT

AGENCY
JUXT Interactive/
Newport Beach

CLIENT
Glue Network

DESIGNERS
see index

ART DIRECTOR
Todd Purgason

PROGRAMMERS
Victor Allen
Khanh Nguyen
Nate Cavanaugh
Casey Corcoran

CONTENT STRATEGIST
Ann-Marie Harbour

CREATIVE DIRECTOR
Todd Purgason

ANNUAL ID
07188N

URL
bridge.theglue
network.com/

BRAND GAMING/APPLICATIONS: ONLINE

MERIT

AGENCY
AKQA/London

CLIENT
Unilever/Lynx

ART DIRECTOR
Miles Unwin

WRITER
Colin Byrne

DESIGNERS
James Capp
Will Cookson

PROGRAMMERS
Dan Wood
David Wiltshire

CREATIVE DIRECTOR
James Hilton

ANNUAL ID
07190N

URL
awards.akqa.com/
awards2006/axe/click/
creative.html

199

BRAND GAMING/APPLICATIONS: ONLINE

MERIT

AGENCY
COG1/San Francisco

CLIENT
Independent Film Channel

WRITER
Jeffrey Hyman

PROGRAMMER
Adam Pasztory

MULTIMEDIA ARTISTS
Mike Rodda
Justin Metros
David Winn

CONTENT STRATEGISTS
Ann Rizzuto
Angel Stokes

CREATIVE DIRECTOR
Jeffrey Hyman

ANNUAL ID
07192N

URL
www.cog1.com/
awards/2007/
samurai.html

MERIT

AGENCY
Forsman & Bodenfors/
Gothenburg

CLIENT
TELE2

ART DIRECTORS
Martin Cedergren
Karin Jacobsson

WRITER
Martin Ringqvist

DESIGNER
Lars Jansson

PRODUCTION COMPANY
Frost New Media

ANNUAL ID
07193N

URL
demo.fb.se/e/tele2/
friendnetwork/

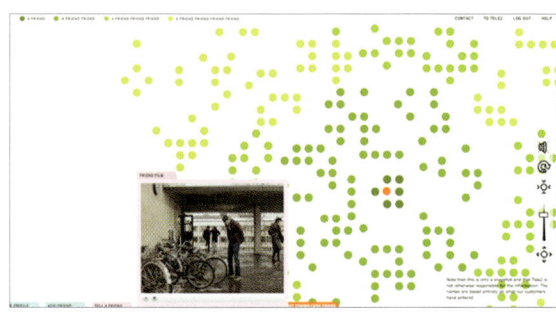

200

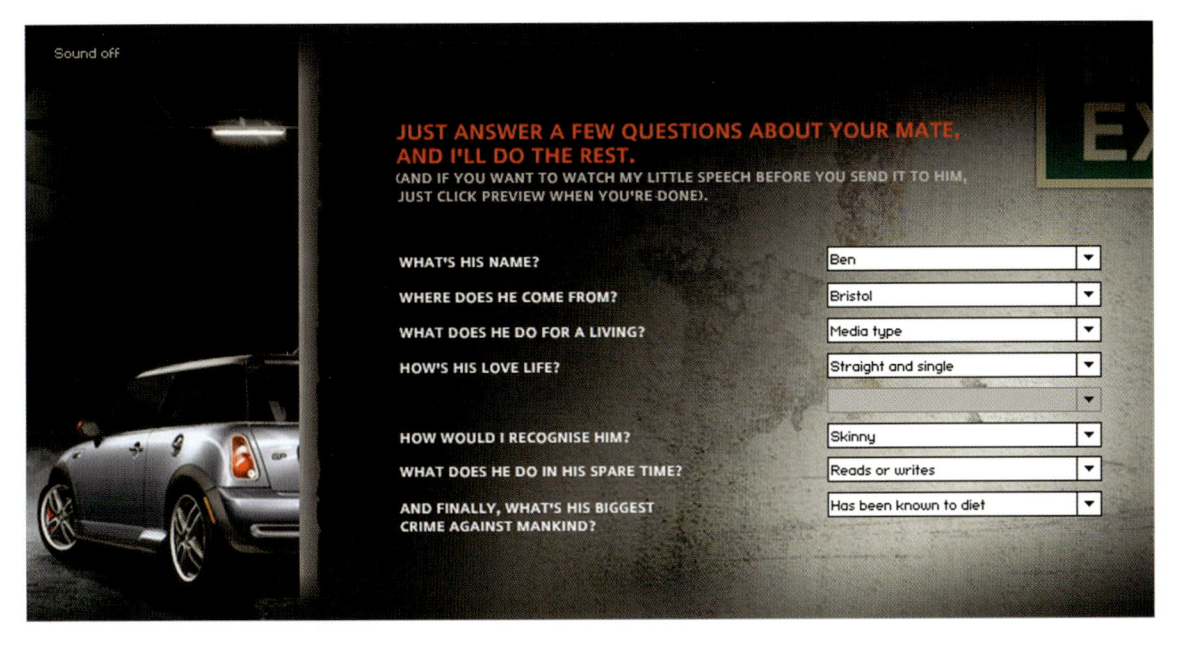

BRAND GAMING/APPLICATIONS: ONLINE

MERIT

AGENCY
glue/London

CLIENT
MINI

ART DIRECTORS
Sally Skinner
Dave Martin

WRITERS
Sally Skinner
Dave Martin

DESIGNERS
Leon Ostle
Simon Cam

PRODUCTION COMPANY
Idiotlamp

CONTENT STRATEGISTS
see index

CREATIVE DIRECTOR
Seb Royce

ANNUAL ID
07194N

URL
bestofg.com/one
show/mini_aveaword_
overview.html

MERIT

AGENCY
Hyper Happen/
London

CLIENT
Nokia

ART DIRECTORS
Arev Manoukian
Cyrus Hogg

MULTIMEDIA ARTIST
Pat Lau

CONTENT STRATEGISTS
Lawrence Weber
Sam Ashken
Tom Johnson

CREATIVE DIRECTORS
Cyrus Hogg
Dave Ozipko

ANNUAL ID
07195N

URL
www.the-passenger.
com/awards/

201

BRAND GAMING/APPLICATIONS: ONLY

MERIT

AGENCY
Jung von Matt/Hamburg

CLIENT
Kozerthaus Dortmund

WRITERS
Melanie Mader
Robert Ehlers

DESIGNERS
Lena Kessel
DAIM

MULTIMEDIA ARTIST
giraffentoast

PROGRAMMERS
see index

CONTENT STRATEGIST
Bernd Kraemer

CREATIVE DIRECTOR
Sven Loskill

ANNUAL ID
07196N

URL
award.jvm.de/one show/popmich/

MERIT

AGENCY
Ogilvy & Mather/Frankfurt

CLIENT
www.stayingalive.org

ART DIRECTOR
Christian Seifert

WRITER
Christian Seifert

ANNUAL ID
07197N

URL
www.ourwork.de/international/staying-alive/film.mov

BRAND GAMING/APPLICATIONS: ONLINE

MERIT

AGENCY
R/GA/New York

CLIENT
Verizon

ART DIRECTOR
Douglas Dauzier

WRITER
Nicole Possin

DESIGNERS
see index

DIRECTOR
Ben Mor

MUSIC & SOUND
Ariel Rechtshaid

CREATIVE DIRECTORS
Douglas Dauzier
Jay Zasa
Chris Hinkle

ANNUAL ID
07199N

URL
www.rga.com/award/beatbox.html

MERIT

AGENCY
Tribal DDB/London

CLIENT
Hasbro

ART DIRECTORS
Ben Clapp
Simon Richings

WRITERS
Simon Richings
James Leach

DESIGNER
Paul Robinson

CREATIVE DIRECTOR
Ben Clapp

ANNUAL ID
07200N

URL
awards.digivault.co.uk/cluedo

WIRELESS/MOBILE ADVERTISING: BUSINESS TO CONSUMER

MERIT

AGENCY
R/GA/New York

CLIENT
Nokia

WRITER
Dov Zmood
Eric Walker

DESIGNERS
Nina Schlechtriem
Brian Votaw
Racha Tarazi

PROGRAMMERS
Randall Loffelmacher
Judy Martinez

AGENCY PRODUCERS
see index

CREATIVE DIRECTORS
Winston Thomas
Carlos Gomez de Llarena
Sara Golding
Martin Legowiecki
Steve Levit

ANNUAL ID
07201N

URL
www.rga.com/award/
bluecasting.html

MERIT

AGENCY
Saatchi & Saatchi/
Torrance

CLIENT
Toyota

ART DIRECTORS
Conan Wang
Juan Bobillo

WRITER
Greg Wells

CONTENT STRATEGIST
Christiana Messina

PRODUCTION COMPANY
Famous Group

CREATIVE DIRECTORS
Greg Wells
Peter Kang

ANNUAL ID
07202N

URL
www.saatchila.com/
yaris_mobisodes/

EMAIL MARKETING: BUSINESS TO CONSUMER

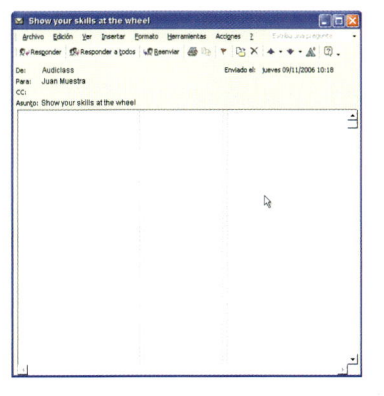

MERIT

AGENCY
*CP PROXIMITY/
Barcelona*

CLIENT
Audi

ART DIRECTOR
Rubén Martínez

WRITER
Nerea Cierco

PROGRAMMER
Marc Martínez

CONTENT STRATEGIST
Juan Manuel Ramírez

CREATIVE DIRECTOR
Enric Nel-lo

ANNUAL ID
07203N

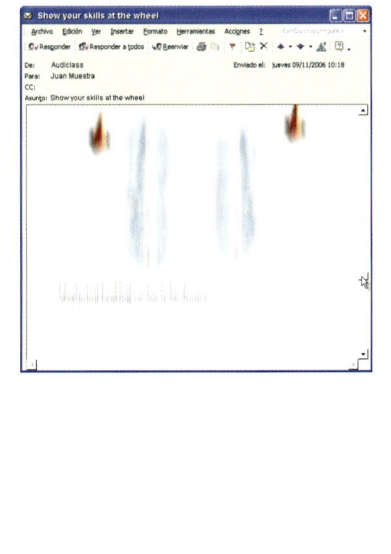

URL
*www.thisismywork.com/
oneshow/control*

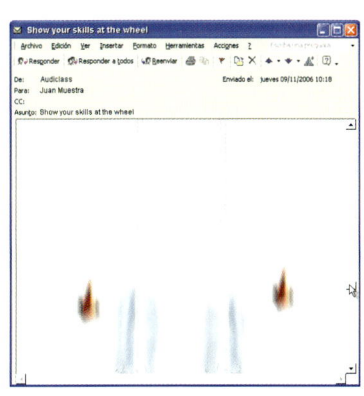

MERIT

AGENCY
*HAKUHODO i-studio/
Tokyo*

CLIENT
GE Consumer Finance

ART DIRECTOR
Tadaaki Harada

WRITER
Jyunya Masuda

DESIGNERS
*Shigeki Takeguchi
Takanobu Otsuka
Yosuke Sasagaki*

MULTIMEDIA ARTIST
Shigeki Takeguchi

CONTENT STRATEGISTS
see index

PRODUCTION COMPANY
777 Interactive

CREATIVE DIRECTOR
Tadaaki Harada

ANNUAL ID
07204N

URL
*www.777interactive.jp/
awards/2006/mail/e/*

205

EMAIL MARKETING: PUBLIC SERVICE/NON-PROFIT/EDUCATIONAL

MERIT

AGENCY
JWT/Quarry Bay

CLIENT
Friends of the Earth

ART DIRECTORS
Fei Leung
Chi Kit Kwong

WRITERS
Rachel Lo
Steven Lee

CREATIVE DIRECTORS
Rachel Chau
Angela Pong
Steven Lee
Chi Kit Kwong

ANNUAL ID
07205N

URL
www.foe.org.hk/christmas/2006/foehk/Xmas_pointer1.html

MERIT

AGENCY
McCann Erickson/São Paulo

CLIENT
Fundacao Dorina Nowill

ART DIRECTOR
Max Chanan

WRITER
Ricardo Sciammarella

PROGRAMMER
Daniel Alegretti

CREATIVE DIRECTORS
Adriana Cury
Max Chanan

ANNUAL ID
07206N

URL
www.ourluggage.com.br/2006/ing/braille/

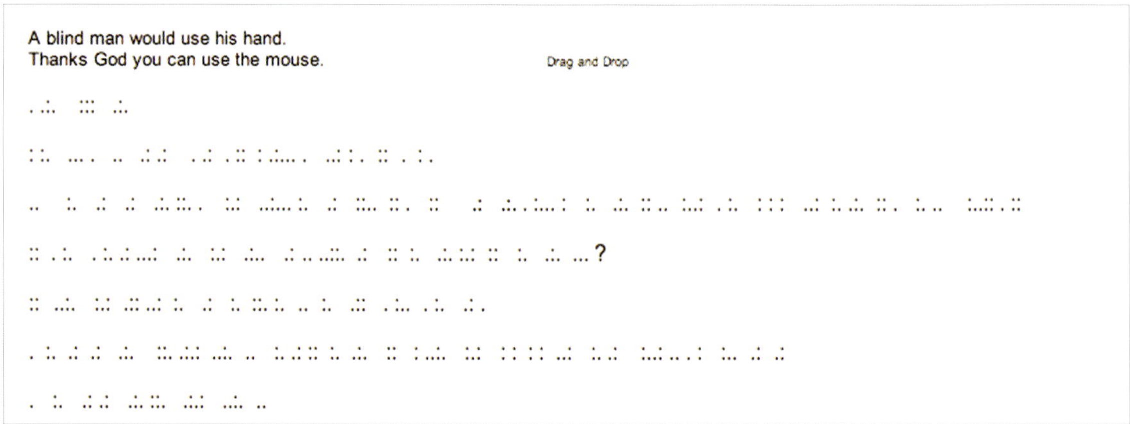

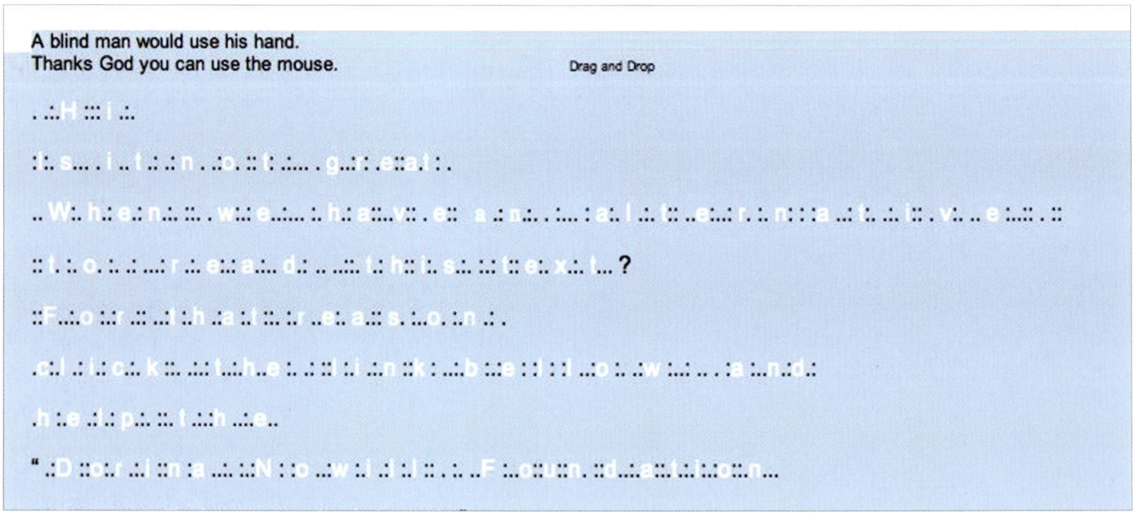

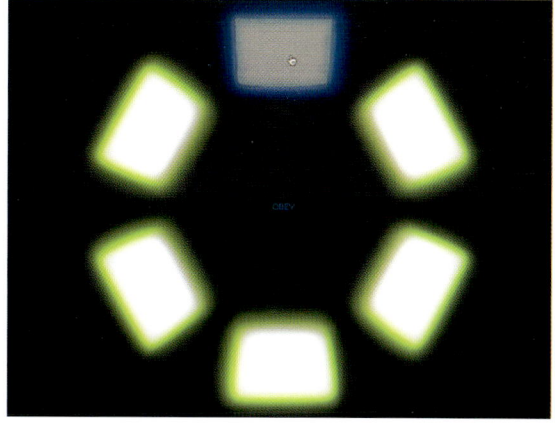

ONLINE BRANDED CONTENT: BUSINESS TO CONSUMER

MERIT

AGENCY
AKQA/San Francisco

CLIENT
The Coca-Cola Company

ART DIRECTOR
Karishma Mehta

WRITER
Dominick Walker

PROGRAMMERS
Michelle Murata
Guillermo Torres
Steven Sherwood

CREATIVE DIRECTORS
PJ Pereira
Rei Inamoto
Adam Lau

ANNUAL ID
07207N

URL
awards.sf.akqa.com/
creative/sprite/lost_
experience/

MERIT

AGENCY
AKQA/San Francisco

CLIENT
NASP (National
Association of
Staredown Professionals)

ANNUAL ID
07208N

URL
awards.sf.akqa.
com/creative/2006/
unflinchingtriumph/

207

ONLINE BRANDED CONTENT: BUSINESS TO CONSUMER

MERIT

AGENCY
Atmosphere BBDO/
New York

CLIENT
Master Foods/Snickers

ART DIRECTORS
Donovan Goodly
Matt Nuzzi

WRITER
Chris Stevenson

PROGRAMMERS
Emily Reed
Cesar Munoz

CREATIVE DIRECTORS
Arturo Aranda
Jimmy Smith

ANNUAL ID
07209N

URL
www.atmospherebbdo.com/IQwork/2006/instantdef/index.asp

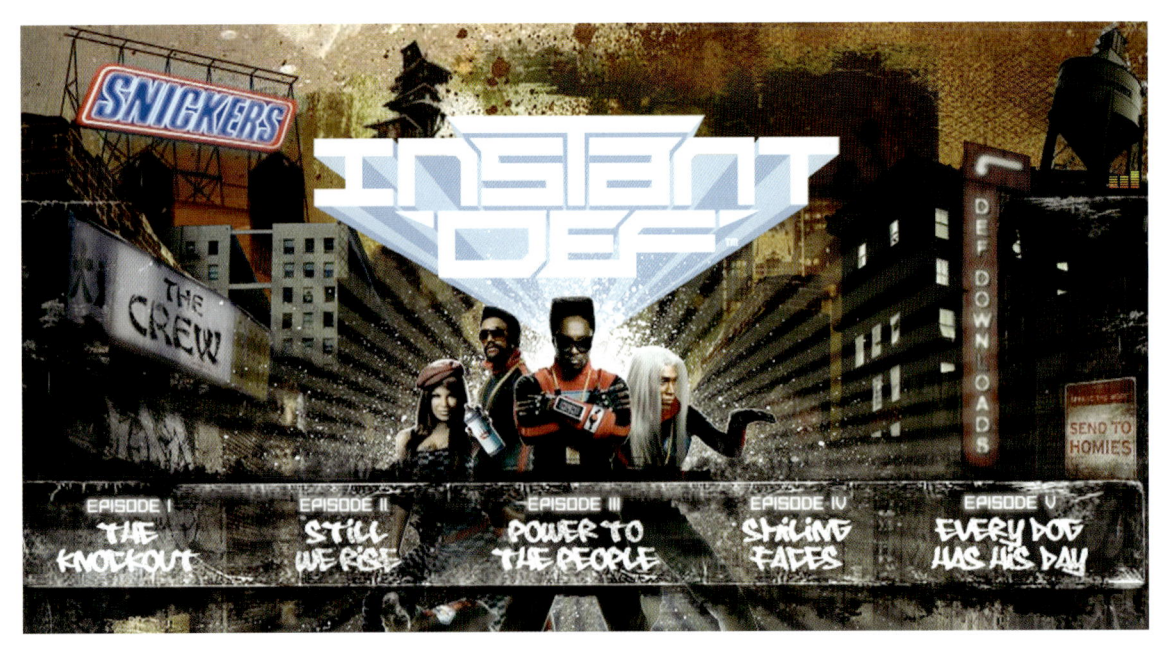

MERIT

AGENCY
Bartle Bogle Hegarty/
New York

CLIENT
Unilever/Axe

ART DIRECTOR
Jon Randazzo

WRITERS
Amir Farhang
The Glue Society

AGENCY PRODUCER
Katherine Cheng

PRODUCTION COMPANY
Radical Media

DIRECTOR
The Glue Society

CREATIVE DIRECTOR
William Gelner

ANNUAL ID
07210N

URL
www.gamekillers.com/films/load/quicktime/earlydetection.html

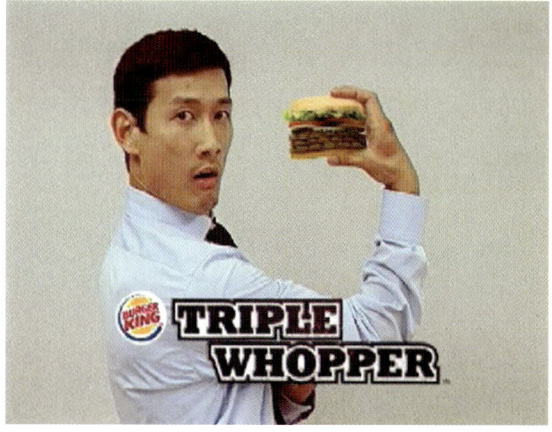

ONLINE BRANDED CONTENT: BUSINESS TO CONSUMER

MERIT

AGENCY
Crispin Porter + Bogusky/Miami

CLIENT
Burger King

ART DIRECTOR
James Dawson-Hollis

WRITER
Bob Cianfrone

PRODUCTION COMPANIES
see index

DIRECTOR
Kinka Usher

MUSIC & SOUND
see index

CREATIVE DIRECTORS
see index

ANNUAL ID
07211N

URL
www.cpbgroup.com/awards/eatlikesnaketv.html

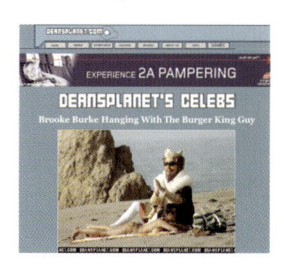

MERIT

AGENCY
Crispin Porter + Bogusky/Miami

CLIENT
Burger King

ART DIRECTOR
Mark Taylor

CREATIVE DIRECTORS
Alex Bogusky
Rob Reilly
Bob Cianfrone
James Dawson-Hollis

ANNUAL ID
07212N

URL
www.cpbgroup.com/awards/burgerkingandbrooke.html

209

ONLINE BRANDED CONTENT: BUSINESS TO CONSUMER

MERIT

AGENCY
Dare/London

CLIENT
Vodafone

ART DIRECTOR
Alex Braxton

WRITER
Alistair Robertson

PRODUCTION COMPANY
Jo Rae-Chodan

DIRECTOR
Andy Welch

CREATIVE DIRECTORS
James Cooper
Flo Heiss

ANNUAL ID
07213N

URL
www.daredigital.com/
oneshow07/online/coins

MERIT

AGENCY
Droga5/New York

CLIENT
Ecko Unltd.

ART DIRECTOR
Duncan Marshall

PRODUCTION COMPANY
Sally Ann Dale
Patrick Milling Smith
Brian Carmody
Allison Kunzman

DIRECTOR
Randy Krallman

CREATIVE DIRECTOR
David Droga

ANNUAL ID
07214N

URL
www.smugglersite.
com/mov/krallman_
stillfree.mov

210

ONLINE BRANDED CONTENT: BUSINESS TO CONSUMER

MERIT

AGENCY
Fallon/Minneapolis

CLIENT
Garmin

ART DIRECTOR
Kris Wixom

WRITERS
Alisa Sengel Wixom
Brian Tierney

PRODUCTION COMPANY
Smith and Sons Films

DIRECTOR
Ulf Johansson

MUSIC & SOUND
Pat Weaver
Ken Chastain

CREATIVE DIRECTORS
Kerry Feuerman
Brian Tierney

ANNUAL ID
07215N

URL
awards.iti.fallon.com/06/garmin_musicvideo/

MERIT

AGENCY
Goodby, Silverstein & Partners/San Francisco

CLIENT
California Milk Board

ART DIRECTOR
Rob Perkins

WRITER
Rob Perkins

DIRECTOR
Rob Perkins

CONTENT STRATEGIST
Mike Geiger

CREATIVE DIRECTORS
Feh Tarty
Jeff Goodby
Pat McKay

ANNUAL ID
07216N

URL
www.goodbysilverstein.com/awards/one_show_07/farmers_video.html

211

ONLINE BRANDED CONTENT: BUSINESS TO CONSUMER

MERIT

AGENCY
Goodby, Silverstein & Partners/San Francisco

CLIENT
Specialized

ART DIRECTORS
Jason Warne
Aaron Dietz
Kevin Jordan

WRITERS
Bob Winter
Nick Prout

CONTENT STRATEGISTS
see index

PRODUCTION COMPANY
FaceFaceFace

CREATIVE DIRECTORS
Rich Silverstein
Steve Simpson
Keith Anderson

ANNUAL ID
07217N

URL
www.goodbysilverstein.com/awards/one_show_07/specialized_movies.html

MERIT

AGENCIES
McCann Worldgroup/
Mekanism/San Francisco

CLIENT
Microsoft/Windows Vista

ART DIRECTOR
Troy Cooper

WRITERS
Rob Bagot
Demetri Martin
Tommy Means

MULTIMEDIA ARTIST
Michael Gillette

PRODUCTION COMPANY
Mekansim

DIRECTOR
Tommy Means

CREATIVE DIRECTORS
Rob Bagot
Tommy Means
John McNeil

ANNUAL ID
07218N

URL
www.clearification.com

ONLINE BRANDED CONTENT: BUSINESS TO CONSUMER

MERIT

AGENCIES
McCann Worldgroup/
Mekanism/San Francisco

CLIENT
Microsoft/Windows Vista

ART DIRECTOR
Troy Cooper

WRITERS
Rob Bagot
Demetri Martin
Tommy Means

PRODUCTION COMPANY
Mekansim

DIRECTOR
Tommy Means

CREATIVE DIRECTORS
Rob Bagot
Tommy Means
John McNeil

ANNUAL ID
07219N

URL
www.clearification.com

MERIT

AGENCIES
McCann Worldgroup/
Mekanism/San Francisco

CLIENT
Microsoft/Windows Vista

ART DIRECTOR
Troy Cooper

WRITERS
Rob Bagot
Demetri Martin
Tommy Means

MULTIMEDIA ARTIST
Michael Gillette

PRODUCTION COMPANY
Mekansim

DIRECTOR
Tommy Means

CREATIVE DIRECTORS
Rob Bagot
Tommy Means
John McNeil

ANNUAL ID
07220N

URL
www.clearification.com

213

ONLINE BRANDED CONTENT: BUSINESS TO CONSUMER

MERIT

AGENCIES
McCann Worldgroup/
Mekanism/San Francisco

CLIENT
Microsoft/Windows Vista

ART DIRECTOR
Troy Cooper

WRITERS
Rob Bagot
Demetri Martin
Tommy Means

PRODUCTION COMPANY
Mekansim

DIRECTOR
Tommy Means

CREATIVE DIRECTORS
Rob Bagot
Tommy Means
John McNeil

ANNUAL ID
07221N

URL
www.clearification.com

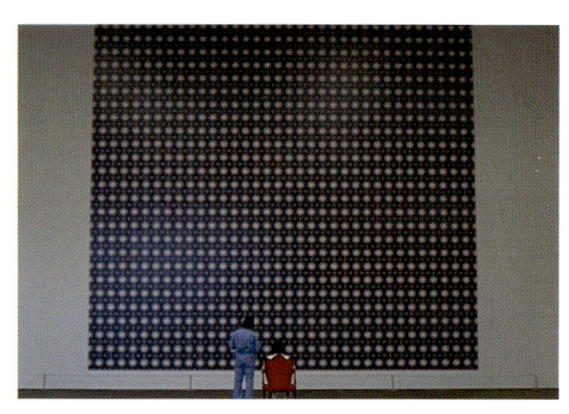

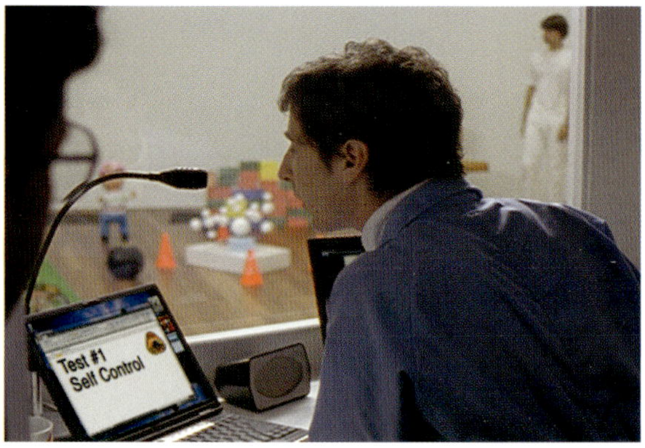

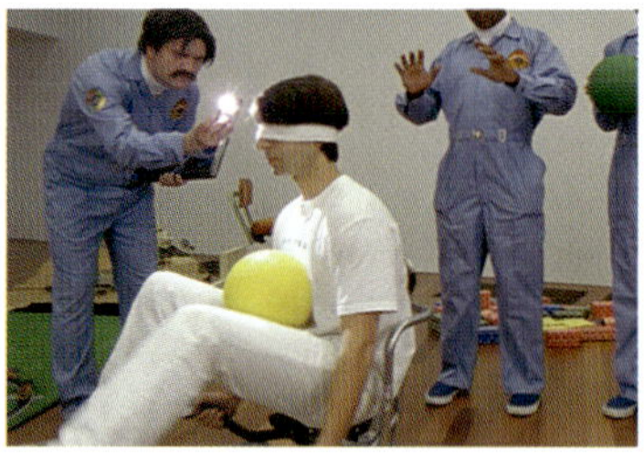

MERIT

AGENCIES
McCann Worldgroup/
Mekanism/San Francisco

CLIENT
Microsoft/Windows Vista

ART DIRECTOR
Troy Cooper

WRITERS
Rob Bagot
Demetri Martin
Tommy Means

MULTIMEDIA ARTIST
Michael Gillette

PRODUCTION COMPANY
Mekansim

DIRECTOR
Tommy Means

CREATIVE DIRECTORS
Rob Bagot
Tommy Means
John McNeil

ANNUAL ID
07222N

URL
www.clearification.com

214

ONLINE BRANDED CONTENT: BUSINESS TO CONSUMER

MERIT

AGENCIES
McCann Worldgroup/
Mekanism/San Francisco

CLIENT
Microsoft/Windows Vista

ART DIRECTOR
Troy Cooper

WRITERS
Rob Bagot
Demetri Martin
Tommy Means

PRODUCTION COMPANY
Mekansim

DIRECTOR
Tommy Means

CREATIVE DIRECTORS
Rob Bagot
Tommy Means
John McNeil

ANNUAL ID
07223N

URL
www.clearification.com

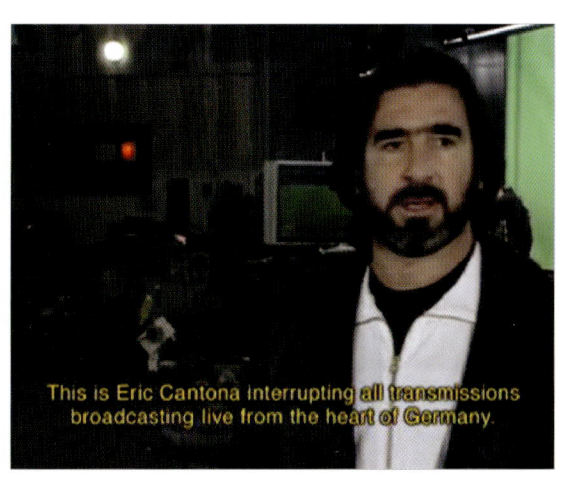

MERIT

AGENCY
Odopod/San Francisco

CLIENT
Nike

ART DIRECTOR
Josh Lowman

PROGRAMMER
Steve Mason

MULTIMEDIA ARTISTS
Curtis Nishimura
Xande Amacedo
Roger Scott
Steve Mason

INFORMATION ARCHITECT
Tim Gasperak

PRODUCTION COMPANY
Maven Networks

CREATIVE DIRECTORS
Tim Bliss
David Bliss
Jacquie Moss

ANNUAL ID
07224N

URL
jogatv.odopod.com

215

ONLINE BRANDED CONTENT: BUSINESS TO CONSUMER

MERIT

AGENCY
Ogilvy & Mather/Toronto

CLIENT
Unilever/Dove

ART DIRECTORS
Tim Piper
Mike Kirkland

WRITERS
Janet Kestin
Tim Piper

PRODUCTION COMPANY
Reginald Pike

DIRECTOR
Yael Staav

CREATIVE DIRECTORS
Janet Kestin
Nancy Vonk

ANNUAL ID
07225N

URL
www.campaignfor
realbeauty.ca/film_
fullscreen.html

ONLINE BRANDED CONTENT: BUSINESS TO BUSINESS

MERIT

AGENCY
Saatchi & Saatchi/
Frankfurt

CLIENT
A.R.T. Studios

ART DIRECTOR
Nicole Groezinger

WRITER
Alexander Priebs-
Macpherson

AGENCY PRODUCER
Michael M. Maschke

PRODUCTION COMPANY
Element-E

DIRECTOR
Alex Feil

CREATIVE DIRECTOR
Burkhart von Scheven

ANNUAL ID
07227N

URL
www.art-studios.de

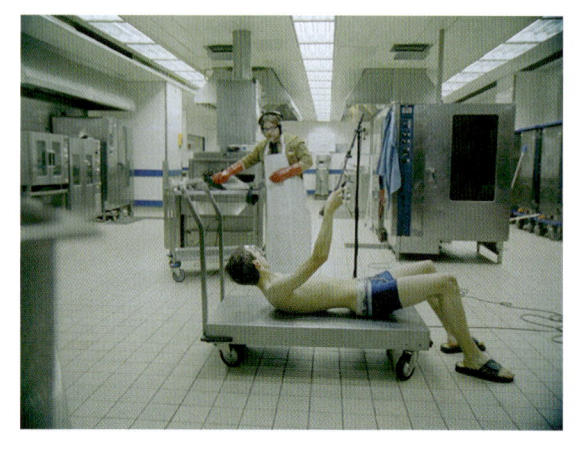

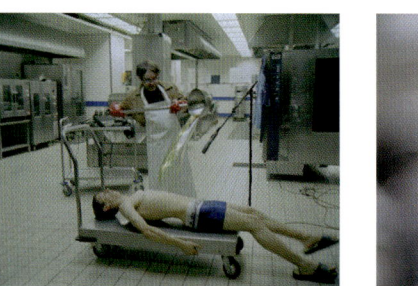

216

ONLINE BRANDED CONTENT: BUSINESS TO BUSINESS

MERIT

AGENCY
strawberryfrog/
New York

CLIENT
Microsoft

ART DIRECTORS
Tricia Ting
Jed Grossman

WRITER
Brian Platt

PRODUCTION COMPANY
Driver

DIRECTOR
Tomorrows Brightest Minds

CREATIVE DIRECTOR
Kevin McKeon

ANNUAL ID
07228N

URL
froglillypad.com/
ny/kyle/

NEW MEDIA INNOVATION & DEVELOPMENT

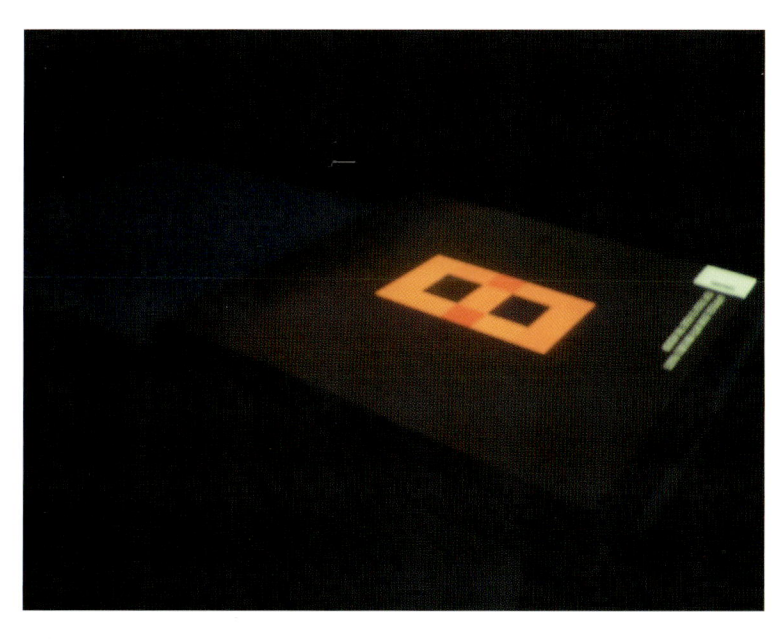

MERIT

AGENCY
(if) Interactive/
Kuala Lumpur

CLIENT
MIDI Conventions

PROGRAMMER
LeeSeng Kong

CREATIVE DIRECTOR
Sanyen Liew

ANNUAL ID
07229N

URL
if.net.my/awards/
index.htm#visible

217

NEW MEDIA INNOVATION & DEVELOPMENT

MERIT

AGENCY
777interactive/Tokyo

CLIENT
Association of Shopping Center Promotions Omotesando

ART DIRECTOR
Rikako Nagashima

WRITER
Genki Kimura

MULTIMEDIA ARTISTS
see index

CONTENT STRATEGISTS
see index

PRODUCTION COMPANIES
see index

CREATIVE DIRECTOR
Junya Masuda

ANNUAL ID
07230N

URL
www.777interactive.jp/awards/2007/akarium/e/index_w.html

MERIT

AGENCY
AgênciaClick/São Paulo

CLIENT
Fiat Automóveis

WRITERS
Ricardo Figueira
Gabriela Hunnicut
Juliana Constantino

CREATIVE DIRECTOR
Ricardo Figueira

ANNUAL ID
07231N

URL
www.okiki.net/2006/fiatideaadventure/acaocinema/en

NEW MEDIA INNOVATION & DEVELOPMENT

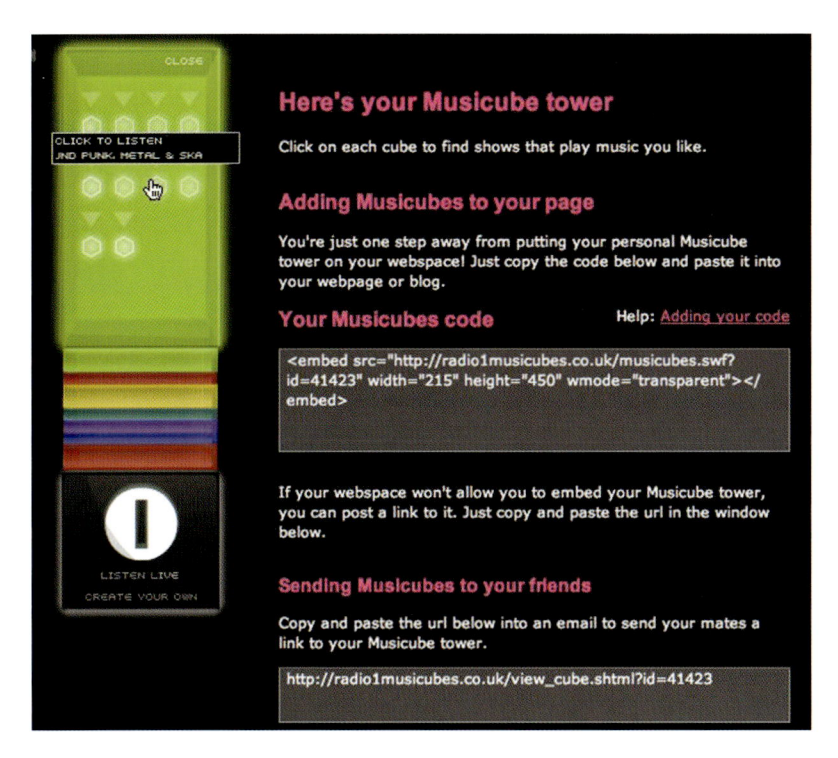

MERIT

AGENCY
Agency Republic/
London

CLIENT
BBC

ART DIRECTOR
Gemma Butler

WRITER
Gavin Gordon-Rodgers

DESIGNER
Dilesh Lalloo

MULTIMEDIA ARTIST
Robin Wong

PROGRAMMER
Richard Lainchbury

CREATIVE DIRECTOR
Andy Sandoz

ANNUAL ID
07232N

URL
www.agencyrepublic.
net/awards/one_
show/radio1.php

MERIT

AGENCY
Crispin Porter +
Bogusky/Miami

CLIENT
Volkswagen

ART DIRECTORS
Conor McCann
John Antoniello

PRODUCTION COMPANY
Domani Studios

CREATIVE DIRECTORS
Alex Bogusky
Andrew Keller
Tony Calcao
Rob Strasberg
Jeff Benjamin

ANNUAL ID
07233N

URL
www.cpbgroup.com/
awards/vwrabbit
widget.html

219

NEW MEDIA INNOVATION & DEVELOPMENT

MERIT

AGENCY
Dare/London

CLIENT
Unilever/Lynx

ART DIRECTOR
Matt Firth

DESIGNER
David Boleas

MULTIMEDIA ARTISTS
David McNulty
Kooch Chung

PROGRAMMER
Wesley Swanepoel

CREATIVE DIRECTORS
Flo Heiss
James Cooper

ANNUAL ID
07234N

URL
www.daredigital.com/
oneshow07/
newmedia/blow

MERIT

AGENCY
delvico/Madrid

CLIENT
Hermann Brown

PROGRAMMER
Manuel Alvarez

CREATIVE DIRECTORS
Juan Silva
Juan Garcia Escudero
Mariano Klein

ANNUAL ID
07235N

URL
www.delvico.es/
festivals/2007/
en/hermann
brown/index.html

NEW MEDIA INNOVATION & DEVELOPMENT

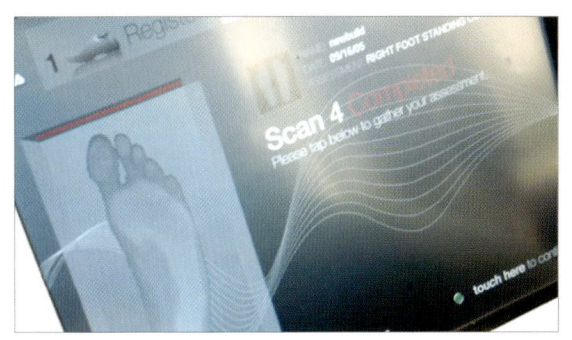

MERIT

AGENCY
Firstborn/New York

CLIENT
Fila

DESIGNER
Matt Sung

PROGRAMMERS
Roger Braunstein
Robert Forras
Jason Horwitz

CONTENT STRATEGIST
Craig Elimeliah

CREATIVE DIRECTOR
Vas Sloutchevsky

ANNUAL ID
07238N

URL
www.firstborn
multimedia.com/
projCaseStudy.
asp?projID=124

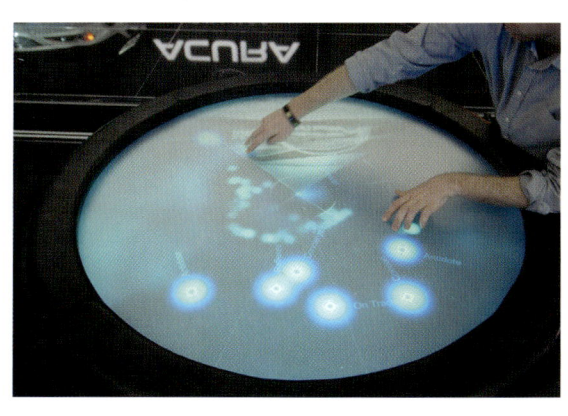

MERIT

AGENCY
George P. Johnson/
Torrance

CLIENT
Acura

ART DIRECTOR
Noah Costello

WRITER
Geoff Mye

DESIGNERS
Woo Sung Kim
Sebastian Bettencourt

PROGRAMMER
Chris Kief

PRODUCTION COMPANY
Mindflood

CREATIVE DIRECTORS
Geoff Mye
Chris Lund
Nikolai Cornell

ANNUAL ID
07239N

URL
www.interactive
oracles.com

221

NEW MEDIA INNOVATION & DEVELOPMENT

MERIT

AGENCY
Jung von Matt/
Stuttgart

CLIENT
Sixt

ART DIRECTOR
Matthias Erb

DESIGNERS
Matthias Erb
Daniel Bretzmann

PROGRAMMER
Daniel Bretzmann

CREATIVE DIRECTOR
Holger Oehrlich

ANNUAL ID
07240N

URL
www.jvm.de/oneshow/
interactive/sixt-ascii

MERIT

AGENCY
Toy/New York

CLIENT
OfficeMax

PRODUCTION COMPANIES
EVB
Grow Interactive
Mindflood
Hello Design
Struck
Templar Studios
The Vacuum Design
WDDG
Biscuit Filmworks
Reginald Pike
Kinetic Pictures
Final Cut

ANNUAL ID
07242N

URL
www.agiftfrom
officemax.com

222

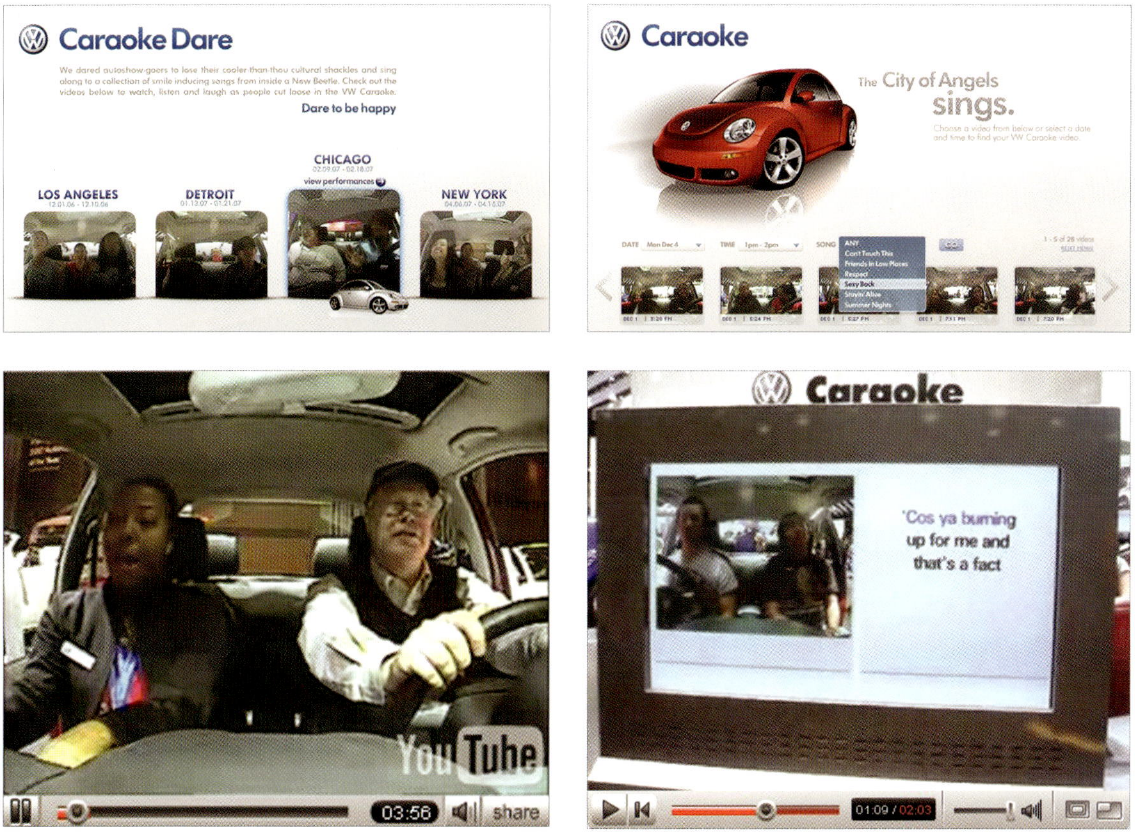

OTHER INTERACTIVE DIGITAL MEDIA

MERIT

AGENCY
Crispin Porter + Bogusky/Miami

CLIENT
Volkswagen

ART DIRECTORS
DJ Neff
John Antoniello

WRITER
Jason Wolske

DESIGNER
Marc Staubitz

PROGRAMMER
Howard Luby

PRODUCTION COMPANY
Mediascape

CREATIVE DIRECTORS
see index

ANNUAL ID
07244N

URL
www.cpbgroup.com/awards/vwcareoke.html

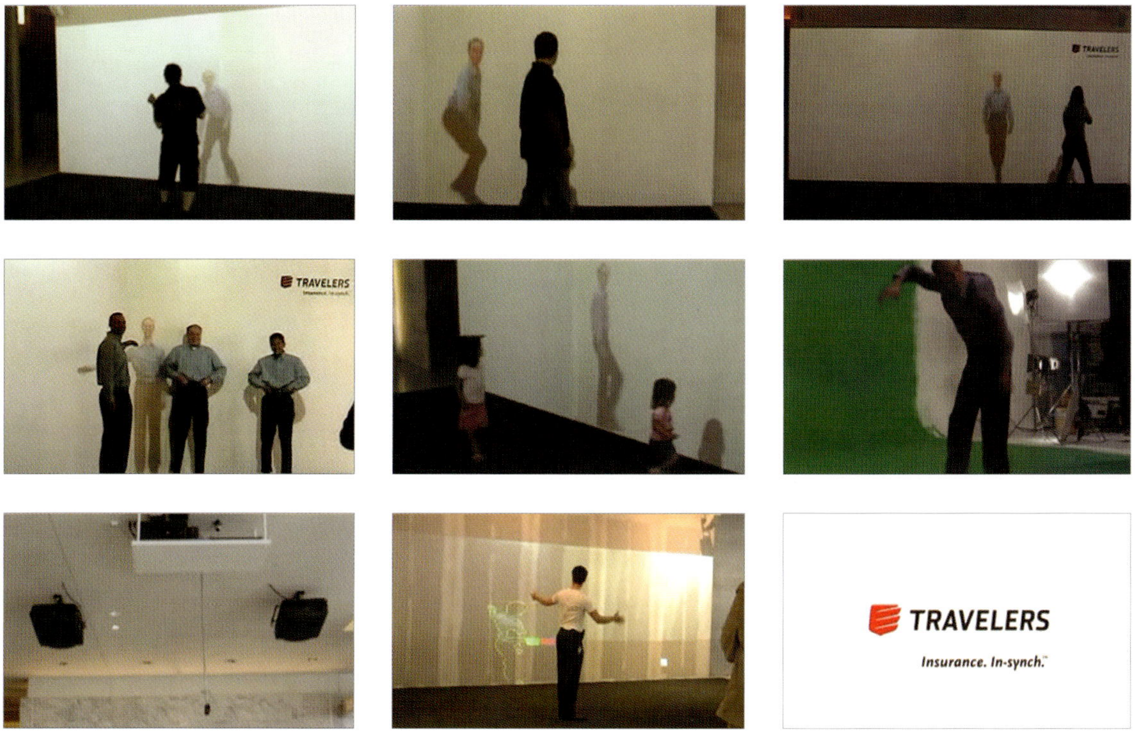

MERIT

AGENCY
Fallon/Minneapolis

CLIENT
Travelers

ART DIRECTOR
James Zucco

WRITER
Brian Tierney

DESIGNER
Freeset

PROGRAMMER
Freeset

PRODUCTION COMPANIES
Freeset
Blue 60

CREATIVE DIRECTOR
Todd Riddle

ANNUAL ID
07245N

URL
awards.iti.fallon.com/06/travelers_wall/

OTHER INTERACTIVE DIGITAL MEDIA

MERIT

AGENCY
OgilvyOne/
São Paulo

CLIENT
Hellmanns

ART DIRECTORS
Mariana Costa
Andre Levy

WRITER
Carol Saraiva

DESIGNERS
see index

PROGRAMMERS
see index

PRODUCTION COMPANY
Cubo

CREATIVE DIRECTORS
Angela Bassichetti
Tete Pacheco
Marco Antonio de Almeida

ANNUAL ID
07246N

URL
www.ourwork.com.br/
screensaver/

MERIT

AGENCY
Ziba Design/
Portland

CLIENT
Bellevue Towers
Investors

ANNUAL ID
07247N

URL
www.ziba.com/
movies/01

INTEGRATED BRANDING CAMPAIGN

MERIT

AGENCY
AKQA/San Francisco

CLIENT
Palm

ART DIRECTOR
Thiago Zanato

WRITER
Joe Sayaman

DESIGNERS
Hoj Jomehri
Terry Lee
Jeremy Gray
Stephen Clements
Caio Lazzuri
Alexandre Torres Ramos

CREATIVE DIRECTORS
Bob Pullum
Adam Lau
PJ Pereira
Rei Inamoto

ANNUAL ID
07249N

URL
awards.sf.akqa.com/
ontreo/creative

MERIT

AGENCY
AlmapBBDO/São Paulo

CLIENT
Audi

ART DIRECTORS
Felipe Lima
Rodrigo Almeida
Sergio Mugnaini
Arne Stach

WRITERS
Moacyr Netto
Roberto Pereira

PROGRAMMER
Rodrigo Frana

PRODUCTION COMPANY
AdMotion

CREATIVE DIRECTORS
Sergio Mugnaini
Marcello Serpa
Rodrigo Almeida
Roberto Pereira

ANNUAL ID
07250N

URL
200.185.34.146/
awards/2007/
audi/robots

INTEGRATED BRANDING CAMPAIGN

MERIT

AGENCY
Clemenger BBDO/
Wellington

CLIENT
Land Transport NZ

ART DIRECTORS
Mark Harricks
Mark Forgan

WRITERS
Paul Nagy
Jamie Standen
Annabelle Gazley

PROGRAMMER
Lisa Scott

PRODUCTION COMPANY
Run the Red

CREATIVE DIRECTORS
Mark Harricks
Philip Andrew

ANNUAL ID
07251N

URL
www.interactiveawards.
co.nz/bloody-legends/

MERIT

AGENCY
Crispin Porter +
Bogusky/Miami

CLIENT
Burger King

ART DIRECTORS
John Parker
Mark Taylor

WRITERS
Evan Fry
Bob Cianfrone

DESIGNERS
Chean Wei Law
Thomas Rodgers

ILLUSTRATOR
Angus Strathie

PRODUCTION COMPANY
EVB

CREATIVE DIRECTORS
see index

ANNUAL ID
07252N

URL
www.cpbgroup.com/
awards/whopperettes
integrated.html

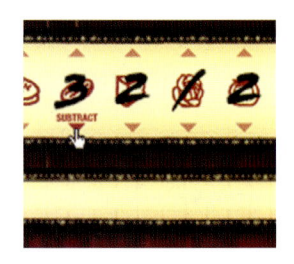

226

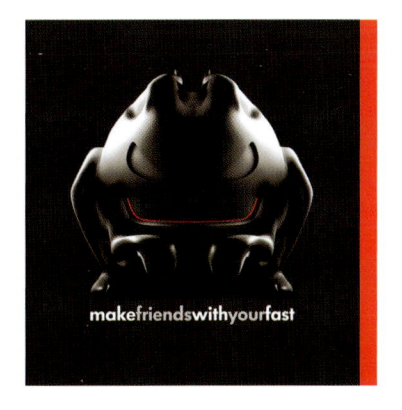

INTEGRATED BRANDING CAMPAIGN

MERIT

AGENCY
Crispin Porter +
Bogusky/Miami

CLIENT
Volkswagen

ART DIRECTORS
Anja Duering
Rahul Panchal

WRITER
Mike Howard

AGENCY PRODUCERS
see index

PRODUCTION COMPANIES
see index

DIRECTORS
Rocky Morton
Randy Krallman

CREATIVE DIRECTORS
see index

ANNUAL ID
07253N

URL
www.cpbgroup.com/
awards/gtifast
integrated.html

MERIT

AGENCY
Crispin Porter +
Bogusky/Miami

CLIENT
Burger King

ART DIRECTORS
Vivienne Wan
Olivier Rabenschlag

WRITERS
Dave Banta
Edu Pou

ILLUSTRATOR
SporkUnltd

AGENCY PRODUCERS
see index

DIRECTOR
Paul Middleditch

CREATIVE DIRECTORS
see index

ANNUAL ID
07254N

URL
www.cpbgroup.com/
awards/bkstackers
integrated.html

227

INTEGRATED BRANDING CAMPAIGN

MERIT

AGENCY
Crispin Porter +
Bogusky/Miami

CLIENT
Volkswagen

ART DIRECTORS
Tiffany Kosel
Conor McCann
Kat Morris
John Antoniello
Kevin Koller

WRITERS
Scott Linnen
Rob Thompson
Claire Sims

AGENCY PRODUCERS
see index

CREATIVE DIRECTORS
see index

ANNUAL ID
07255N

URL
www.cpbgroup.com/
awards/vwfeatures
rabbit.html

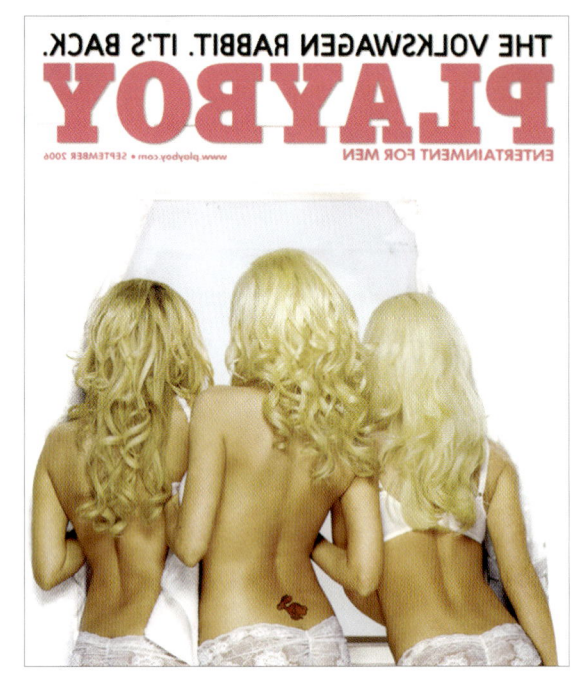

MERIT

AGENCY
McKinney/Durham

CLIENT
Oasys Mobile

ART DIRECTORS
Owen Tingle
Ryan O'Hara Theisen
Justin Smith
Jason Musante

WRITERS
Colin Dodd
Matt Fischvogt

AGENCY PRODUCERS
see index

DIRECTOR
Henry Littlechild

CREATIVE DIRECTORS
David Baldwin
Dave Cook
Matt Fischvogt
Jason Musante

ANNUAL ID
07257N

URL
www.awardshowsub
missions.com/PHERO
TONES_integrated.html

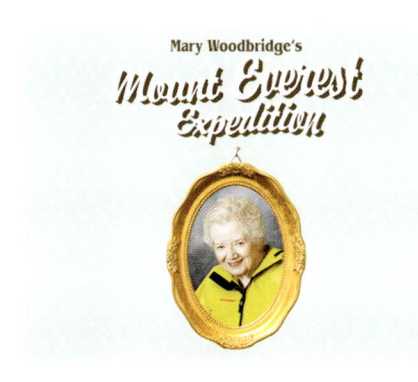

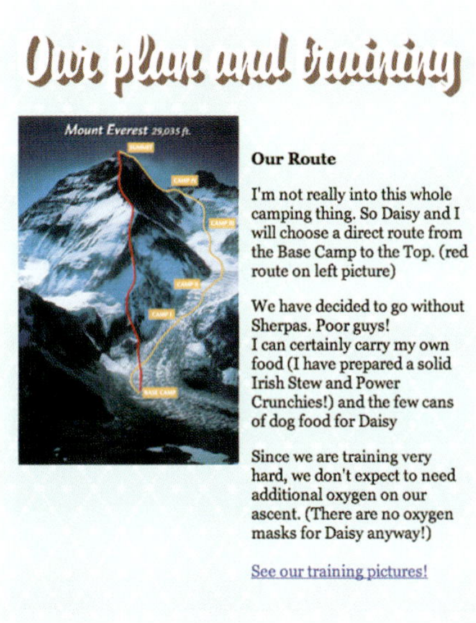

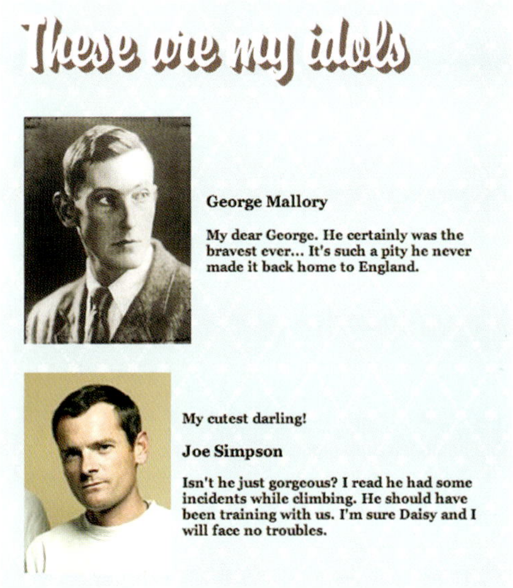

INTEGRATED BRANDING CAMPAIGN

MERIT

AGENCY
Spillmann/Felser/
Leo Burnett/Zurich

CLIENT
Mammut Sports
Group

ART DIRECTOR
Raul Serrat

WRITER
Peter Brönnimann

AGENCY PRODUCER
Sebahat Derdiyok

PRODUCTION COMPANY
Plan B Films

DIRECTOR
Chris Niemeyer

CREATIVE DIRECTOR
Martin Spillmann

ANNUAL ID
07258N

URL
snipurl.com/mary_woodbridge

MERIT

AGENCY
WONGDOODY/Seattle

CLIENT
Washington State
Department of Health

ART DIRECTORS
Mark Watson
Tony Zimney

WRITERS
Matt McCain
Noah Will

AGENCY PRODUCER
Dax Estorninos

DIRECTORS
Geordie Stephens
World Famous
Craig Tanimoto

CREATIVE DIRECTOR
Tracy Wong

ANNUAL ID
07259N

URL
www.nostankyou.com

229

SELF-PROMOTION: WEB SITES

MERIT

AGENCY
(if) Interactive/
Kuala Lumpur

WRITER
Weina Ha

CREATIVE DIRECTOR
Sanyen Liew

ANNUAL ID
07260N

URL
if.net.my/awards/
index.htm#manifesto

MERIT

AGENCY
amautalab/
Buenos Aires

ANNUAL ID
07261N

URL
www.amautalab.com

230

SELF-PROMOTION: WEB SITES

MERIT

AGENCY
Dare/London

DESIGNER
Adrian Rowbotham

MULTIMEDIA ARTISTS
*David McNulty
Kooch Chung*

CREATIVE DIRECTORS
*Flo Heiss
James Cooper*

ANNUAL ID
07262N

URL
www.daredigital.com/oneshow07/selfpromotion/dareschool

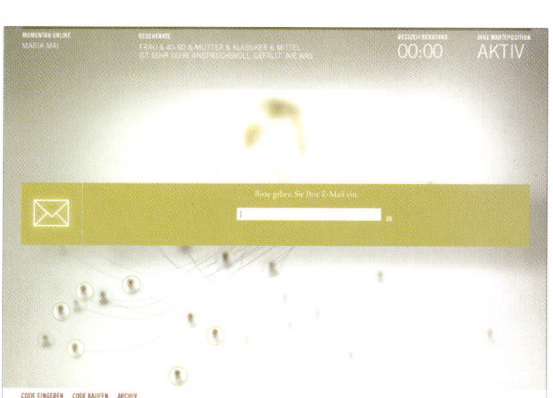

MERIT

AGENCY
Scholz & Volkmer/Wiesbaden

ART DIRECTOR
Dominik Lammer

WRITERS
*Andreas Henke
Tim Sobczak
Eva Kuemml*

DESIGNERS
*Melanie Lenz
Matthias Zosel
Steffen Baerenfaenger*

PROGRAMMERS
*Robert Fred Corporaal
Peter Reichard*

CONTENT STRATEGISTS
see index

CREATIVE DIRECTOR
Heike Brockmann

ANNUAL ID
07264N

URL
www.s-v.de/projects/geschenkedenken

SELF-PROMOTION: WEB SITES

MERIT

AGENCY
Urban Silo/
San Francisco

CLIENT
Jim Elliott

WRITER
Jim Elliott

DESIGNER
Craig Erickson

PROGRAMMER
Jason Kiemig

ANNUAL ID
07265N

URL
www.urbansilo.com

MERIT

AGENCY
WM Team/
Hannover

ANNUAL ID
07266N

URL
www.wmteam.com

232

SELF-PROMOTION: BRANDED CONTENT

MERIT

AGENCY
TYO Interactive Design/
Tokyo

DESIGNER
Yuka Taniguchi

PROGRAMMERS
Yukio Sato
Jun Mitomo
Tomoyuki Tada

INFORMATION ARCHITECTS
Kenji Morimoto
Tomohiro Suzuki
MC Takashi

CREATIVE DIRECTORS
Takayoshi Kishimoto
Issaku Masuda

ANNUAL ID
07267N

URL
www.tyo-id.co.jp/
tyoid/game/

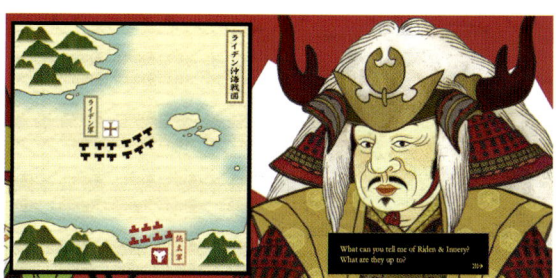

MERIT

AGENCY
Yomiko Advertising/
Tokyo

ART DIRECTORS
Mayo Tobita
Makoto Takeuchi
Shu Omori

WRITERS
Nobuyuki Ishii
Ren Sukegawa
Ken Fujino
Nirei Tanimoto

DESIGNERS
Makoto Takeuchi
Shu Omori

MULTIMEDIA ARTIST
Shigeo Sugiyama

CREATIVE DIRECTORS
Nobuyuki Ishii
Ren Sukegawa
Ken Fujino

ANNUAL ID
07268N

URL
www.yomiko.co.jp/
bushido/concept/
index.html

INDEX
PG:235-246

INDEX

AGENCY

#
(if) Interactive / Kuala Lumpur: 138, 217, 230
777interactive / Tokyo: 218

A
ADK / Tokyo: 126
AgênciaClick / São Paulo: 27, 142, 218
Agency Republic / London: 163, 219
Åkestam.Holst / Stockholm: 86
AKQA / London: 106, 148, 152, 185, 199
AKQA / San Francisco: 88, 108, 153, 163, 164, 207, 225
AKQA / Washington: 164, 196
AlmapBBDO / São Paulo: 32, 225
amautalab / Buenos Aires: 230
ARC Worldwide / Singapore: 197
argonauten G2 / Düsseldorf: 110
Arnold / Boston: 96, 197
Atmosphere BBDO / New York: 36, 208

B
Bartle Bogle Hegarty / New York: 100, 165, 186, 208
Big Spaceship / Brooklyn: 66
BLITZ / Los Angeles: 165
BLOC / London: 166
Butler, Shine, Stern & Partners / Sausalito: 153, 154, 166

C
Cactus Marketing Communications / Denver: 198
Clemenger BBDO / Wellington: 226
Clemmow Hornby Inge/ London: 150
Code and Theory / New York: 167
COG1 / San Francisco: 200
CONTRAPUNTO / Madrid: 40
CP PROXIMITY / Barcelona: 56, 167, 205
Crispin Porter + Bogusky / Miami: 37, 38, 46, 50, 122, 124, 130, 143, 144, 145, 154, 155, 168, 169, 170, 186, 209, 219, 223, 226, 227, 228

D
Daddy / Gothenburg: 155, 170
Dare / London: 183, 210, 220, 231
DDB / São Paulo: 31, 184
DDB / Seattle: 33
Del Campo Nazca Saatchi & Saatchi / Martinez: 145
delvico / Madrid: 220
Dentsu / Tokyo: 156
devilfish / London: 102
Domani Studios / Brooklyn: 171
DoubleYou / Barcelona: 187
DraftFCB / Toronto: 187, 188
Droga5 / New York: 210

E / F
Euro RSCG 4D / Amstelveen: 82
EVB / San Francisco: 171
F/Nazca Saatchi & Saatchi / São Paulo: 28, 156
Fallon / Minneapolis: 172, 211, 223
Farfar / Stockholm: 26, 60, 78, 172, 173, 174
Firstborn / New York: 198, 221
FORM::PROCESS / Tokyo: 70
Forsman & Bodenfors / Gothenburg: 72, 174, 175, 188, 200
Framfab Denmark / Copenhagen: 58

G–J
George P. Johnson / Torrance: 221
glue / London: 29, 157, 201
Goodby, Silverstein & Partners / San Francisco: 39, 48, 118, 148, 149, 175, 176, 177, 211, 212
Great Works / Stockholm: 68, 189, 190
Grupo W / Saltillo: 76, 80, 177
GT / Tokyo: 116
HAKUHODO i-studio / Tokyo: 205
Hyper Happen / London: 201
IMG SRC / Tokyo: 190
Interone Worldwide / Munich: 90
Jonathan Yuen / Singapore: 136
Jung von Matt / Hamburg: 92, 202
Jung von Matt / Stuttgart: 35, 222
juxt interactive / Newport Beach: 199
JWT / Quarry Bay: 206
JWT / New York: 132, 191

K–M
Kinetic / Singapore: 54, 178
Lean Mean Fighting Machine / London: 30, 161
Leo Burnett / Singapore: 197
Leo Burnett / Sydney: 34, 151
Lowe Brindfors / Stockholm: 178
Lowe / New York: 195
Marketel / Montreal: 158
McCann Erickson / São Paulo: 206
McCann Norway / Oslo: 179
McCann Worldgroup / San Francisco: 179, 212, 213, 214, 215
McKinney / Durham: 120, 128, 228
mono / Minneapolis: 134

N–P
NEUE DIGITALE / Frankfurt: 191
Nordpol+ / Hamburg: 146
North Kingdom / Skellefteå: 180
Odopod / San Francisco: 215
Ogilvy / San Francisco: 146
Ogilvy & Mather / Toronto: 98, 216
Ogilvy & Mather / Frankfurt: 202
Ogilvy / Singapore: 112
OgilvyInteractive / Madrid: 149, 150
OgilvyOne Worldwide / São Paulo: 224
OgilvyOne Worldwide / Hong Kong: 147
OgilvyOne Worldwide / Bangkok: 158, 159
OgilvyOne Worldwide / Frankfurt: 52
Plan.Net Concept / Munich: 161
Poke / London: 185
Profero / London: 41, 114
Projector /Tokyo: 180
Publicis / New York: 181
Pyramid Film / Tokyo: 192

Q–S
qubibi / Tokyo: 42
R/GA / New York: 74, 94, 104, 192, 203, 204
Rethink / Vancouver: 193
Rich Creative / Richmond: 196
Saatchi & Saatchi / Singapore: 151, 159
Saatchi & Saatchi / Frankfurt: 152, 160, 216
Saatchi & Saatchi / Torrance: 193, 204
Saatchi & Saatchi / Auckland: 195
Savaglio\TBWA / Buenos Aires: 162
Scholz & Volkmer / Wiesbaden: 62, 231
SID LEE / Montral: 181
Spillmann/Felser/Leo Burnett / Zurich: 229
strawberryfrog / New York: 217
Syzygy / London: 160

T–Z
TAXI / Montreal: 182
TAXI / Toronto: 182
TBWA\Chiat\Day / New York: 84
Tequila / Los Angeles: 183
tha / Tokyo: 64
Toy / New York: 222
Tribal DDB / New York: 44
Tribal DDB / Mumbai: 162
Tribal DDB / London: 203
TYO Interactive Design / Tokyo: 233
Urban Silo / San Francisco: 232
Vodafone Group / Newbury: 184
Wieden + Kennedy / Portland: 194
WM Team / Hannover: 232
WONGDOODY / Seattle: 229
Wunderman / São Paulo: 147
Wysiwyg Comunicación Interactiva / Madrid: 194
Yomiko Advertising / Tokyo: 233
Ziba Design / Portland: 224

AGENCY PRODUCER

A / B
Al-Kadiri, Zu: 132
Allen, Jennifer: 192
Alvarez, Marcelino: 228
Anderson, Cheri: 130
Arcey, Jessica: 227
Bamberg, Barrie: 130
Beck, Rich: 120
Beltramo, Aymi: 227
Binch, Winston: 124, 130, 226, 227, 228
Blitzer, Peter: 203
Bonin, Matt: 124, 226, 228
Bosak, Stafford: 228
Burtch, Anson: 120
Busby, Brock: 104

C–H
Colombo, Paola: 204
Cheng, Katherine: 208
D'Amico, Neil: 130, 228
DeBruler, Meghan: 130, 227
Derdiyok, Sebahat: 229
Dierauer, Jessica: 227
Dold, Jurgen: 122
Estorninos, Dax: 229
Ferguson, Laura: 84
Fierro, Yajaira: 227
Fukuda, Takeshi: 126
Garetti, Anthony: 132
Himebrook, Darren: 130, 226, 227
Hoffman, Jessica: 124, 130
Hosoike, Yasutoshi: 126
Howell, Matt: 104

I–L
Ingle, Toni: 228
Jacobs, Letitia: 130
Jenkins, Melissa: 120
Jurow, Daniel: 104
Kakinami, Shunsuke: 126

INDEX

Kuo, James: *104*
Lewis, Cathy: *228*
Lyons, Sean: *104*

M
Machado, Ana Maria: *225*
Maschke, Michael M.: *216*
Mateu, Rebekah: *130, 227*
McHugh, Spencer: *204*
Meadows, Bill: *122, 124, 130, 227*
Mee, Chaz: *192*
Minowa, Mits: *126*
Mishriky, Nora: *128, 228*
Moore, Suzanne: *128*

N–Y
Nelson, Anthony: *228*
Niblick, David: *130*
Pelleck, Robin: *132*
Radel, Sheri: *122*
Rasco, Eric: *122*
Rasul, Sumeera: *204*
Rekasis, Brian: *122*
Reznick, Jessica: *122*
Rose, Susanna: *227*
Ross, David: *104*
Ruth, Dan: *124, 130*
Samuel, Rupert: *122, 124, 130, 226, 227, 228*
Schneider, Philip: *132*
Setten, Lisa: *100*
St. Luc, Ronelle: *192*
Sutton, Paul: *124, 130, 226, 227, 228*
Vega, Luna: *204*
Wegner, Mitch: *203*
Wilson, Cathy: *128, 228*
Youssef, Ameer: *74*

ART DIRECTOR

A
Åström, Jacob: *189*
Alda, Ramiro: *149*
Almeida, Rodrigo: *225*
Almgren, Lovisa: *172*
Amadeo, Andy: *172*
Ameron, Graham: *187*
Anderle, Martin: *152*
Antoniello, John: *144, 145, 219, 223, 228*
Anweiler, Dominik: *146*
Appelblad, Mathias: *174, 175, 188*
Augusto, Rafael: *142*

B
Back, Steve: *195*
Baibich, Roberto: *182*
Balin, Liz: *171*
Barragán, Alberto: *40*
Bartsch, Christian: *160*
Batchelor, Bart: *193*
Bedford, Scott: *160*
Bergdahl, John: *72*
Bergen, Jeannette: *92*
Bergstrom, Nicke: *78*
Besada, Kike: *194*
Bobillo, Juan: *204*
Bowman, Dave: *195*
Braga, Mateus: *142*
Brattberg, Ake: *173*
Braxton, Alex: *210*
Brunetti, Victor: *198*
Budye, Anis: *162*
Burton, Matty: *195*
Butler, Gemma: *219*

C
Cabral, Daniel: *142*
Caguin, Mike: *166*
Calderon, Miguel: *80, 177*
Capp, James: *108, 152*
Cedergren, Martin: *72, 200*
Chanan, Max: *206*
Chaubet, Patrick: *182*
Clapp, Ben: *203*
Clark, Scott: *114*
Clemens, Dave: *130*
Cockburn, Georg: *160*
Cole, Joe: *171*
Collins, Paul: *86*
Cook, Simon: *185*
Cooper, Troy: *179, 212, 213, 214, 215*
Copiz, Stefan: *176*
Costa, Mariana: *224*
Costello, Mike: *96*
Costello, Noah: *221*
Coyne, Michael: *39, 148*

D
da Silva e Silva, Vicente: *142*
Daum, Nik: *194*
Dauzier, Douglas: *203*
Davies, Robert: *112*
Dawson-Hollis, James: *209*
Delgado, Ana: *187*
del Rizzo, Anthony: *188*
de Moraes, Thiago: *150*
de Queiroz, Fabiano: *27*
Dibona, Dylan: *167*
Dietz, Aaron: *149, 212*
DiLallo, Andy: *195*
Di Lorenzo, Steve: *187, 188*
Duering, Anja: *227*

E/F
Eghammer, Johan: *175*
Eklind, Anders: *174, 175*
Eneroth, Paul: *188*
Erb, Matthias: *222*
Ewart, DaYoung: *37, 38, 154*
Ferrare, Mike: *50, 124, 130, 168, 169, 186*
Ferreira, Nuno: *182*
Firth, Matt: *220*
Ford, Bryce: *196*
Forgan, Mark: *226*
Frandsen, Rasmus: *58*
Frisell, Karin: *174*
Fujimaki, Atsushi: *190*

G
García, Pablo: *194*
García, José María: *150*
Gaulin, Stéphane: *158*
Giacomo, Guiga: *32*
Godoi, Vagner: *28*
Golden, Virginia: *196*
Gonzalez, Diego: *150*
Goodly, Donovan: *208*
Gravena, Pedro: *184*
Groezinger, Nicole: *216*
Grossman, Jed: *217*
Gugel, Andy: *172*
Gursky, Scott: *181*

H
Harada, Tadaaki: *205*
Harricks, Mark: *226*
Harris, Cameron: *195*
Hays, David: *183*
Hedeback, Jonas: *155*
Hermanas, David: *128*
Hinrichs, Oliver: *110*
Hiram, Rodrigo: *142*
Hogg, Cyrus: *201*
Horn, Patrick: *168*
Hughes, Mike: *166*

I–K
Israel, Aramis: *122, 124, 169, 186*
Ito, Naoki: *126*
Jacobsson, Karin: *200*
Jakob, Uwe: *52*
Jespersen, Paul: *188*
Jiménez, Javier: *194*
Jones, Chris: *195*
Jordan, Kevin: *212*
Joven, Gloria: *56*
Kim, Thibault: *147*
King, Adam: *157*
Kirkland, Mike: *98, 216*
Kliebe, Kelly: *193*
Koller, Kevin: *38, 130, 144, 168, 228*
Kosel, Tiffany: *124, 169, 186, 228*
Kreutzer, Tobias: *62*
Kwong, Chi Kit: *206*

L
Lam, Sean: *78, 154*
Lambert, Brian: *166*
Lammer, Dominik: *231*
Larsson von Reybekiel, Max: *68*
Lee, David: *153*
Lee, Robert: *158*
Leis, Jaume: *167*
Leong, Alan: *197*
Leung, Fei: *206*
Levy, Andre: *224*
Lima, Felipe: *225*
Lindstrom, Robert: *48, 176, 184*
Lloyd, Simon: *29, 157*
Loskill, Sven: *92*
Lowman, Josh: *215*

M
Machado, Maggi: *195*
Makoto, Ricardo: *142*
Malm, Andreas: *174, 188*
Manoukian, Arev: *201*
Marshall, Duncan: *210*
Martínez, Rubén: *56, 205*
Martin, Dave: *201*
Martinez, Jose Luis: *171*
Martis, James: *37, 143, 155*
Matthews, Jennifer: *128*
McCann, Conor: *143, 144, 169, 186, 219, 228*
Mehta, Karishma: *148, 207*
Merrifield, Brian: *195*
Mochizuki, Kaori: *156*
Modell, Daniel: *44*
Moliterno, Eco: *147*
Moreno, Cesar: *76*
Morris, Kat: *169, 228*
Morton, John: *195*
Mugnaini, Sergio: *225*
Musante, Jason: *228*

INDEX

N–P

Nagashima, Rikako: 218
Nakade, Masaya: 106
Nakamura, Yugo: 64
Neff, DJ: 223
Ng, Jay: 195
Nielsen, Jakob: 179
Nitipanont, Anuwat: 158
Novoa, Conchi: 194
Nuzzi, Matt: 208
O'Hara Theisen, Ryan: 120, 228
Ohrn, Johan: 26, 174
Omori, Shu: 233
Ots, Kieran: 34, 151
Owen, Ian: 41
Page, Ray: 33
Panchal, Rahul: 124, 169, 170, 186, 227
Parker, John: 46, 226
Pedersen, Doug: 168
Perkins, Rob: 211
Piera, Blanca: 187
Piper, Tim: 98, 216
Poopuu, Jimmy: 190
Pridgen, Scott: 128
Przekop, Dan: 191
Purgason, Todd: 199

R

Rabenschlag, Olivier: 227
Ral, Brandon: 167
Ramón, Jordi: 167
Randazzo, Jon: 165, 186, 208
Rasmussen, Robert: 132
Richings, Simon: 203
Rodgers, Thomas: 37, 143
Rosa, Sandro: 31
Roy, Paul: 171
Rufo, Lucio: 156

S

Scott, Keith: 144
Seifert, Christian: 202
Selimi, Bejadin: 191
Sengers, Martijn: 82
Serrat, Raul: 229
Shah, Amee: 100
Sharkey, Devin: 176
Shay, Kate: 146
Siegal, Meghan: 96, 197
Sikes, Mark: 175
Simon, Brett: 36
Skinner, Sally: 201
Smith, Justin: 228
Soh, Jae: 151, 159
Sommer, Christian: 161
Sperduti, Anthony: 84
Spirkovski, Michael: 34, 151
Stach, Arne: 225
Stanfield, Jason: 33
Stephens, Geordie: 170
Stewart, Nik: 102
Stump, Jim: 163
Suárez, Nicolás: 162
Suarez, David: 132
Swartz, Dave: 145
Swinburne, Matt: 195

T

Tagger, Andreas: 153, 154
Tajer, Pablo: 145
Takeuchi, Makoto: 233
Tan, Francis: 54
Tan, Robin: 151, 159
Tarty, Feh: 48, 176

Tavares, Liliana: 56
Taylor, Mark: 46, 112, 122, 209, 226
Tellving, Mats: 170
Teo, Xavier: 112
Tesch, Johan: 178
Teshigawara, Kazumasa: 42
Timonen, Mikko: 175
Ting, Tricia: 217
Tingle, Owen: 228
Tipton, Franklin: 170
Tobita, Mayo: 233
Toda, Yoshihiro: 180
Treichel, Daniel: 132
Turner, Christine: 29, 157

U–Z

Unwin, Miles: 199
Valencius, Chris: 118
Vernon, January: 44
Versfeld, Jesper: 189
Vorranartpankul, Ekalak: 159
Wahlgren, Daniel: 179
Wakeland, Robert: 146
Wall, Daniel: 172, 173
Wan, Vivienne: 227
Wang, Conan: 204
Warne, Jason: 177, 212
Watson, Mark: 229
WeePeng, Ho: 197
Westerdahl, Patrik: 178
Whitson, Micah: 128
Williams, Megan: 189
Wixom, Kris: 172, 211
Wojciewski, Doug: 191
Yagi, Takaaki: 70
Yemma, Dawn: 50, 130, 186
Yuen, Jonathan: 136
Yip, Garman: 183
Zanato, Thiago: 88, 163, 225
Zimney, Tony: 229
Zucco, James: 223
Zukoski, Tom: 124, 169, 186

CLIENTS

/ A

(if) interactive: 230
A.R.T. Studios: 216
Acura: 221
adidas: 157, 191
Adobe: 165, 175
Advertising Women of New York: 195
Aktionsbündnis Landmine.de: 161
amautalab: 230
American Legacy Foundation / truth: 96, 197
Amp'd Mobile: 182
Answer Seguro On Line: 145
Apoteket: 72
Arcadia Festival: 181
Arno: 28
Association of Shopping Center Promotions Omotesando: 218
Audi: 9, 20, 110, 205, 225
AWARE: 151

B / C

BBC: 219
Bellevue Towers Investors: 224
Bond: 159
Brastemp: 27
Brynild: 179

Burger King: 11, 14, 18, 46, 122, 145, 209, 226, 227
Cacique Rum: 187
Caixa Economica Federal: 142
California Milk Board: 48, 176, 211
Canadian College of English Language: 193
Carlsberg: 170
Casio Computer: 192
Cisco Systems: 9, 52
COI / Home Office: 41
Colorado State Tobacco Education and Prevention Partnership, STEPP: 198
Comcast: 148, 149, 176

D–F

Dare: 231
Dea Planeta: 167
Dermtek Reversa: 182
Diageo: 112
Diesel: 11, 13, 60, 194
DJ Blink: 138
ECKO Unltd.: 210
Edison Innovation Foundation: 198
EMI Records: 166
ESPN: 164
Everyman Institute of Cancer Research: 185
FedEx: 36
Fiat Automoveis: 218
Fila: 221
Flowers Feed The Soul: 178
Ford: 191
Foster Farms: 177
Friends of the Earth: 206
Full Frame Documentary Film Festival: 120
Fundação Dorina Nowill: 206
Fundacion Natura: 56

G–J

Garmin: 211
GE Consumer Finance: 205
Georgia Pacific / Brawny: 172
Getty Images: 68
Glue Network: 199
Greenpeace: 32, 162
Haggar: 168
Hasbro: 203
HD DVD: 39
Hellmanns: 224
Henkel: 31
Hermann Brown: 220
Hewlett-Packard: 159, 188
Hitachi: 167
IAB: 150
Ikea: 174
Independent Film Channel: 200
Infopresse: 158
JetBlue: 132
Jim Elliott: 232
Jonathan Yuen: 136
Kabel Deutschland RedX Club: 35
Konzerthaus Dortmund: 202

L–M

Lamton: 158
Land Rover: 147
Land Transport NZ: 226
Levi Strauss Japan: 190
Mammut Sports Group: 229
Masp Museum: 184
Master Foods: 208
Mazda: 160
Mercedes-Benz: 163
Microsoft: 116, 217
Microsoft / Windows Vista: 12, 21, 179, 212, 213, 214, 215

INDEX

MIDI Conventions: 217
Miller Lite: 170
MINI: 29, 90, 114, 153, 154, 166, 201
mono: 134
Motorola Motofone: 187
MTV: 162

N–R

NASP (National Association of Staredown Professionals): 15, 207
Nastuh Abootalebi: 62
Neo Quimica: 156
Nike: 11, 15, 16, 17, 23, 58, 66, 74, 104, 106, 126, 164, 192, 215
Nokia: 172, 173, 201, 204
Oasys Mobile: 228
OfficeMax: 222
Old Spice: 194
Optimo: 10, 70
Orbit White: 171
P&G / Thermacare Menstrual: 181
Palm: 88, 163, 225
Philips Norelco: 44
Polaris Industries: 128
ProSieben Television: 92
R/GA: 94
Red Bull: 155
RememberSegregation.org: 19, 33
Renault: 146

S / T

Samaritans of Singapore: 197
Saturn: 118
Schirn Kunsthalle: 152
Scholz & Volkmer: 231
Semillero, Creatives School: 76
Sixt: 222
Sky One: 102
Slim Jim: 144
Smirnoff: 18, 100
Sony PlayStation: 183
Specialized: 212
Spring Mobile: 86
Sprint: 84
Stadium: 188
Stella Artois / InBev: 178
T-Mobile: 160
T2: 196
TELE2: 200
Telefonica: 149
The Coca-Cola Company: 16, 20, 142, 148, 185, 207
The Economist: 147, 161
The Global Fund to Fight AIDS, TB and Malaria: 196
The Hear and Be Heard Fund Centre for Hearing Intervention & Language Development: 54
The Roy Castle Foundation: 150
The Swedish Alcohol Committee: 78
TOTO: 156
Toyota: 180, 193, 204
Travelers: 223
TYO Interactive Design: 233

U–Y

Unilever / Axe: 165, 186, 199, 208
Unilever / Lynx: 220
Unilever / Dove: 14, 98, 216
Unilever / Rexona: 80, 177
UNIQLO: 17, 18, 64, 180
V&S Absolut Spirits: 189, 190
Verizon: 203
Virgin Games: 30
Virgin Money: 157

Visit Sweden: 174, 26
Vodafone: 183, 184, 210
Volkswagen: 37, 38, 50, 124, 130, 143, 144, 154, 155, 168, 169, 186, 219, 223, 227, 228
Volvo: 82, 175
Washington State Department of Health: 229
Weave Toshi: 14, 17, 22, 42
WM Team: 232
World Wildlife Fund: 34, 40, 151
www.stayingalive.org: 202
Xbox: 153
Yahoo!: 146
Yell.com: 108, 152
Yomiko Advertising: 233
Young Guns: 195

CONTENT STRATEGIST

A–G

Albrycht, Peter: 148
Andersson, Jonas: 78
Ashken, Sam: 201
Blumenthal, Adam: 128
Bradley, Hilary: 118
Carlsson, Anne Gro: 179
Carton, Greg: 147
Chan, Jennifer: 147
Charlebois, Brit: 39, 118, 176
Clark, Brian: 191
Cornell, Nikolai: 221
Costello, Noah: 221
Courtial, Jerome: 201
Duffy, Shannon: 193
Elimeliah, Craig: 221
Enander, Ulf: 180
Eriksson, David: 48, 176
Forslund, Marten: 26, 173, 174
Frick, Anna: 172
Geiger, Mike: 39, 48, 118, 148, 149, 175, 176, 177, 211, 212
German, Robert: 155

H–K

Harbour, Ann-Marie: 199
Hayashi, Yoshibumi: 218
Head, Carey: 212
Henke, Andreas: 231
Hori, Hiroshi: 218
Horn, Ines: 160
Iwasaki, Toru: 156
Johnson, Tom: 201
Kamogawa, Norie: 205
Kelso, Amanda: 149
Khanna, Brinda: 187
Kraemer, Bernd: 202
Kraft, Manfred: 62
Kreutzer, Tobias: 62

L–R

LaCivita, Dan: 198
Le Bas, Julien: 221
Lee, Dora: 148
Lee, Jon: 196
Leidich, Kim: 188
Mártín, Beatriz: 187
Macdonald, Alan: 187, 188
Martner, Gustav: 170
Masuda, Jyunya: 205
Messina, Christiana: 204
Mizutani, Michitaka: 156

Morton, Sara: 228
Mye, Geoff: 221
Okudaira, Keitaro: 156
Percy, Jonathan: 177
Ramírez, Juan Manuel: 205
Reichard, Peter: 231
Rizzuto, Ann: 200
Rooke, Chris: 196
Rosenstein, Aaron: 33
Ross, Miranda: 29, 157, 201

S–Z

Sahara, Michio: 156
Schamber, Sandra: 152
Schjøtt, Anniken: 179
Scholz, Tobias: 231
Schulz, Wolfgang: 110
Sherain, Bettina: 58
Stefansson, Simon: 180
Stighall, Roger: 48, 176
Stokes, Angel: 200
Strehle, Patrick: 161
Sugano, Mai: 156
Swartz, John: 187
Swirla, Paula: 187
Takahashi, Kenna: 175
Tannenberger, Pia: 62
Taylor, James: 149
Tei, Akimichi: 156
Waern, Robert: 170
Watanabe, Saori: 156
Weber, Lawrence: 201
Winbolt, Eric: 166
Yanagita, Satoshi: 156
Yeung, Fiona: 147
Zachariasen, Marius: 179
Zafra, Iciar: 167

CREATIVE DIRECTOR

A

Abe, Yuki: 156
Adams, Tom: 96, 144, 197
Almeida, Rodrigo: 225
Alshin, Adam: 84
Anderson, Keith: 118, 175, 177, 212
Andrew, Philip: 226
Aranda, Arturo: 208
Ashoff, Simone: 92
Ault, Andrew: 132

B

Bagot, Rob: 167, 179, 212, 213, 214, 215
Baldwin, David: 120, 128, 228
Ball, Sam: 30, 161
Banks, Jon: 122
Barlow, Toby: 191
Barrett, Jamie: 149, 176
Bassichetti, Angela: 224
Bedford, Scott: 160
Bedwood, Dave: 30, 161
Beech, Peter: 185
Beerda, Sicco: 82
Benjamin, Jeff: 37, 38, 46, 50, 122, 124, 130, 143, 144, 145, 154, 155, 168, 169, 170, 186, 209, 219, 223, 226, 227, 228
Bergstrom, Nicke: 26, 78, 172, 173, 174
Best, Wayne: 182
Bigio, Gastón: 145
Billig, Noel: 74
Bliss, David: 215

239

INDEX

Bliss, Tim: 215
Bogusky, Alex: 37, 38, 46, 50, 96, 122, 124, 130, 143, 144, 145, 154, 155, 168, 169, 170, 186, 197, 209, 219, 223, 226, 227, 228
Boivin, Sue: 188
Bonner, Daniel: 106, 108, 152
Borchert, Gui: 104
Brockmann, Heike: 62, 231
Brugge, Sabine: 161
Bull, Matthew: 178
Butler, Gemma: 163
Butler, John: 153, 154, 166

C

Calcao, Tony: 37, 38, 50, 124, 130, 143, 144, 154, 155, 168, 169, 186, 219, 223, 227, 228
Calderon, Miguel: 76, 80, 177
Camp, Roger: 172
Caputo, Steve: 192
Cartman, Joseph: 192
Castaño, Marga: 194
Ceria, Arthur: 146
Chávarri, Jaime: 40
Chanan, Max: 206
Chandra, Meera: 162
Chapman, Nick: 188
Charier, Stephane: 182
Chau, Rachel: 206
Cheng, Valerie: 197
Cianfrone, Bob: 209
Clapp, Ben: 203
Collis, Mark: 34, 151
Conforme, Johann: 193
Cook, Dave: 228
Cooper, James: 183, 210, 220, 231
Cornell, Nikolai: 221
Corrales, Juan: 40
Cortsen, Lars: 58
Costa, Fabio: 146
Cury, Adriana: 206

D–G

Dangel, Gabriele: 184
Dauzier, Douglas: 203
Davidge, Nick: 183
Dawson-Hollis, James: 145, 209, 227
de Almeida, Marco Antonio: 224
de Dios, Iván: 40
de Llarena, Carlos Gomez: 204
Denton, John: 166
Dibona, Brendan: 164
Dibona, Dylan: 167
di Lorenzo, Steve: 187, 188
Dr. Schmidt, Ulf: 52
Droga, David: 210
Eriksson, David: 184
Favat, Pete: 96, 197
Fernandes, Fabio: 28, 156
Feuerman, Kerry: 211
Figueira, Ricardo: 27, 142, 218
Fischvogt, Matt: 228
Fitzloff, Mark: 194
Francisco, Judith: 187
Fritz, Ingo: 146
Frost, Eric: 172
Fry, Evan: 168
Fujino, Ken: 233
Garcia Escudero, Juan: 220
Gassner, Martin: 90
Gelner, William: 165, 186, 208
Graf, Gerry: 84
Gnomes, Karl: 162
Golding, Sara: 204

Goodby, Jeff: 48, 118, 176, 211
Gordon-Rodgers, Gavin: 163
Grais, Ian: 193
Greenaway, Andy: 151, 159
Greenstein, Keith: 128
Gunn, Kirt: 181
Gurvit, Jonathan: 145
Gutierrez, Eric: 33

H–I

Höglund, Björn: 170
Harada, Tadaaki: 205
Harricks, Mark: 226
Heiss, Flo: 183, 210, 220, 231
Hermanas, David: 128
Hilton, James: 199
Hinkle, Chris: 203
Hogg, Cyrus: 201
Holman, Richard: 102
Hollester, Jeremy: 132
Holzman, Jason: 82
Huesmann, Bernd: 161
Huschka, Peter: 152, 160
Hyman, Jeffrey: 200
Inamoto, Rei: 88, 153, 163, 164, 207, 225
Ingram, Karen: 181
Ishii, Nobuyuki: 233
Ito, Takeharu: 190
Ito, Naoki: 126
Itzkoff, Maxi: 162

K–L

Küster, Sven: 110
Kang, Peter: 193, 204
Kearse, John: 96, 197
Keister, Paul: 170
Keller, Andrew: 37, 38, 46, 50, 124, 130, 143, 144, 145, 154, 155, 168, 169, 186, 209, 219, 223, 226, 227, 228
Kestin, Janet: 98, 216
Kiger, Kris: 104
Kishimoto, Takayoshi: 233
Klein, Mariano: 220
Klinkhammer, Elke: 191
Koike, Hiroshi: 190
Kutschinski, Michael: 52
Kwong, Chi Kit: 206
Lam, Natalie: 104
Lam, Sean: 54, 178
Lau, Adam: 88, 163, 207, 225
Law, Nick: 74, 104
Lee, David: 164
Lee, Steven: 206
Legowiecki, Martin: 204
Levit, Steve: 204
Liew, Sanyen: 138, 217, 230
Linnen, Scott: 124, 144, 169, 186
Livengood, John: 33
Loskill, Sven: 202
Lund, Chris: 221
Lundy, Brook: 44

M

Manchester, Kristian: 181
Martínez, Nuria: 194
Masuda, Issaku: 233
Masuda, Junya: 218
Mazzariol, Mauricio: 31, 184
McCann, Jason: 182
McGinness, Will: 39, 48, 118, 148, 149, 176
McKay, Pat: 211
McKeon, Kevin: 217
McNeil, John: 167, 179, 212, 213, 214, 215
Means, Tommy: 179, 212, 213, 214, 215

Miron, Normand: 158
Moliterno, Eco: 147
Montague, Ty: 132, 191
Montero, Antonio: 40
Moss, Jacquie: 215
Moss, Peter: 112
Mugnaini, Sergio: 32, 225
Musante, Jason: 228
Mye, Geoff: 221
Mykolyn, Steve: 182

N–P

Nagasaki, Yoshiaki: 180
Nel-lo, Enric: 56, 167, 205
Nesle, Stephen: 44
Nicholson, Peter: 132
Northrop, Ronny: 39
Norton, Cabot: 36
Nussbaum, Jill: 104
Nyström, Mattias: 68
O'Sullivan, Mike: 195
Oehrlich, Holger: 35, 222
Olivera, Hugo: 56
Otto, Mike John: 90
Ozipko, Dave: 201
Pacheco, Tete: 224
Paradise, Liz: 128
Paterson, Ewan: 150
Peck, Tony: 147
Pereira, PJ: 88, 148, 153, 163, 164, 207, 225
Pereira, Roberto: 225
Persson, Ted: 189, 190
Pinto, Fabio Simões: 28, 156
Pong, Angela: 206
Postaer, Jeremy: 132
Powell, Matt: 41, 114
Pueyo, Emma: 187
Pullum, Bob: 88, 163, 225,
Purgason, Todd: 199

R

Ralph, Brandon: 167
Rasines, Jess: 149, 150
Rasmussen, Robert: 132
Reilly, Rob: 46, 122, 145, 168, 209, 226, 227
Rico, Marta: 187
Riddle, Todd: 223
Robinson, Neil: 164
Roddy, Kevin: 100
Romano, Fernanda: 195
Royce, Seb: 29, 157, 201
Rudy, Peter: 167

S

Sandoz, Andy: 219
Sato, Tatsuro: 126
Sato, Kashiwa: 64
Savaglio, Ernesto: 162
Sawadatikom, Saharath: 158, 159
Schier, Sebastian: 152, 160
Seifert, Christian: 202
Serkin, Mariano: 162
Serpa, Marcello: 225
Shine, Mike: 153, 154, 166
Siegal, Meghan: 96, 197
Silburn, Paul: 172
Silva, Juan: 220
Silverstein, Rich: 177, 212
Simpson, Steve: 212
Sloutchevsky, Vas: 221
Smiley, Rob: 189
Smith, Jimmy: 208

INDEX

Sobral Caetano da Silva, Nei: *153, 154, 166*
Solana, Daniel: *187*
Speidel, Doug: *183*
Sperduti, Anthony: *84*
Spiegel, Michael: *104*
Spillmann, Martin: *229*
Staples, Chris: *193*
Strasberg, Rob: *37, 38, 50, 124, 130, 143, 144, 154, 155, 168, 169, 186, 219, 223, 227, 228*
Sukegawa, Ren: *233*

T–Z

Tait, Iain: *185*
Talbot, Toby: *195*
Tanaka, Koichiro: *180*
Tarty, Feh: *211*
Taylor, Mark: *172*
Taylor, Monica: *194*
Teshigawara, Kazumasa: *42*
Thomas, Winston: *204*
Thompson, Kim: *122*
Tierney, Brian: *211*
Ting, Richard: *104, 192*
Trudeau, Dominique: *182*
Vacherot, Sebastien: *189, 190*
Valencia, Ulises: *80*
Valente, Sergio: *31, 184*
Vasconcellos, Raphael: *142*
Vonk, Nancy: *98, 216*
Von Scheven, Burkhart: *216*
Watt, Bruce: *159*
Wellfare, Judy: *132*
Wells, Greg: *204*
Wenneker, Mark: *176*
Wiggins, Chris: *172*
Wnek, Mark: *195*
Wong, Tracy: *229*
Wright, Bill: *170*
Yasuda, Masahiko: *156*
Zada, Jason: *171*
Zasa, Jay: *203*
Zoelch, Michael: *35*

DESIGNER

A / B

Abrams, Rachel: *74, 203*
Andersson, Nina: *72, 174*
Arlig, Johan: *114*
Badía, Lisi: *187*
Balin, Liz: *153*
Bang, Andy: *199*
Barragán, Alberto: *40*
Bassichetti, Angela: *224*
Baxter, Jeff: *74, 104*
Beacock, Mark: *30, 161*
Berger, Chris: *165, 186*
Bernett, Claudia: *104*
Bernard, Justin: *199*
Bessen, Neal: *197*
Blouse, Dustin: *164*
Boleas, David: *220*
Bourguignon, André: *191*
Bretzmann, Daniel: *222*
Burneiko, Pedro: *142*

C

Calderon, Miguel: *177*
Calleja, Jorge: *199*
Camacho, Enrique: *199*
Capp, James: *199*
Castro, Miguel: *199*
Christensen, Dennis: *183*
Cina, Mike: *199*
Convay, Wade: *74, 104*
Cook, Simon: *185*
Cookson, Will: *199*
Corotan, Mark: *203*
Costa, Mariana: *224*
Cuban Council: *96*

D–G

da Costa, Antonio: *82*
DAIM: *202*
Daum, Nik: *194*
Davis, Jeremy: *167*
del Marmol, Mike: *122*
Dolling, Lotta: *72*
Duffney, Craig: *172*
Ekman, Malin: *170*
Erb, Matthias: *222*
Erickson, Craig: *232*
Fino, Jorge: *199*
Frandsen, Rasmus: *58*
Freeset: *223*
Fujimaki, Atsushi: *190*
Funck, Isabelle: *78*
Futamura, Kojiro: *64*
Godoi, Vagner: *28*
Gray, Jeremy: *88, 225*
Grove Moeller, Kristian: *58*
Gugel, Andy: *172*
Gutierrez, Jezreel: *80, 177*

H–K

Hansen, Mike: *199*
Hansson, Hampus: *199*
Hansson, Per: *26, 172, 173, 174*
Hello Design: *193*
Hellström, Andreas: *180*
Holzenkamp, Nicole: *52*
Hostetler, Jemma: *199*
Hsieh, Kevin: *164, 171*
Ilizarbe, Alvaro: *122*
Irdel, Mehmet: *203*
Jankowski, Adam: *191*
Jansson, Lars: *175, 200*
Jomehri, Hoj: *88, 225*
Kamikanda, Saiko: *126*
Kania, Dave: *181*
Karpinska, Aya: *74*
Kayal, Brad: *96*
Kessel, Lena: *202*
Kiemann, Fite: *161*
Kim, Ed: *104*
Kim, Woo Sung: *221*
Kloostra, Feike: *82*
Kurihara, Keigo: *70*

L / M

Lalloo, Dilesh: *219*
Lamm, Staffan: *180*
Lange, Carlos: *122*
Lanne, Emil: *165, 186*
Larson, Adam: *197*
Lee, Jiwon: *122*
Lee, Terry: *88, 225*
Lenz, Melanie: *231*
Leung, Carrie: *147*
Levy, Andre: *224*
Li, ShuZeng: *192*
Liao, Daniel: *195*
Long, Jamie: *114*
Lundberg, Rickard: *173*

Martelius, Simon: *173*
Martis, James: *130*
MAS Design: *132*
Matsukawa, Sayaka: *64*
Matsuura, Toshinori: *126*
McCann, Conor: *38, 50, 122, 124, 130, 169, 186*
McCracken, Tim: *120, 128*
Melin, Bjarne: *180*
MESH Architects: *132*
Miller, Brian: *199*
Miranda, Joe: *122*
Mistry, Nitin: *157*
Mohr, Martin: *58*
Moon, Cindy: *197*
Moreno, Cesar: *76*
Mustacich, Alex: *199*

N–R

Nedebock, Jurgen: *82*
Nikkels, Edwin: *82*
Noe, Christoph: *62*
Oderwald, Ben: *74*
Omori, Shu: *233*
Ostle, Leon: *29, 157, 201*
Otsuka, Takanobu: *205*
Peddie, Stuart: *41*
Perryer, Justin: *160*
Persson, Jonas: *30*
Poopuu, Jimmy: *190*
Pridgen, Scott: *128*
Queen, William: *28, 156*
Reger, Michael: *104*
Robinson, Paul: *203*
Rodgers, Thomas: *46, 130, 226*
Rodriguez, Johnny: *199*
Rodriguez, Pres: *122*
Rose, Will: *183*
Rowbotham, Adrian: *231*
Russel, Boyd: *160*

S

Sakevich, Elena: *104*
Sasagaki, Yosuke: *205*
Sasikumar, Deepu: *162*
Sato, Tomohiro: *70*
Schlechtriem, Nina: *204*
Schlierkamp, Martin: *92*
Schulwitz, Silja: *90*
Seale, Rob: *36*
Seki, Yosuke: *70*
Siegal, Meghan: *197*
Slapgård, Kathrine: *179*
Smith, Craig: *172*
Smith, Dave: *199*
Smith, Nate: *199*
Staubitz, Marc: *223*
Stoerlein, Serena: *52*
Sung, Matt: *221*

T–Z

Takeguchi, Shigeki: *205*
Takeuchi, Makoto: *233*
Tan, Robin: *151, 159*
Taniguchi, Yuka: *233*
Tarazi, Racha: *204*
Thamrin, Christine: *197*
Thomas, Andy: *196*
Timonen, Mikko: *174, 188*
Tindale, Dave: *199*
Ting, Birdie: *138*
Tobens, Joe: *104*
Valdivieso, Eduardo: *199*
Valencius, Chris: *197*

INDEX

Van Dzura, Gary: *104*
Verity, Matt: *29, 157*
Votaw, Brian: *204*
Wass, Jerry: *188*
Wei Law, Chean: *46, 124, 169, 186, 226*
Wendling, Andrew: *167*
Williams, Chris: *108, 152*
Williford, Scott: *120*
Wojciewski, Doug: *191*
Wood, Graham: *191*
Wright, Dan: *108, 152*
Wu, Yu-Ming: *192*
Yeretsky, Kiril: *203*
Yoshimori, Takeshi: *190*
Yuen, Jonathan: *136*
Zosel, Matthias: *231*

DIRECTOR

A–L
Akerlund, Jonas: *124*
Aselton, Matt: *130*
Bahry, Chris: *225*
Ebeling, Mick: *225*
Eguchi, Kan: *126*
Ewing, Larry: *225*
Feil, Alex: *216*
Godsall, Tim: *84*
Greenstein, Keith: *128*
Hermanas, David: *128*
Hobbyfilm: *60*
Israel, Aramis: *122*
Johansson, Ulf: *211*
Krallman, Randy: *210, 227*
Littlechild, Henry: *228*
Lutz, Julien Christian: *100*

M–R
Means, Tommy: *212, 213, 214, 215*
Middleditch, Paul: *227*
Mor, Ben: *203*
Morrison, Phil: *130*
Morton, Rocky: *227*
Niemeyer, Chris: *229*
Palmer, Chris: *102*
Perkins, Rob: *211*
Piper, Tim: *98*
Prindle, Scott: *130*
Rasco, Eric: *122*
Ruth, Dan: *122*

S–Y
Staav, Yael: *98, 216*
Stephens, Geordie: *229*
Tanimoto, Craig: *229*
Terashima, Toru: *126*
The Glue Society: *208*
Tomioka, Toshihiro: *126*
Tomorrows Brightest Minds: *217*
Usher, Kinka: *209*
Van Osdale, Steve: *128*
Walsh, Matt: *124, 130*
Welch, Andy: *210*
Yamanaka, Yasuhiro: *126*

INFORMATION ARCHITECT

A–M
Alvarez-Borrás, Ignacio: *194*
Antonuccio, Joe: *197*
Bessa, Alexandre: *28, 156*
Christiansen, Jens: *58*
Corbacho, Luis M.: *194*
Dull, Matthew: *191*
Gasperak, Tim: *215*
Goldstein, Melissa: *197*
Gustavsson, Anders: *78*
Heathcott, Adam: *169*
Hori, Takeo: *156*
Kief, Chris: *221*
Kvart, Rebekah: *180*
Llarena, Oscar: *186*
Lundqvist, Marielle: *26, 172, 173*
Mc Takashi: *233*
Miller, Heidi: *74*
Morimoto, Kenji: *233*

N–Y
Nakayama, Yukinori: *156*
Obata, Paula: *28, 156*
Söderlind, Bitte: *180*
Sakai, Chiemi: *156*
Schulz, Wolfgang: *110*
Stephens, Danielle: *196*
Suzuki, Tomohiro: *233*
Tanizawa, Nobuyuki: *156*
Watanabe, Tomohiro: *156*
Westman, Sofie: *173*
Yang, Lawrence: *88, 163, 225*

MULTIMEDIA ARTIST

A–G
Abraham, Leif: *92*
Amacedo, Xande: *215*
Atlin, Dov: *187*
Baerenfaenger, Steffen: *231*
Bartsch, Christian: *160*
Bates, Daniel: *80, 177*
Berglund, Henrik: *86*
Bessen, Neal: *197*
Bettencourt, Sebastian: *221*
Bruket, Anders o Mille: *180*
Cam, Simon: *29, 157, 201*
Cha, Edward: *98*
Chaffee, Eben: *197*
Chi, Henry: *188*
Chiyoda, Hiroki: *156*
Chung, Kooch: *183, 220, 231*
Church, Odin: *163*
Clavijo, Vanessa: *227*
Clements, Stephen: *88, 163, 225*
Cloutier, Marie-Michèle: *158*
Darling, Jim: *183*
DJ Hiro: *70*
Doherty, Jason: *188*
Drilon, Mark: *203*
Ewart, Dayoung: *130*
Fischer, Jens: *62*
Forsgren, Mikael: *180*
Gibson, Kevin: *98*
Gillette, Michael: *179, 212, 213, 214, 215*

giraffentoast: *202*
Gray, Jeremy: *163*
Guilln, Daniel: *187*
Gustavsson, Anders: *172*

H–L
Hansson, Per: *78*
Hawley, Jacob: *171*
Hello Design: *193*
Hernndez, Ral: *187*
Hoefler, Mark: *146*
Hosoya, Shota: *156*
Howell, Lisi: *171*
Hunter, Erik: *166*
Iida, Ken'ichi: *126*
Isaksson, Daniel: *178*
Jaquet, Holger: *92*
Jerrems, Sacha: *196*
Joelson, Oskar: *155*
Johnson, Paul: *170*
Jomehri, Hoj: *163*
Kjaergaard, Josef: *198*
Lam, Sean: *178*
Lamont-Havers, Ian: *132*
Lanju, Arai: *197*
Lau, Pat: *201*
Law, Matthew: *88, 163*
Lazzuri, Caio: *88, 163, 164, 225*
Lechner, Ralf: *92*
Lee, Terry: *163*
Lindgren, Mathias: *180*
Loar, Reed: *203*
Local Projects: *132*

M–R
Maeschig, Christoph: *92*
Mahalem, Felipe: *224*
Makila, Eric: *98, 216*
Mandaji, Marcelo: *32*
Mariscal, Sebastian: *76, 80, 177*
Martins, Ricardo: *147*
Martis, James: *38, 50, 170, 186*
Mason, Steve: *215*
Masuda, Junya: *218*
McDougall, Hamish: *157*
McKenna, Ryan: *132*
McNulty, David: *183, 220, 231*
Meld Media: *182*
Metros, Justin: *200*
Misirlioglu, Can: *192*
Moreno, Cesar: *76*
Mullen, Greg: *106*
Murata, Michelle: *148*
Nishimura, Curtis: *215*
Norin, Erik: *173, 173*

O–S
Olson, Amariah: *120*
Olson, Larry: *120*
Olson, Obin: *120*
Pence, Laura: *203*
Petrocci, Matthew: *171*
Pomerantz, Seth: *132*
Pretty Production: *180*
Purdy, Dan: *187, 188*
Reiling, Jon: *164*
Rodda, Mike: *200*
Rodgers, Thomas: *50, 170, 186*
Santi, Luis: *38*
Santiesteban, Eduardo: *227*
Schulz, Felix: *92*
Scott, Roger: *215*
Sembo, Kensuke: *218*
Shimazaki, Jun: *156*

242

Sterner, Erik: *155, 170*
Sugai, Toshiyuki: *218*
Sugiyama, Shigeo: *233*

T–Z
Takeguchi, Shigeki: *205*
Tan, Francis: *54*
Tanaka, Ryoji: *218*
Teso, Chris: *197*
The Quarry: *102*
Torres, Guillermo: *148*
Torres Ramos, Alexandre: *225*
Uchida, Ikuo: *218*
Ushiyama, Hitoshi: *156*
Valencia, Ulises: *76, 80, 177*
Valle, Stephanie: *158*
Vellasco, Felipe: *224*
Voelpel, Mark: *104*
Wallström, Daniel: *180*
Whitelaw, Andrew: *171*
Wills, Alex: *106*
Winn, David: *200*
Wong, Robin: *219*
Woode, Victor: *157*
Yeretsky, Kiril: *104*
Z4: *32*
Zagorskis, Bob: *98*
Zwirner, Kaspar: *35*

MUSIC & SOUND

B–M
Beacon Street Studios: *209*
Chastain, Ken: *211*
Critchlow, Taj: *100*
Diggz, J: *100*
LaPlaca, Dan: *94*
Feltenstein, Andrew: *209*
Friedman, Alan: *132*
Green, Andy: *132*
Meadows, Bill: *209*

O–W
Ortega, Lindi: *216*
Rechtshaid, Ariel: *203*
Scramble: *102*
Studio Apollo: *181*
Studio La Majeure: *181*
Technicolour: *216*
Vapor Music Group: *98*
Weaver, Pat: *211*

PRODUCTION COMPANY

A–C
777interactive: *205*
AdMotion: *225*
Against All Odds: *178*
Agency Net: *198*
Area 52: *209*
Avenue A Razorfish: *156*
B-Reel: *72, 188*
Biscuit Filmworks: *84, 222*
Blitz Games: *122*
Blue 60: *223*
Booker: *40*
Bridge Design: *156*
Carmody, Brian: *210*
Colony: *26, 172, 173, 174*
Cubo: *224*

D–F
Dale, Sally Ann: *210*
Dandelion: *181*
Dentsu Tec: *156*
Digital Domain: *169, 186*
digital egg: *156*
Doke, Yusuke: *218*
Domani Studios: *37, 38, 130, 143, 154, 194, 219*
Driver: *217*
DV3 Productions: *120*
Element-E: *216*
Effekt-Etage Berlin: *191*
Eriksson, Anton: *180*
Epoch Films: *130*
EVB: *46, 222, 226*
Evolution Engine: *122*
FaceFaceFace: *212*
Famous Group: *204*
Final Cut: *222*
FramFab: *82*
Freecloud: *26, 172, 173*
Freeset: *223*
Frost New Media: *200*

G–K
George P. Johnson: *221*
Gorgeous: *102*
Grow Interactive: *222*
Grupo W: *76, 80, 177*
Hanson Dodge: *50, 130, 186*
H.S.I. Productions: *100, 227*
Harakiri: *26, 172, 174*
Hello Design: *193, 222*
House of Usher: *209*
Idiotlamp: *201*
IQ Interactive: *124, 169, 186*
juxt interactive: *199*
JWTwo: *132*
Kamiya, Syuhei: *218*
Keytoon: *171*
Kinetic Pictures: *222*
Kitchen: *156*
Klipmart: *153, 154*
Kokokaka: *174, 175*
Kramgo: *72*
Kunzman, Allison: *210*

L–O
La Fabrique d'Image: *181, 182*
Lim, Pervyn: *112*
Mad Cat Studios: *155*
Maven Networks: *215*
Mecano: *182*
Mediascape: *223*
Mekansim: *179, 212, 213, 214, 215*
MFX: *175*
Milling Smith, Patrick: *210*
Mindflood: *168, 221, 222*
MJZ: *227*
Monster Films: *180*
Natzke Design: *149*
Next: *202*
North Kingdom: *48, 168, 176, 184*
Nozaki, Satomi: *218*
Number-9: *176*
Obscura Digital: *118*
Ong, Kenny: *112*

P–Z
Palmer, Rick: *166*
Paragraph: *180*
Plus Et Plus: *132*
Plus Productions: *122*
Projector: *180*
Radical Media: *208*
Rae-Chodan, Jo: *210*
Ralph, Brandon: *227*
Reginald Pike: *98, 216, 222*
Riot: *209*
Rock Fight: *171*
Root Communications: *126*
RSA: *124, 169, 186*
Run the Red: *226*
S., Celica: *112*
Sammarco Productions: *174*
Smith and Sons Films: *211*
Smoke: *209*
Squarewave: *144, 145*
Struck Design: *44, 222*
Suzuki, Hiroo: *218*
Templar Studios: *148, 222*
Tequila Creative Technology: *183*
The Barbarian Group: *118, 176*
The Vacuum Design: *222*
The Viral Factory: *228*
TYO Productions: *126*
Unit-9: *39, 148, 175, 177*
Upset TV: *29, 157*
Villains: *170*
Visual Art: *173*
WDDG: *222*
Zugara: *37, 143, 155*

PROGRAMMER

A–C
Alan, Brad: *74*
Albuquerque, Carolina: *142*
Alegretti, Daniel: *206*
Allen, Victor: *199*
Alvarez, Manuel: *220*
Ambrose, Aaron: *74, 104*
Anderson, Russ: *203*
Aoude, Dani: *191*
Banks, Lee: *106*
Bartsch, Philip: *202*
Bechmann, Yasmine: *92*
Braunstein, Roger: *221*
Bretzmann, Daniel: *222*
Brewer, Joshua: *166*
Brown, Laurie: *172*
Brunetta, Andre: *27, 142*
Cardozo, Andre: *27, 142*
Cavanaugh, Nate: *199*
Chan, Jason: *178*
Cinicola, André: *28*
Corcoran, Casey: *199*
Coronges, Nick: *104*
Corporaal, Robert Fred: *231*
Cox, Dave: *30, 161*
Cuban Council: *96*

D–J
Decaix, Patrick: *90*
Delia, Chris: *167*

INDEX

Denken: 162
Duangsong, Seksun: 158
Duncan, Charles: 164
Elwin, Matthew: 106
Fernandez, Juan Carlos: 194
Forras, Robert: 221
França, Rodrigo: 32, 225
Franzen, Liv: 173
Freeset: 223
García, Oscar: 149, 150
Gargan, Andy: 196
Gauthier, Dominique: 158
Gessner, Sven: 110
Gonzalo, Enrique: 149, 150
Gordon, Larry: 169
Gosselin, Robert: 181
Guelensoy, Kerem: 62
Gustavsson, Bo: 26, 78, 172, 173, 174
Hader, Matthias: 104
Hafiz, Nauman: 104
Haughie, John: 128
Hayes, Steve: 166
Hello Design: 193
Hermann, Florian: 62
Herrmann, Sven: 202
Hezinger, Stefanie: 35
Hinkle, Chris: 203
Hoffman, Bob: 203
Horwitz, Jason: 221
illianced: 189
Joelson, Oskar: 155, 170
Johansson, Bjorn: 78, 172
Johnson, Scott: 146
Junk, Thomas: 191

K / L

Karthik, CK: 162
Keegan, Andrew: 183
Kengle, Carrie: 192
Khoo, Aaron: 197
Kief, Chris: 221
Kiemig, Jason: 232
Kitamura, Keita: 64
Knott, Andrew: 185
Knott, Mike: 164
Kong, LeeSeng: 217
Kohno, Asako: 104
Kraft, Manfred: 62
Kraftsow, Dave: 170
Kreuder, Timm: 62
Kroon, Klas: 48, 176, 180
Laham, Tarik: 120
Lainchbury, Richard: 219
Lam, Sean: 178
Larios, Hector: 203
Lechner, Ralf: 202
Lee, Gicheol: 198
Lee, Terry: 164
Lee, William: 104
LeeSeng: 138
Leggett, Richard: 106
Lemay, Andy: 172
Liang, Shang: 112
List, Oliver: 110
Liszewski, Paul: 164
Lobb, Iain: 166
Loeffler, Jens: 74
Luby, Howard: 223
Ludvigsen, Martin: 58

M

Macedo, Marcelo: 142
Maeschig, Christoph: 202
Mainguy, Bob: 158
Manderson, Cam: 196
Mann, Craig: 120
Maraschin, Vincent: 224
Martínez, Carlos: 194
Martínez, Marc: 56, 205
Mason, Steve: 215
Massaia, Mauricio: 184
Mastri, John: 46, 226
Mathew, Ebbey: 96, 197
Miranda, Helio: 142
Mito, Tetsuya: 70
Mitomo, Jun: 233
Monvoisin, Xavier: 166
Moscardó, Juan Carlos: 56, 167
Mosley, Michael: 104
Mualim, Teguh: 170
Mueller, Oliver: 35
Munoz, Cesar: 208
Murata, Michelle: 207

N–P

Nan, Sunny: 192
Nguyen, Alex: 196
Nguyen, Khanh: 199
Nunes, Wagner: 31, 184
O'Byrne, Chris: 114
O'Reilly, Dave: 112
Oliveira, Ary: 224
Orefjerd, Andre: 179
Ortchanian, Paul: 176
Ortega, Jordi: 143, 169, 170
Ortiz, Edgar: 80, 177
Pacheco, Paulo: 28, 156
Park, Jim: 134
Pasztory, Adam: 200
Patterson, Brad: 128, 228
Perry, Richard: 191
Peterson, Justin: 171
Piccuirro, Michael: 104, 192
Piro, Joseph: 166
pixelpusher.ca: 182
Ploj, Michael: 90
Prindle, Scott: 168, 169, 170

R / S

Rauch, Wolf: 62
Reed, Emily: 208
Reichard, Peter: 62, 231
Roberston, Adam: 163
Rocasalbas, Dani: 167
Roman, Michele: 104, 192
Roy, Dorian: 110
Roth, Geoffrey: 74, 104
Rubio, Jose: 187
Rundgren, Per: 155, 170
Sanchez, Ricardo: 194
Sandoval, Álvaro: 187
Santi, Luis: 170
Sato, Yukio: 233
Schweickhardt, Heiko: 191
Scott, Lisa: 226
Sherwood, Steven: 88, 148, 163, 207, 225
Shuman, Lucas: 46, 226
Smith, Aaron: 170
Smith, Stephen: 106
Sosinski, Ben: 104
Ström, Martin: 189
Striegel, Jason: 172, 211
Studt, Jan-M.: 92
Suerek, Eva: 90
Sundberg, Oskar: 68
Swanepoel, Wesley: 220
Swartz, Mike: 33
Sweeney, Clive: 120, 128, 228

T–Y

Tada, Tomoyuki: 233
Tan, Francis: 54
Tan, Robin: 151, 159
Teshigawara, Kazumasa: 42
Teso, Chris: 197
Three Melons: 145
Torres, Guillermo: 207
Trahey, Scott: 191
Tubert, John: 104
Uranga, Raul: 76, 80, 177
Valdez, Rick: 170
Van Malsen, Marcus: 196
Vine, Billy: 157
Volume One: 186
Wahlgren, David: 179
Walsh, Matt: 168, 169, 170, 228
Warren, Steve: 74
Wessels, Stefan: 112
Wiechers, Stan: 104
Williford, Scott: 120
Wiltshire, David: 199
Wissing, Jocke: 189, 190
Wiström, Isak: 180
Wood, Dan: 199
Yang, August: 74, 104

WRITER

A / B

Åsman, Maria: 170
Alshin, Adam: 84
Adams, Tom: 168
Amorin, Francisco: 162
Anderson, Keith: 33
Andersson, Mikael: 170
Ault, Andrew: 132
Baños, Elena: 194
Bagot, Rob: 179, 212, 213, 214, 215
Bailey, Nick: 106
Baker, Claire: 30
Banta, Dave: 145, 227
Bartholf, Martin: 178
Baudry, Nicolas: 158
Bauer, Dominik: 152
Benjamin, Jay: 195
Bergeron, Guillaume: 181
Berglof, Henrik: 78, 172
Bletterman, Josh: 104
Blanco, Mari Carmen: 149, 150
Blink: 138
Bowler, Sarah Jane: 188
Bowman, Dave: 195
Brönnimann, Peter: 229
Burrough, Vicky: 34, 151
Burton, Matty: 195
Byrne, Colin: 199

C–E

Chávarri, Jaime: 40
Charney, Paul: 48, 176
Cianfrone, Bob: 46, 122, 209, 226
Cierco, Nerea: 56, 205
Cochrane, Ryan: 146
Coelho, Soraya: 142
Conde, Paco: 187
Constantino, Juliana: 218
Cooper, Nathan: 185
Corbitt, Carl: 38, 130, 168
Dasgupta, Chaitali: 162
Davidge, Nick: 183

INDEX

Dawe, Linda: 158
de Rooij, Bram: 82
de Tilly, Elyse Noel: 182
Dietz, Mandy: 149
di Gangi, Madeleine: 182
Dodd, Colin: 228
Ehlers, Robert: 92, 202
Einhorn, Marc: 96, 197
Elliott, Jim: 232
Emery, Toria: 118
Eriksen, Tom: 26, 174
Escuadra, Jose: 150

F / G

Farhang, Amir: 165, 186, 208
Figueira, Ricardo: 218
Fischvogt, Matt: 228
Frost, Eric: 172
Fry, Evan: 46, 226
Fujino, Ken: 233
Gazley, Annabelle: 226
Gill, Brian: 182
Gillette, Jeff: 122, 124, 143, 169, 186
Ginsberg, Scott: 44
Gjaerum, Jorgen: 188
Goh, Alex: 54
Gonzalez, Daniel: 132
Gonzalez, Ivan: 80, 177
Gordon-Rodgers, Gavin: 219
Greenstein, Keith: 128
Gribel, Cristiane: 28, 156
Gunn, Kirt: 181
Guynn, John: 128

H

Ha, Weina: 230
Hall, Bob: 164
Hancock, Chris: 153, 154
Harris, Ben: 163
Hasan, Mona: 128
Hazledine, Tom: 195
Heath, John: 36
Hegerfors, Anders: 174
Henderson, Brandon: 82
Henke, Andreas: 231
Herbstman, Ed: 181
Hess, Alison: 104
Hillman, Mark: 160
Horovitch, David: 187
Hough, Zoe: 30
Howard, Mike: 37, 124, 143, 154, 155, 169, 186, 227
Hunnicut, Gabriela: 218
Husband, Eric: 166
Hyman, Jeffrey: 200

I – L

Ian, Matt: 100
Ishii, Nobuyuki: 233
Israel, Aramis: 122
Ito, Naoki: 126
James, Stephen: 90
Jansson, Fredrik: 174
Kestin, Janet: 216
Kimura, Genki: 218
Klump, Val: 194
Krahl Jr., Jones: 27
Kramm, Justin: 153
Kruse, Johan: 155, 170
Kubitz, Matthias: 35
Kuemml, Eva: 231
Kutscher, Ryan: 122, 124, 168, 169, 186
Kyeli, Mak: 197
Laurent, Filip: 86

Lawlor, Nat: 148, 176
Leach, James: 203
Leahan, Jonny: 191
Ledoux, Matt: 96
Lee, Justine: 151, 159
Lee, Steven: 206
Lidzell, Anders: 180
Lieberman, Karl: 82
Linnen, Scott: 124, 169, 186, 228
Lloyd, Simon: 29, 157
Lo, Rachel: 206
Lundy, Brook: 44
Lynch, Chad: 120

M

Mader, Melanie: 202
Makak, Roger: 151, 159
Martin, Dave: 201
Martin, Demetri: 179, 212, 213, 214, 215
Masuda, Jyunya: 205
Mathisen, Nick: 166
McAloon, Grant: 34, 151
McCain, Matt: 229
McKay, Pat: 48, 176
McLeod, James: 195
Means, Tommy: 179, 212, 213, 214, 215
Medina, Angela: 150
Mikosh, Jake: 122
Milardo, Michael: 193
Molinillo, Daniel: 194
Moliterno, Eco: 147
Murray, Brian: 128
Mye, Geoff: 221

N – P

Nagy, Paul: 226
Nakajima, Satoshi: 156
Nelson, Jacob: 175
Netto, Moacyr: 32, 225
Nielsen, Jakob: 179
Nilsson, Filip: 175
Nishihara, Mikiko: 156
Northrop, Ronny: 48, 176
Olivera, Hugo: 167
Olivero, Johan: 72
Osvald, Rebecka: 188
Parker, Jonny: 102
Paterson, Ewan: 150
Pegler, Ben: 195
Pereira, Roberto: 225
Perkins, Rob: 211
Piper, Tim: 98, 216
Platt, Brian: 217
Possin, Nicole: 203
Pou, Edu: 227
Price, Stephanie: 195
Priebs-Macpherson, Alexander: 216
Prout, Nick: 212
Pueyo, Emma: 187

Q / R

Qvennerstedt, Anna: 72
Raven, Lewis: 157
Richings, Simon: 203
Ringqvist, Martin: 200
Riviera, Spencer: 39, 175
Robertson, Alistair: 210
Robson, Thomas: 58
Rollman, Dan: 176
Rooke, Guy: 144
Roper, Tim: 130
Rudy, Peter: 167
Ruiz, Ruben: 76
Russell, Steven: 181

S

Sacroisky, Daniel: 145
Salomonsson, Jeff: 173
Sanders, Glenn: 183
Saraiva, Carol: 224
Sayaman, Joe: 163, 225
Sciammarella, Ricardo: 206
Scott, John: 112
Seifert, Christian: 202
Sengel Wixom, Alisa: 172, 211
Sherman, Scott: 181
Sims, Claire: 186, 228
Skinner, Sally: 201
Sobczak, Tim: 62, 231
Sommer, Christian: 161
Spelliscy, Ryan: 178
Standen, Jamie: 226
Steemson, Helen: 195
Stevenson, Chris: 208
Sukegawa, Ren: 233
Sweeney, Mike: 177

T

Taiar, Rafael: 31
Talbot, Toby: 195
Tan, Eugene: 178
Tan, Grace: 112
Tanimoto, Nirei: 233
Taylor, James: 41
Thanasilpisan, Vichai: 159
The Glue Society: 208
Thompson, Rob: 122, 169, 186, 228
Tierney, Brian: 211, 223
Toledo, Keke: 184
Topol, Lisa: 132
Torrón, Lis: 40
Tsujino, Yutaka: 50, 130, 186
Turner, Christine: 29, 157
Tyler, Alexandra: 171

W

Wahlgren, Daniel: 179
Walker, Dominick: 148, 207
Walker, Eric: 204
Weiner, Clay: 100, 165
Wells, Anthony: 193
Wells, Greg: 204
Wilce, Phil: 108, 152
Will, Noah: 229
Winter, Bob: 212
Witting, John: 183
Wolffe, Chris: 172
Wolske, Jason: 50, 130, 186, 223
Wong, Houston: 147

Y / Z

Youngleib, Ken: 183
Yuen, Jonathan: 136
Zmood, Dov: 204